Lecture Notes in Economics and Mathematical Systems

Managing Editors: M. Beckmann and W. Krelle

301

J. Kacprzyk M. Roubens (Eds.)

Non-Conventional Preference Relations in Decision Making

Springer-Verlag Berlin Heidelberg GmbH

Managing Editors

Prof. Dr. M. Beckmann
Brown University
Providence, RI 02912, USA

Prof. Dr. W. Krelle
Institut für Gesellschafts- und Wirtschaftswissenschaften
der Universität Bonn
Adenauerallee 24–42, D-5300 Bonn, FRG

Editors

Dr. Janusz Kacprzyk
Systems Research Institute, Polish Academy of Science
ul. Newelska 6, 01-447 Warsaw, Poland

Prof. Dr. Marc Roubens
Faculté Polytechnique de Mons
rue de Houdain, 9, B-7000 Mons, Belgium

ISBN 978-3-540-18954-1 ISBN 978-3-642-51711-2 (eBook)
DOI 10.1007/978-3-642-51711-2

Originally published by Springer-Verlag, Berlin· Heidelberg in 1988.

PREFACE

Bernard ROY
Professor, University of Paris-Dauphine
Director of LAMSADE

Il is not unusual for a dozen or so loosely related working papers to be published in book form as the natural outgrowth of a scientific gathering. Although many a volume of collected papers has come into point in this way, the homogeneity of the articles included will often be more apparent than real. As the reader will quickly observe, such is not the case with the present volume. As one can judge from its title, it is in fact an outcome of an editorial project by J. Kacprzyk and M. Roubens. They asked contributing authors to submit recent works which would examine, within a non-traditional theoretical framework, preference analysis and preference modelling in a fuzzy context oriented towards decision aid.

The articles by J.P. Doignon, B. Monjardet, T. Tanino and Ph. Vincke emphasize the analysis of preference structures, mainly in the presence of incomparability, intransitivity, thresholds and, more generally, inaccurate determination. Considerable attention is devoted to the analysis of efficient and non-dominated (in Pareto's sense of the term) decisions in the four papers presented by S. Ovchinnikov and M. Ozernoy, V.E. Zhukovin, Z. Switalski, and M. Roubens and Ph. Vincke. The theory of social choice and the problems of voting have not been neglected as witnessed in the two papers submitted by M. Fedrizzi and J. Kacprzyk, and H. Nurmi. Finally, the very restrictive nature of the classical axiomatics of preference modelling under risk and uncertainty, as well as recent efforts to extend this area and, as much as possible, to enlarge the limits it has set for a large number of theoretical works is the topic of P.C. Fishburn's masterly introductory article.

The above considerations give only the barest outline of this volume's contents. In fact, these eleven articles provide a large panoramic view of the most advanced recent work in decision aid selected on the basis of an intention that emerges quite clearly. Namely, in the face of the inadequacies of classical decision theory, the editors have endeavored to show what fuzzy sets theory (and, more specifically, fuzzy numbers) can contribute to analysing, modelling and justifying preferences and to using these procedures to best advantage, both in an individual and collective setting, within the context of decision aid. It is true that in this area, more than in many others, information of a linguistic nature abounds. In this connection we immediately think of the all-important yet vague notion related to the specificity of the role which different criteria can play in the formation of preferences, that specificity sought in quantifying weights, substitution rates, importance coefficients, veto thresholds, ..., the quantities which are used highly contingent upon the types of models for multicriteria aggregation used. Perhaps a twelfth article could have been devoted to this topic but however vast a panoramic view might be, it will always leave some features of the landscape in shadow.

While exploring the different articles included in this volume, I was struck by the rigour and precision which characterize most of them. However, if we try to situate these works, above all theoretical in nature, in the realm of real works preferences to which they refer in order to gain legitimacy we see that this rigour is actually quite relative, based as it is on a number of presuppositions which cannot be all made explicit. I believe, however, that if this were not so, these articles would be of little interest. In fact, following R. Thom, I am convinced that "l'absolue rigueur n'est possible que dans et par l'insignifiance" (*).

Preferences are formed, transformed, justified, for a given actor, not only with reference to his own value system and to his criteria at a particular moment, but also under the influence of his perception of the objects compared, of his judgment on the quality of this perception, and of any interactions which may emerge between himself and other actors. Thus conflicting systems of logic, uncertain knowledge, and necessarily ambiguous positions are always present. In the face of such complexity, the treatment of preference relations, even on an essentially theoretical level, implies that one aspect or another is given greater consideration. One of the merits of this book is that it puts forth some of those aspects which during recent years have both revealed certain inadequacies in the classical theories and made possible the introduction of original approaches based on the concept of fuzzy relations.

This volume, which is - to the best of my knowledge - the only one of its kind at the present time, is in many respects a remarkable instrument for reflection. The authors are involved in a search for useful tools and techniques, good operators, and fruitful concepts which make it possible to comprehend ambiguity and inaccurate determination as they stand, that is without reducing them in the imprecision or randomness of a probabilistic type. In our view, a scientific approach to what can appropriately be called "preferences" should come to terms with this irreductibility and give recognition to ambiguity and inaccurate determination among those values on which any body of scientific knowledge must be founded. Can current developments under the label of "fuzzy sets" fulfil by their very nature this expectation, both at

(*) "absolute rigour is possible only in and through insignificance".

the mathematical and conceptual level ? The question must remain open. We have a long way to go before we shall be able to see clearly the interrelations between the processes through which preferences, convictions, and choices are developed and set forth on the one hand and the mathematics of "min" and "max" operators or of Zadeh's extension principle on the other.

In conclusion, I would like to underline another of this collection's strong points. Through the problems it takes up, the book makes us more fully aware of the limits on objectivity encountered in the field of decision aid and, consequently, of the virtual impossibility of giving an optimal decision a truly scientific foundation (with the exception of hypotheses which are so particular that they put us considerably far away from the real world which serves us as a reference). All this goes well beyond the book's intended scope. These limits explain the diversity of approaches and emphasize the necessity of accepting the principle by which different approaches may lead to significantly different results. Our concepts, our tools, and our procedures cannot be understood from the perspective of discovering (with more or less approximation) preexisting truths which can be universally imposed.

Those who read these lines and who will then, hopefully, go on to read the entire volume may wonder what, precisely, it is that decision aid helps us to do. Some may answer that it helps us to make better decisions, but how should we interpret that response (what meaning for "better") ? Personally, I would answer in a different way : decision aid and the preference analysis upon which it is based enable us to enhance the degree of conformity and coherence between the evolution of a decision-making process, and the value systems and the objectives of those involved in this process. The purpose of decision aid is, therefore, to help us make our way in the presence of ambiguity, uncertainty and an abundance of bifurcations.

CONTENTS

NORMATIVE THEORIES OF DECISION MAKING UNDER RISK AND UNDER UNCERTAINTY

P. C. Fishburn AT&T Bell Laboratories Murray Hill, New Jersey 07974

ABSTRACT. Theories of rational preference and choice in situations of decision making under risk and under uncertainty that were developed during the 1940's and 1950's have come under increasing fire because of their inability to model certain types of reasonable and persistent patterns of preference. This essay outlines the standard theories, discusses defenses and criticisms of their axioms, and reviews recent efforts to generalize them in such a way that the new theories model a wider spectrum of reasonable behaviors without giving up too much of the mathematical convenience and elegance of the earlier theories.

1. Introduction

Normative decision theory is the study of guidelines for right action. It involves the formulation and defense of principles of comparative evaluation and choice among competing alternatives, proposed as rules that individuals or societies ought to — or perhaps would want to — follow. It deals also with the implications of these principles both on an abstract level and in reference to particular types of decision situations. The general subject is vast since it covers numerous ethical and normative social theories developed during the past few millenia.

The aim of the present essay is exceedingly narrow in view of the larger perspective of the subject. It is to discuss a comparatively recent episode in the history of normative decision theory that has been heavily influenced by eighteenth century Enlightenment thought and the subsequent ascendancy of rationalism and scientific method in the analysis of human behavior. The principals in this episode are, with few exceptions, twentieth-century mathematicians, economists, and statisticians. The exceptions include Daniel Bernoulli (1738), who proposed a theory to explain why choices of prudent individuals among risky monetary options often violate the principle of expected profit maximization, and the Rev. Thomas Bayes (1763), who helped to pioneer the notion of probability as a theory of rational degrees of belief.

The theory I wish to describe is most succinctly known as expected utility theory. This is actually a family of related theories that divide into two subfamilies differentiated by the phrases (Luce and Raiffa, 1957) "decision making under risk" and "decision making under uncertainty."

The first of these pertains to decisions that yield various outcomes with known probabilities: if you choose \$2,000 outright over a 50-50 gamble between \$0 or \$5,000, you have made a decision under "risk." The second applies to the more general case in which outcomes are tied to uncertain events whose probabilities are not known: if you decide to eat a serving of mushrooms of questionable toxicity, you have made a decision under "uncertainty."

The primitive notions of a theory of expected utility are an individual's preference relation $>$ ("is preferred to") on a set of risky — or uncertain — decision alternatives. The guidelines or principles of the theory are statements about $>$ that are commonly referred to as axioms. The implications of the axioms are further statements about $>$ that are deduced from the axioms. As we shall see, some of these show how preferences correspond to a numerical structure that gives rise to an expectation operator that lies behind the name "expected utility."

A main theme of the essay is that part of the expected utility episode has yet to be written. The reason is that some of the axioms of the standard theories — due to John von Neumann and Oskar Morgenstern (1944) in the case of risk and Frank P. Ramsey (1931) and Leonard J. Savage (1954) in the case of uncertainty — have come under severe criticism as general principles of rational choice. As a consequence, more-general theories that retain some of the standard axioms but relax others to accommodate reasonable patterns of preference and choice that conflict with standard theories are being developed. It seems likely that another decade or two will pass before the shifting foundations settle.

My account of foundations adheres to the risk-uncertainty dichotomy. The next four sections focus on the risk category; the final three sections deal with uncertainty. In each part I will first review the standard theory. Examples that challenge the axioms as principles of rational choice will then be given. Finally, we shall look at new directions in the axiomatic foundations.

2. The Theory of von Neumann and Morgenstern

The standard expected utility theory of von Neumann and Morgenstern (1944) was formulated as an adjunct to their theory of games. Others soon recognized it in its own right as an important foundation for decision making under risk. Through the years it has been refined and applied to many areas of economic analysis. A thorough technical account, including extensions and generalizations, is given in Fishburn (1982a).

Abstract versions of von Neumann-Morgenstern expected utility theory, as in the original presentation and elsewhere (Herstein and Milnor, 1953; Fishburn, 1970, 1982a), apply $>$ to a set endowed with convexity-like properties. For expository purposes, it will suffice in the present section to work with a convex set P of probability distributions $p,q,\ldots$ defined on a set X of outcomes. Each $p \in P$ can be viewed as a risky alternative that yields outcome $x \in X$ with probability $p(x)$, with the $p(x)$ summing to unity.

Convexity of P means that if $p,q \in P$ and $0 \leqslant \lambda \leqslant 1$, then $\lambda p + (1-\lambda)q$ is in P. Convexity is defined pointwise so that $(\lambda p + (1-\lambda)q)(x) = \lambda p(x) + (1-\lambda)q(x)$ for all $x \in X$. If we begin with a set of distributions that is not convex, it can always be extended to a convex set in an obvious way. For interpretive purposes, the probabilities $\lambda, \lambda_1, \lambda_2, \ldots$ used in such an extension can be thought of as objective probabilities associated with a precisely calibrated random mechanism.

The standard theory uses three axioms that formalize notions of order, independence, and continuity. They apply to all $p,q,r \in P$ and all $0 < \lambda < 1$.

AXIOM A1 (order). *$>$ on P is asymmetric and negatively transitive. That is, $p > q \Rightarrow$ not $(q > p)$; $p > q \Rightarrow (p > r$ or $r > q)$.*

AXIOM A2 (independence). $[p > q,\ 0 \leqslant \lambda \leqslant 1] \Rightarrow \lambda p + (1-\lambda)r > \lambda q + (1-\lambda)r$.

AXIOM A3 (continuity). $[p > q,\ q > r] \Rightarrow [\alpha p + (1-\alpha)r > q$ *and* $q > \beta p + (1-\beta)r$ *for some α and β in $(0,1)$*].

The asymmetry part of axiom A1, $p > q \Rightarrow$ not $(q > p)$, makes it clear that $>$ stands for *strict preference*. It simply says that the individual will not both prefer p to q *and* prefer q to p, or, in the language of normative theory, that it is unreasonable or irrational to hold a definite preference for p over q and a definite preference for q over p at the same time. It leaves open the possibility that neither p nor q is preferred to the other, and in this case we write $p \sim q$ and say that the individual is *indifferent* between p and q:

$$p \sim q \Leftrightarrow \text{neither } p > q \text{ nor } q > p .$$

An operational definition of the indifference relation $\sim$ is that if $p \sim q$ and the individual must choose one or the other, then he would be quite happy to let anyone else make the choice for him. The union of $>$ and $\sim$ is denoted by $\succsim$ ("is preferred or indifferent to"), defined by

$$p \succsim q \Leftrightarrow p > q \text{ or } p \sim q .$$

Asymmetry implies that, for any distinct $p,q \in P$, exactly one of $p > q$, $q > p$ and $p \sim q$ holds, and at least one of $p \succsim q$ and $q \succsim p$ holds. In addition, if $p = q$ then $p \sim q$.

The negative transitivity part of axiom A1, $p > q \Rightarrow (p > r$ or $r > q)$, or, equivalently [not $(p > r)$ and not $(r > q)$] $\Rightarrow$ not $(p > q)$, says that if p is (strictly) preferred to q, and if r is any distribution in P, then either p is preferred to r or r is preferred to q (possibly both). In particular, given $p > q$, this rules out the combination of $r \succsim p$ *and* $q \succsim r$. It is usually held to be self-evident that any reasonable person who definitely prefers one risky alternative to a second risky alternative will either prefer the first to a third or, failing that, will surely prefer the third to the second.

It is easily proved that, given asymmetry, negative transitivity holds if and only if both $>$ and $\sim$ are *transitive*, i.e., for all $p,q,r \in P$,

$$(p > q \text{ and } q > r) \Rightarrow p > r; \quad (p \sim q \text{ and } q \sim r) \Rightarrow p \sim r .$$

Although these might be violated in several ways, the most flagrant violation occurs when preferences form a cyclic pattern, say with $p > q$, $q > r$ and $r > p$. Such a pattern is held to be irrational or foolish since it induces a money pump. If the individual presently has title to q then, since he prefers p to q, he will pay at least a small sum to exchange q for p; then, given p, he will pay something more to exchange it for the preferred r; finally, given r, he will again pay to exchange r for the preferred q. Thus, he begins and ends at q, but is poorer in the process.

Axiom A1 implies that P can be partitioned into indifference classes that are totally ordered in preference. All distributions in one class are indifferent to one another, and all in a "higher" class are preferred to all in a "lower" class. It follows that if Q is any nonempty finite subset of P, then there is at least one $q^* \in Q$ such that $q^* \gtrsim q$ for all $q \in Q$. Hence, every finite Q contains a maximally preferred distribution, thus providing an appealing basis for choice from finite subsets. If $Q = \{p_1, p_2, \ldots, p_n\}$ and A1 is violated by the preference cycle $p_1 > p_2 > \cdots > p_n > p_1$, then $>$ gives little guidance for a choice from Q. Thus A1 supplies a reasonable criterion of choice based solely on the binary relation $>$ that may be inoperative if the axiom fails.

This completes the main arguments for the acceptance of Axiom A1 as a principle of sound judgment and choice.

The usual defense of axiom A2 adopts a two-stage argument for $\lambda p + (1-\lambda)r$ and $\lambda q + (1-\lambda)r$. Probabilistically, $\lambda p + (1-\lambda)r$ is tantamount to the choice of p or r with respective probabilities λ and $1-\lambda$, followed by the choice of $x \in X$ according to the one of p and r selected in the first stage — and similarly for $\lambda q + (1-\lambda)r$. Since both distributions yield r with probability $1-\lambda$, it is held that preference between $\lambda p + (1-\lambda)r$ and $\lambda q + (1-\lambda)r$ ought to be independent of r and depend entirely on preference between p and q so long as $\lambda > 0$. Thus, if $p > q$ and $\lambda > 0$, then $\lambda p + (1-\lambda)r > \lambda q + (1-\lambda)r$.

Herstein and Milnor (1953) use a slightly different continuity axiom than axiom A3 that enables them to use the following indifference-independence axiom instead of A2:

$$p \sim q \Rightarrow (1/2)p + (1/2)r \sim (1/2)q + (1/2)r \,.$$

This can be defended by an argument like that given for A2. Neither it nor A2 appears among von Neumann and Morgenstern's own axioms. This is due to their peculiar treatment of indifference as true identity (Appendix, second edition of 1947), which subsumes axioms like $p \sim q \Rightarrow \lambda p + (1-\lambda)r \sim \lambda q + (1-\lambda)r$ under their identity relation.

Although axiom A3 might be more of a mathematical convenience than a rationality postulate, it too has a cogent rationale. In particular, since the difference between p and $\alpha p + (1-\alpha)r$ seems negligible if α is nearly 1, it is hard to imagine that $\alpha p + (1-\alpha)r$ will not be preferred to q for some $0 < \alpha < 1$ whenever p is preferred to q. A symmetric argument with β near 0 supports $q > \beta p + (1-\beta)r$ when $q > r$.

Failures of A3 might possibly arise from qualitative differences, as when

$$p = \text{win } \$2$$

$$q = \text{win } \$1$$

$$r = \text{be executed.}$$

The mathematical implications of not adopting A3 or a related continuity postulate have been examined (Hausner, 1954; Chipman, 1960; Fishburn, 1974), but I shall not discuss them here since continuity has not been a major point of contention in recent reexaminations of the foundations.

It should be evident that the axioms under discussion have very little to do with ethical issues that are often addressed by normative theory. They only provide internal consistency and coherence to systems of preferences and say nothing otherwise about what ought to be preferred or chosen. As such, they reflect the strain of scientific rationalism in the present age, but are not in conflict with most systems of ethics. For example, similar axioms of individual preferences have been used within normative theories of fairness and justice in social decision making — a topic I shall comment on briefly in section 5.

Axioms A1 through A3 have several important implications, such as monotonicity ($p \succ q$ and $\beta > \alpha \Rightarrow \beta p + (1-\beta)q \succ \alpha p + (1-\alpha)q$) and others we shall meet later, but all of these are captured in an elegant mathematical representation for $(P, \succ)$. In particular, A1 through A3 hold for $(P, \succ)$ if and only if there is a real valued function u on P such that, for all $p, q \in P$ and all $0 \leqslant \lambda \leqslant 1$,

$$p \succ q \Leftrightarrow u(p) > u(q),$$

(1) $$u(\lambda p + (1-\lambda)q) = \lambda u(p) + (1-\lambda)u(q).$$

Thus, the numerical *utility function* u preserves the preference order $\succ$ and is *linear* in convex combinations as expressed by the equation "the utility of a convex combination equals the convex combination of the utilities of its parts." Moreover, given that u has these properties, so does v on P if, and only if, there are numbers $a > 0$ and b such that, for all $p \in P$,

$$v(p) = au(p) + b.$$

Thus, von Neumann-Morgenstern utilities are unique up to the choice of scale unit and origin.

The notion of expected utility is a direct consequence of the linearity property (1). Suppose P contains every single-outcome distribution, and define u on X from u on P by

$$u(x) = u(p) \quad \text{when} \quad p(x) = 1.$$

It then follows from (1) that if $p(x) > 0$ for at most a finite number of $x \in X$, then

$$u(p) = \sum_X p(x)\, u(x),$$

i.e., the utility of a risky alternative is the expectation of the utilities of its possible outcomes. If P contains other types of distributions or probability measures, then one or more additional axioms to take care of the technical details (Blackwell and Girshick, 1954; Fishburn, 1970, 1982a) yield the more general integral form

$$u(p) = \int_X u(x)\, dp(x) \, .$$

The von Neumann-Morgenstern theory thus leads to the existence of a utility function u on outcomes that satisfies

$$p > q \Leftrightarrow \int u(x)\, dp(x) > \int u(x)\, dq(x)$$

and is supported by an appealing rationale.

3. Problems in the Foundations

Criticisms of the axioms, and experiments to test their descriptive plausibility, began to appear in the late 1940's (Preston and Baratta, 1948; Mosteller and Nogee, 1951). In the early 1950's, Allais (1953, 1979a) demonstrated systematic violations of independence, and May (1954) gave sensible reasons why transitivity might fail. For the most part, phenomena like independence violations and distortions of probabilities (Edwards, 1954) were seen as evidence against expected utility as an adequate descriptive theory of actual behavior, but not as evidence against its normative validity. Consequently, alternative descriptive-explanatory models were proposed and tested (Edwards, 1954; Slovic, 1967; Payne, 1973; Libby and Fishburn, 1977; Kahneman and Tversky, 1979) while the status of expected utility as a normative theory remained largely intact.

I believe that the latter situation is now changing, but before looking at new axiomatic proposals I shall briefly cite reasons why transitivity and independence are not inviolable normative principles. Some of these reasons are motivated by empirical evidence and illustrate the potentially fine line between descriptive and normative theory, while others seem more directly normative. I shall begin with the transitivity part of A1, then turn to A2.

Simple examples with monetary outcomes challenge the reasonableness of transitive indifference. For example, a person may be indifferent between \$367 and an even-chance gamble for \$1000 or \$0, indifferent between the gamble and \$368, yet prefer \$368 to \$367. While this could be attributed to limited discriminatory ability, I see no sense in calling it irrational or nonnormative.

More serious violations of transitivity occur when preferences cycle. The most plausible examples of cyclic preferences arise in multiple criteria situations (May, 1954; Tversky, 1969). To illustrate, suppose a person receives three employment offers with the following characteristics:

	Salary	Location	Work Quality
x:	Excellent	Satisfactory	Good
y:	Good	Excellent	Satisfactory
z:	Satisfactory	Good	Excellent

On the basis of binary comparisons he prefers x to y, y to z, and z to x. In each comparison, he prefers the offer that is better on two of the three criteria and is quite comfortable with the idea of choosing between any two according to his preferences if the third should be withdrawn. Is this irrational?

Other examples of cyclic preferences arise in connection with the phenomenon known as "preference reversals" for pairs of lotteries. This is discussed from several perspectives by Loomes and Sugden (1983), Fishburn (1985), and Slovic and Lichtenstein (1983).

What about the money pump? The first thing to be said about that is that the money pump concept envisions a dynamic situation with elements of strategy and deception that transcend the basic choice problem. It is a game that a sensible person with cyclic preferences would eschew if he knew what was involved. Thus, I do regard willing participation as a money pump as irrational, or at least naive, but see this as no reason against the admissibility of cyclic preferences in certain situations as reasonable patterns of judgment.

What, then, about the failure of $>$ to provide a clear choice when preferences cycle? Obviously, with $x > y > z > x$, there is no transparent way for our person to make a choice from $\{x,y,z\}$ on the basis of his preferences on this set. This does not, however, prevent him from considering his preferences on the set P of probability distribution on $\{x,y,z\}$ — a proposal that is very much in the spirit of decision making under risk. And, if there is a $p^* \in P$ such that $p^* \gtrsim p$ for all $p \in P$, then, from an ex ante perspective, he has a maximally preferred choice. The possibility of an axiomatic theory that implies the existence of such a p^* in cyclic-preference situations has in fact been realized, as we shall see in the next two sections.

Several people, including Allais (1953, 1979b), Morrison (1967), MacCrimmon (1968), MacCrimmon and Larsson (1979), and Kahneman and Tversky (1979), have convincingly demonstrated systematic failures of independence in simple monetary settings. The empirical fact is that the nature of r or the size of λ can make a difference in preference between $\lambda p + (1-\lambda)r$ and $\lambda q + (1-\lambda)r$, and it is hard to ignore this in assessing the normative adequacy of independence. Moreover, the standard defense of A2 (see Figure 1) may be based on an illusion created by separating $\lambda p + (1-\lambda)r$ and $\lambda q + (1-\lambda)r$ into parts. When the distributions are viewed holistically, important comparative aspects may appear that could be disguised by the two-stage separation argument. A typical example will illustrate the situation.

Let

$$p(\$300) = 1;$$

$$q(\$400) = 0.90,\ q(\$0) = 0.10;$$

$$r(\$0) = 1,$$

and consider $\lambda p + (1-\lambda)r$ versus $\lambda q + (1-\lambda)r$. When $\lambda = 1$, the choice is between \$300 and a gamble that pays \$400 with probability 0.90 (nothing otherwise). Many people prefer the sure thing and therefore have $p > q$.

As λ decreases, both distributions increase the chance of getting \$0, and preference may switch to $\lambda q + (1-\lambda)r$ at some point. For example, when $\lambda = 0.10$,

$\lambda p + (1-\lambda)r$ gives \$300 with prob. 0.10 (\$0 otherwise),

$\lambda q + (1-\lambda)r$ gives \$400 with prob. 0.09 (\$0 otherwise),

and now many people with $p > q$ will prefer $\lambda q + (1-\lambda)r$ to $\lambda p + (1-\lambda)r$ since the latter distribution has only a slightly larger probability of winning a positive amount that is substantially less than what might be won with $\lambda q + (1-\lambda)r$.

If λ is kept at 0.10 but r is changed from $r(\$0) = 1$ to $r(\$5{,}000) = 1$, then it seems likely that $\lambda p + (1-\lambda)r$ will be preferred to $\lambda q + (1-\lambda)r$.

Here is an example with the Herstein-Milnor axiom

$$p \sim q \Rightarrow 2^{-1}p + 2^{-1}r \sim 2^{-1}q + 2^{-1}r\,[\,\cdots \Rightarrow 2^{-n}p + (1-2^{-n})r \sim 2^{-n}q + (1-2^{-n})r\,]$$

that you can try on yourself. Let

$$p(\$1{,}000{,}000) = 1;$$

$$q(\$5{,}000{,}000) = \gamma,\ q(\$0) = 1-\gamma;$$

$$r(\$0) = 1.$$

First, determine a γ at which you are indifferent between p and q. Be quite sure that you would be happy to let anyone else choose from $\{p,q\}$ on your behalf at this value of γ. With γ thus determined, q is fixed. Now compare $2^{-n}p + (1-2^{-n})r$ and $2^{-n}q + (1-2^{-n})r$ for one or more values of n, say with $n = 3$ or $n = 10$. Are you indifferent between the two, or do you have a preference? If it is the latter, you violate independence.

Violations of independence, or of transitivity, are often attributed to errors in judgment or classified as inconsistencies, but for the most part I feel that this misses the point. The point is that there are certain patterns of preferences, held by reasonable people for good reasons, that simply do not agree with the axioms of expected utility theory and which suggest the need for serious reappraisal of the normative foundations of decision making under risk.

4. New Directions

Generalizations of the von Neumann-Morgenstern theory can be classified according to whether they focus on monetary outcomes or arbitrary outcomes, and by whether the numerical representation or model for preference between risky alternatives is supported by an explicit set of axioms for $>$ on P. A distinction may also be made between generalizations intended primarily as descriptive theories (Kahneman and Tversky, 1979), and those proposed as normative theories (Allais, 1979a, 1979b). However, sometimes this distinction is avoided altogether (Fishburn, 1982b, 1983a), and in other cases both descriptive and normative significance are suggested (Bell, 1982; Machina, 1982a; Chew, 1982; Loomes and Sugden, 1982).

The theories cited here fall into three of the four categories under our initial classification as follows:

money, no axioms: Allais, Bell, Loomes-Sugden, Machina;

money, axioms: Kahneman-Tversky;

arbitrary, axioms: Chew, Fishburn.

Because of the present focus on axiomatic foundations for normative theory in a general setting, I shall restrict my remarks to the final category. Two axiomatizations of $>$ on P will be noted. The first, due to Fishburn (1982b), uses neither the transitivity nor independence axioms of von Neumann and Morgenstern, yet renders utility measurable in a well-defined sense. The second, due to Chew and MacCrimmon (1979) and refined by Chew (1982) and Fishburn (1983a), restores the transitivity axiom and obtains a representation that uses two linear functions. All of the theories mentioned above avoid the implications of independence, and all except Loomes and Sugden (1982) and Fishburn (1982b) presume that $\sim$ and $>$ are transitive.

Fishburn (1982b) refers to his theory as the SSB theory because its numerical representation for preference uses a skew-symmetric bilinear (SSB) functional ϕ on $P \times P$. This means that ϕ is a real valued function that, for all $p,q,r \in P$ and all $0 \leqslant \lambda \leqslant 1$, satisfies

$$\phi(p,q) = -\phi(q,p) \quad [skew-symmetry]$$

and

$$\phi(\lambda p + (1-\lambda)q,r) = \lambda\phi(p,r) + (1-\lambda)\,\phi(q,r)\ .$$

The latter property says that ϕ is linear in its first argument. Since this and skew-symmetry imply linearity in the second argument, ϕ is *bilinear*. I shall return to ϕ shortly.

The SSB theory uses three axioms that apply to all $p,q,r \in P$ and all $0 < \lambda < 1$.

AXIOM B1 (continuity). $[p > q, q > r] \Rightarrow q \sim \alpha p + (1-\alpha)r$ *for some* α *in* $(0,1)$.

AXIOM B2 (convexity). $[p > q, p \gtrsim r] \Rightarrow p > \lambda q + (1-\lambda)r$; $[q > p, r \gtrsim p] \Rightarrow \lambda q + (1-\lambda)r > p$; $[p \sim q, p \sim r] \Rightarrow p \sim \lambda q + (1-\lambda)r$.

AXIOM B3 (symmetry). $[p > q, q > r, p > r, q \sim (1/2)p + (1/2)r] \Rightarrow [\lambda p + (1-\lambda)r \sim (1/2)p + (1/2)q \Leftrightarrow \lambda r + (1-\lambda)p \sim (1/2)r + (1/2)q]$.

Axiom B1 is similar to A3. It implies that $>$ is asymmetric, and B1 and B2 together imply that α in B1 is unique.

Axiom B2, which retains some of the flavor of independence, says that if one distribution is preferred to (less preferred than, indifferent to) each of two others, then it will be preferred to (less preferred than, indifferent to) any convex combination of those two. In other words, for each $p \in P$, $\{q \in P: p > q\}$, $\{q \in P: q > p\}$ and $\{q \in P: q \sim p\}$ are convex subsets of P. In addition, the first two parts of B2 cover the $>/\sim$ hypotheses of $[p > q,\ p \sim r]$ and $[q > p,\ r \sim p]$.

I regard B2 as a reasonable principle for preferences and am not aware of data that question its descriptive validity. However, it may be too strong for a general descriptive theory because of the fine line it presumes between preference and indifference. For example, if $p > q$ and $p \sim r$, then some people may be indifferent between p and $\lambda q + (1-\lambda)r$ when λ is near to 0.

Axiom B3 is a symmetry condition, or a principle of balance for the indifference relation. It says that if p, q, and r are ordered in preference as $p > q > r$, and if q is midway in preference between p and r in the sense that $q \sim (1/2)p + (1/2)r$, then the balanced indifference equation $\lambda p + (1-\lambda)r \sim (1/2)p + (1/2)q$ will be preserved when p and r are interchanged throughout. The conclusion of B3 is a special instance of the more general balance conclusion which says that, given $p > q > r$ and $q \sim (1/2)p + (1/2)r$, any indifference equation between convex combinations of distributions in $\{p,q,r\}$ will remain an indifference equation when p and r are interchanged throughout.

As with B2, I regard B3 as an appealing principle of rational judgment and know of no evidence that bears on its descriptive stature. It is hoped that others will consider the matter.

Fishburn (1982b) shows that B1 through B3 hold for $(P, >)$ if and only if there is an SSB functional ϕ on $P \times P$ such that, for all $p, q \in P$,

$$p > q \Leftrightarrow \phi(p,q) > 0 .$$

Thus $>$ is the subset of $P \times P$ on which ϕ is positive, and $\sim$ is the subset of $P \times P$ on which ϕ vanishes. Moreover, given ϕ as indicated, an SSB functional ϕ' on $P \times P$ satisfies the representation if, and only if, there exists $a > 0$ such that

$$\phi'(p) = a\phi(p) \quad \text{for all} \quad p \in P .$$

Consequently, SSB utilities are unique up to the choice of scale unit.

If $(P, >)$ satisfies the von Neumann-Morgenstern axioms, then B1-B3 also hold, and ϕ for the SSB representation can be separably decomposed as

$$\phi(p,q) = u(p) - u(q),$$

with u a linear utility function. This suggests that, in the more general SSB case, $\phi(p,q)$ can be thought of as a nonseparable measure of preference difference between p and q in the risky context. Loomes and Sugden (1982) use a regret-rejoicing interpretation for ϕ.

As with u, ϕ has an "expected utility" form. Suppose P contains every single-outcome distribution, and define ϕ on $X \times X$ from ϕ on $P \times P$ by

$$\phi(x,y) = \phi(p,q) \quad \text{when} \quad p(x) = q(y) = 1 .$$

If $p(x) + q(x) > 0$ for at most a finite number of $x \in X$, then bilinearity yields

$$\phi(p,q) = \sum_{x \in X} \sum_{y \in X} p(x)\, q(y)\, \phi(x,y),$$

so that $\phi(p,q)$ is the expected value of $\phi(x,y)$ under the product measure $p \times q$ on $X \times X$. This is generalized to an integral form in Fishburn (1984a).

The second new theory has slightly different axiomatizations in Chew (1982) and Fishburn (1983a). I shall follow the latter for expositional convenience since it adds only one new axiom,

B4. $\sim$ *on* P *is transitive*,

to B1-B3. Together, B1-B4 imply that $>$ too is transitive, hence that A1 holds.

The utility representation for B1-B4 is intermediate to the SSB representation and the linear representation of von Neumann and Morgenstern. Specifically, B1-B4 hold if and only if there are linear functions u and w on P with w nonnegative such that w is strictly positive if P has both maximal and minimal distributions under $>$, or if it has neither, and such that, for all $p,q \in P$,

$$p > q \Leftrightarrow u(p)\, w(q) > u(q)\, w(p) .$$

If w is strictly positive, the inequality can be written in the ratio form $u(p)/w(p) > u(q)/w(q)$, and if the "weighting function" w is constant, then the representation reduces to that of von Neumann and Morgenstern. In addition, if we define ϕ on $P \times P$ by

$$\phi(p,q) = u(p)\, w(q) - u(q)\, w(p),$$

then ϕ is an SSB functional that represents $>$ in the manner noted above. Thus, the addition of transitivity to the axioms of SSB utility theory implies that $\phi(p,q)$ is separable in p and q according to the preceding equation. Uniqueness conditions for u and w will not be detailed here: see Chew (1982) and Fishburn (1983a).

The "expected utility" form of the (u,w) representation for simple distributions is

$$p > q \Leftrightarrow \left[\sum_X p(x)\, u(x)\right] \left[\sum_X q(x)\, w(x)\right] > \left[\sum_X q(x)\, u(x)\right] \left[\sum_X p(x)\, w(x)\right] .$$

Like preceding cases, this can be extended to an integral form by the addition of a few technical axioms.

5. Applications

Significant efforts have been made to assess the potential of generalizations of expected utilit in areas of economics where the standard theory has proved useful and in areas where i explanatory power has been limited. For example, most of the authors cited in the precedin section show how their generalizations accommodate Allais-type failures of independence, an Chew (1983), Machina (1982a, 1982b), and Loomes and Sugden (1982) examine generalization of the standard theory of risk attitudes (Pratt, 1964; Arrow, 1965) and the phenomenon c simultaneous gambling and insurance-buying (Friedman and Savage, 1948). In addition, Che (1983) and Fishburn (1984a) discuss notions of stochastic dominance (Whitmore and Findla 1978), and Chew (1983), Machina (1982a) and Fishburn (1984b) consider applications of the generalizations to problems in social choice and social welfare theory.

As would be expected, the more general theories are better able than the standard theory t model certain types of economic behavior, and it appears that they lead to results similar to thos obtained from the standard theory in areas where it has been most widely used. Further researc will help to clarify the picture.

I shall conclude the present discussion of decision making under risk by noting a consequenc of the SSB theory and its application to social choice theory. Let ϕ be an SSB functional o $P \times P$ that represents $>$ by $p > q \Leftrightarrow \phi(p,q) > 0$, and let Q be a nonempty subset of P wit convex hull $H(Q) = \{\sum \lambda_i p_i : p_i \in Q$ and $\lambda_i \geqslant 0$ with $\sum \lambda_i = 1$, the sum being finite$\}$. It is the an easy consequence of the von Neumann minimax theorem that there is a $p^* \in H(Q)$ such tha $p^* \gtrsim q$ for all $q \in H(Q)$. Thus, even though the SSB theory allows preference cycles, it implie that the convex hull of every nonempty finite set of distributions contains a distribution that i preferred or indifferent to every other distribution in the hull (Fishburn, 1984a).

An application of this result to voting is suggested in Fishburn (1984b). Suppose a numbe of people vote in an election among the candidates in a finite set X, and let $\phi(x,y)$ equal th number of voters who reveal a preference for x over y, minus the number who reveal a preferenc for y over x. By definition, the plurality function ϕ on $X \times X$ is skew symmetric. Extend ϕ t the set $P \times P$, where P is the set of probability distributions on X, by defining $\phi(p,q)$ a $\sum\sum_{p}(x)\, q(y)\, \phi(x,y)$. It follows that ϕ on $P \times P$ is SSB. The result of the preceding paragrap implies that there is a $p^* \in P$ such that

$$\phi(p^*,q) \geqslant 0 \quad \text{for every } q \in P .$$

If such a p^* is used to select the winning candidate, then the election procedure satisfies both th principle of majority choice and Pareto optimality. That is, if candidate x^* has $\phi(x^*,x) > 0$ fo every $x \neq x^*$, then $p^*(x^*) = 1$. In addition, if voters order the candidates on their ballots, the $p^*(y) = 0$ if there is another candidate x such that at least one voter prefers x to y and no vote prefers y to x.

6. Subjective Expected Utility

The standard subjective expected utility model for decision making under uncertainty is composed of a probability measure ρ defined on the subsets (events) of a set S of *states* of the world and a utility function u defined on a set X of decision outcomes such that, for all functions f and g in the set F of functions from S into X,

$$f > g \Leftrightarrow \int_S u(f(s))\, d\rho(s) > \int_S u(g(s))\, d\rho(s)\,. \tag{2}$$

The states $s \in S$ describe potential realizations of things about which the decision maker is uncertain. They are formulated so that one and only one state will obtain, and, for each event $A \subset S$, $\rho(A)$ is the decision maker's personal probability — conceived of as a measure of rational degree of belief — for the proposition that some $s \in A$ will obtain. The outcomes in X are valued by the decision maker in different degrees that are reflected in the utility function u.

A function $f: S \rightarrow X$ is a potential *act* that assigns an outcome $f(s) \in X$ to each state $s \in S$. To say that act f is preferred to act g is to say that the person would rather take his chances on the state-dependent array of outcomes provided by f than on those provided by g when he is uncertain about which state will obtain. According to the standard model, f is preferred to g if, and only if, f has greater subjective expected utility than g.

The first complete $(F, >)$ axiomatization for this numerical representation of preferences in the face of uncertainty is due to Savage (1954), who drew on earlier ideas of Ramsey (1931), de Finetti (1937), and von Neumann and Morgenstern (1944). Since then, a number of other axiomatizations have been proposed (Fishburn, 1981). Here I shall comment only on Savage's theory and a related approach that has been used as a point of departure for recent generalizations.

Savage uses seven axioms for $(F, >)$. The final three axioms are an uncontroversial nontriviality condition, a continuity axiom based on finite partitions of S (which is necessarily an infinite set in his theory), and an appealing dominance principle that is used to obtain the full integral form. The first four axioms embrace his ordering and independence postulates. To state them, we need a few definitions. First, $f = g$ on A if $f(s) = g(s)$ for all $s \in A$, and $f = x$ on A if $f(s) = x$ for all $s \in A$. Second, event A is *null* if $f \sim g$ whenever $f = g$ on the complement $A^c = S \backslash A$ of A. Third, $f > g$ *given* A if $f' > g'$ whenever $f = f'$ and $g = g'$ on A, and $f' = g'$ on A^c. Finally, $x > y$ if $f > g$ when $f = x$ and $g = y$ on S. The following apply to all f, g, f', $g' \in F$, all $A, B \subseteq S$, and all $x, y, x', y' \in X$.

AXIOM P1. *$>$ on F is asymmetric and negatively transitive.*

AXIOM P2. $[f = f'$ *and* $g = g'$ *on* A; $f = g$ *and* $f' = g'$ *on* $A^c] \Rightarrow [f > g \Leftrightarrow f' > g']$.

AXIOM P3. $[A$ *is not null*; $f = x$ *and* $g = y$ *on* $A] \Rightarrow [x > y \Leftrightarrow f > g$ *given* $A]$.

AXIOM P4. $[x > y,\ x' > y'$; $f = x$ *and* $f' = x'$ *on* A, $f = y$ *and* $f' = y'$ *on* A^c; $g = x$ *and* $g' = x'$ *on* B, $g = y$ *and* $g' = y'$ *on* $B^c] \Rightarrow [f > g \Leftrightarrow f' > g']$.

Axiom P1 is similar to A1. Axiom P2, which is similar in spirit to the independence axiom A2, says that $\succ$ is independent of states in A^c that have identical outcomes for the two acts. That is, if $f \succ g$ when $f = g$ on A^c, and if f and g are modified on A^c but retain $f = g$ on A^c, then $f \succ g$ after the modification. Together, P1 and P2 imply that the conditional relation $\succ$ *given* A has the ordering properties of P1.

Axiom P3 ties $\succ$ *given* A for nonnull events to preferences between outcomes (or constant acts), thus positing a degree of similarity among conditional orders. Savage refers to the combination of P2 and P3 as his "surething principle."

The fourth axiom is used to obtain an unambiguous ordering relation $\succ^*$ ("is more probable than") over the events in S when $\succ^*$ is defined by

$$A \succ^* B \text{ if } f \succ g \text{ whenever } x \succ y,\ f = x \text{ on } A,\ g = x$$

$$\text{on } B,\ f = y \text{ on } A^c,\ g = y \text{ on } B^c .$$

Thus, $A \succ^* B$ if the person would rather take his chances on the occurrence of A than B for the preferred outcome x.

Savage's axioms imply that there is a bounded (Fishburn, 1970, Chapter 14) real valued function u on X and a probability measure ρ on the subsets of S that satisfy (2) for all $f,g \in F$. Moreover, for all $A,B \subseteq S$, ρ satisfies

$$A \succ^* B \Leftrightarrow \rho(A) > \rho(B),$$

$$0 < \lambda < 1 \Rightarrow \rho(C) = \lambda\rho(B) \quad \text{for some} \quad C \subseteq B,$$

so that ρ preserves $\succ^*$ and is continuously divisible. Moreover, ρ is unique, and u is unique up to the choice of scale unit and origin.

Because Savage's axioms imply that S is infinite, others (Anscombe and Aumann, 1963; Pratt, Raiffa, and Schlaifer, 1964; Fishburn, 1967, 1970) have developed theories for finite S that use extraneous scaling properties to construct the set P of probability distributions on X and then apply $\succ$ to the set H of functions from S into P. Each function in H is a *lottery act* that assigns a distribution or lottery in P (rather than a single outcome) to each state. A lottery act corresponds to a Savage act if each assigned distribution has probability 1 for some outcome.

To illustrate further, suppose $S = \{1, \ldots, n\}$ and let

$$H = P^n = \{\underset{\sim}{p} = (p_1, \ldots, p_n) \colon p_i \in P \text{ for each } i\} .$$

Convex combinations of lottery acts are taken statewise:

$$\lambda \underset{\sim}{p} + (1-\lambda)\underset{\sim}{q} = \lambda(p_1, \ldots, p_n) + (1-\lambda)\,(q_1, \ldots, q_n)$$

$$= (\lambda p_1 + (1-\lambda)q_1, \ldots, \lambda p_n + (1-\lambda)q_n) .$$

Because H is convex, axioms A1-A3 can be applied directly to $(H, >)$ rather than to $(P, >)$. When this is done, it follows that for each state i there is a linear function u_i on P such that, for all $\underset{\sim}{p}, \underset{\sim}{q} \in H$,

$$\underset{\sim}{p} > \underset{\sim}{q} \Leftrightarrow \sum_{i=1}^{n} u_i(p_i) > \sum_{i=1}^{n} u_i(q_i) .$$

If it is assumed also that at least one state is not null and — similar to P3 — that the ordering induced by u_i on P is the same for all nonnull i, then there are unique $\rho_i \geqslant 0$ with $\sum \rho_i = 1$ and $\rho_i = 0 \Leftrightarrow i$ is null, and linear u on P, unique except for scale unit and origin, such that, for all $\underset{\sim}{p}, \underset{\sim}{q} \in H$,

$$\underset{\sim}{p} > \underset{\sim}{q} \Leftrightarrow \sum_{i=1}^{n} \rho_i u(p_i) > \sum_{i=1}^{n} \rho_i u(q_i) .$$

When $p_i(x_i) = q_i(y_i) = 1$ for all i, this reduces to the finite version of (2):

$$(x_1, \ldots, x_n) > (y_1, \ldots, y_n) \Leftrightarrow \sum \rho_i u(x_i) > \sum \rho_i u(y_i) .$$

Again, because H is convex, the SSB axioms B1-B3 of section 4 can be applied to $(H, >)$. I shall comment on this in section 8.

7. More Problems in the Foundations

Savage's (1954) proof that (2) follows from his axioms first obtains ρ on events and then uses ρ to construct probability distributions on X that correspond to acts that map S into finite subsets of X. The natural definition of $>$ on these distributions is then shown to satisfy the von Neumann-Morgenstern axioms, and this leads to (2) for such acts. Because of this and the direct use of lottery acts in the finite-states approach, the theories of the preceding section are vulnerable to the criticisms in section 3 of the von Neumann-Morgenstern axioms.

For example, an Allais-type challenge to Savage's independence axiom P2 imagines that S is partitioned into three events, A, B, and C, with $\rho(A)$, $\rho(B)$, and $\rho(C)$ equal respectively to approximately 0.01, 0.09, and 0.90. Outcomes are increments to wealth, and four acts are proposed:

	A	B	C
f:	\$1,000,000	\$1,000,000	\$1,000,000
g:	0	\$5,000,000	\$1,000,000
f':	\$1,000,000	\$1,000,000	0
g':	0	\$5,000,000	0

It is observed that many people have $f > g$ and $g' > f'$, which contradicts P2 when A used there is taken as $A \cup B$ in the present example.

A different criticism of independence among states that depends on a preference for relative specificity, or against ambiguity, is offered by Ellsberg (1961). Suppose an urn contains 30 red balls and 60 others that are solid black and solid yellow in unknown proportion. One ball is to be chosen at random. Four acts are envisioned:

f: win \$1000 if red is chosen (nothing otherwise);

g: win \$1000 if black is chosen;

f': win \$1000 if red or yellow is chosen;

g': win \$1000 if black or yellow is chosen.

Again, many people have $f > g$ and $g' > f'$. In the first comparison, a third of the 90 balls are known to be red; in the second, two-thirds of the 90 are known to be black or yellow. If $p(r)$, $p(b)$ and $p(y)$ are the respective probabilities for drawing the three colors, then the standard model gives $p(r) > p(b)$ on the basis of $f > g$, and $p(b) + p(y) > p(r) + p(y)$, or $p(b) > p(r)$, on the basis of $g' > f'$.

A simplified and rearranged version of the preceding example is more explicit in identifying the states according to the unknown composition of the urn. Suppose there are just three balls. One is red and the other two are black and yellow in unknown proportion; i.e., either both are black (bb = state 1), or one is black and the other is yellow (by = state 2), or both are yellow (yy = state 3). Again, one ball is to be drawn at random. The probabilities of winning the \$1,000 prize for the four acts in the preceding paragraph are shown as follows for each state:

	1(bb)	2(by)	3(yy)
f:	1/3	1/3	1/3
g:	2/3	1/3	0
f':	1/3	2/3	1
g':	2/3	2/3	2/3

If the decision maker prefers the acts with equal chances for the prize under each state to their variable-chance counterparts, then $f > g$ and $g' > f'$, and when this is so it violates the standard model of subjective probability since that model has $f > g \Rightarrow \rho(yy) > \rho(bb)$, whereas $g' > f' \Rightarrow \rho(bb) > \rho(yy)$.

8. More New Directions

There are presently about four approaches being followed (see Fishburn, 1981, for earlier work) that generalize standard theories of subjective expected utility to accommodate violations of independence. All, except a version by Luce and Narens (1985), apply $>$ to the n-state set $H = P^n$ of lottery acts discussed in section 6.

The first, by Loomes and Sugden (1982) and Bell (1982), proposes the representation

$$\underset{\sim}{p} > \underset{\sim}{q} \Leftrightarrow \sum_{i=1}^{n} \rho_i \phi^* (p_i, q_i) > 0,$$

where the ρ_i are state probabilities and ϕ^* is an SSB functional on $P \times P$. Bell, and Loomes and Sugden, do not axiomatize this representation but discuss its logic in detail for the monetary-outcomes setting.

The second, by Fishburn (1984c), applies the SSB axioms B1-B3 of section 4 to $(H, >)$ to obtain

$$\phi(\underset{\sim}{p}, \underset{\sim}{q}) = \sum_{i,j} \phi_{ij} (p_i, q_j),$$

where each ϕ_{ij} is bilinear and $\phi_{ij}(p,q) = -\phi_{ji}(q,p)$ for all $i,j \in S$ and all $p,q \in P$. Effects of within-state and between states consistency axioms are examined. The paper concludes with axioms that are necessary and sufficient for the model of Bell and Loomes-Sugden, i.e., for

$$\phi(\underset{\sim}{p}, \underset{\sim}{q}) = \sum_{i=1}^{n} \rho_i \phi^* (p_i, q_i) .$$

Three axioms besides B1-B3 are used for this. The first says that $>$ on P within state i (a fixed distribution in all other states) is the same for each nonnull i. The second says that some state is not null, and the third is a weak between-states independence axiom.

The preceding work admits nontransitive preferences and accommodates within-state violations of independence. However, its ability to incorporate Ellsberg-type violations of independence is limited (but see Fishburn, 1983b). For example, the preferences in the examples of the preceding section are inconsistent with the Loomes-Sugden model.

A third recent generalization, by Schmeidler (1984) [see also Gilboa (1985)], retains more of the von Neumann-Morgenstern utility structure — it reduces to their theory when $S = \{1\}$ — but weakens subjective probability to a nonadditive form that is more consistent with Ellsberg-type violations of independence. Schmeidler uses the von Neumann-Morgenstern ordering and continuity axioms A1 and A3 for $(H, >)$ along with a consistency principle like Savage's P3 for similar conditional orders for events. He weakens the independence axiom A2 to apply only to lottery acts $\underset{\sim}{p}$, $\underset{\sim}{q}$, and $\underset{\sim}{r}$ that are pairwise comonotonic: $\underset{\sim}{p}$ and $\underset{\sim}{q}$ are *comonotonic* if, for all $i,j \in S$, not $[p_i > p_j$ and $q_j > q_i]$, where $>$ on P is defined in the natural way from preferences between constant lottery acts in H. These four axioms imply the existence of a linear function u on P and a monotonic but not necessarily additive set function ρ^* on events in S such that, for all $\underset{\sim}{p}$, $\underset{\sim}{q} \in H$,

$$\underset{\sim}{p} > \underset{\sim}{q} \Leftrightarrow E^*(u,\underset{\sim}{p};\rho^*) > E^*(u,\underset{\sim}{q};\rho^*),$$

where

$$E^*(u,\underset{\sim}{p};\rho^*) = \sum_{j=1}^{m-1} (\alpha_j - \alpha_{j+1})\rho^* \left(\bigcup_{k=1}^{j} A_k\right) + \alpha_m \rho^*(S)$$

when $\{A_1, \ldots, A_m\}$ is a partition of S and $u(p_i) = \alpha_j$ for all $i \in A_j$ with $\alpha_1 > \ldots > \alpha_m$. If A2 holds completely on H, then ρ^* is additive and we get $\underset{\sim}{p} > \underset{\sim}{q} \Leftrightarrow \sum \rho_i^* u(p_i) > \sum \rho_i^* u(q_i)$.

It should be mentioned that Schmeidler allows S to be infinite, so his results are slightly more general than I have suggested and they provide a basis for extending the nonadditive expectation operator E^* to lottery acts with an infinite number of u values.

A fourth generalization of subjective expected utility, in Fishburn (1986), retains some of the aspects of Fishburn's SSB approach cited above and uses two sets of state parameters. One set is like ordinary state probabilities; the other is designed to accommodate aversion to uncertainty as it arises in Ellsberg's work (1961). A special case of this model is similar to Schmeidler's model.

The recent developments summarized here indicate new directions for normative theories of decision making under uncertainty. I believe that they constitute a nice beginning, but would submit that the greater part of the effort lies ahead.

References

Allais, M. "Le comportement de l'homme rationnel devant le risque: critique des postulats et axiomes de l'ecole Americaine." *Econometrica* 21 (1953), pp. 503-546.

Allais, M. "The Foundations of a Positive Theory of Choice Involving Risk and a Criticism of the Postulates and Axioms of the American School (1952)." In *Expected Utility Hypotheses and the Allais Paradox*, ed. by M. Allais and O. Hagen. Dordrecht, Holland: Reidel, 1979, pp 27-145. a.

Allais, M. "The So-Called Allais Paradox and Rational Decisions Under Uncertainty." In *Expected Utility Hypothesis Utility and the Allais Paradox*, ed. by M. Allais and O. Hagen Dordrecht, Holland: Reidel, 1979, pp. 437-681. b.

Anscombe, F. J., and Aumann, R. J. "A Definition of Subjective Probability." *Annals of Mathematical Statistics* 34 (1963), pp. 199-205.

Arrow, K. J. *Aspects of the Theory of Risk Bearing.* Helsinki: Yrjö Jahssonin Säätiö, 1965.

Bayes, T. "An Essay Towards Solving a Problem in the Doctrine of Chances." *Philosophical Transactions of the Royal Society* 53 (1763), pp. 370-418. Reprinted with comments by E. C

Molina in *Facsimiles of Two Papers of Bayes.* Washington, D.C.: The Graduate School, Department of Agriculture, 1940.

Bell, D. E. "Regret in Decision Making Under Uncertainty." *Operations Research* 30 (1982), pp. 961-981.

Bernoulli, D. "Specimen theoriae novae de mensura sortis." *Commentarii Academiae Scientiarum Imperialis Petropolitanae* 5 (1738), pp. 175-192. Translated by L. Sommer, *Econometrica* 22 (1954), pp. 23-36.

Blackwell, D., and Girshick, M. A. *Theory of Games and Statistical Decisions.* New York: Wiley, 1954.

Chew, S. H. "A Mixture Set Axiomatization of Weighted Utility Theory." College of Business & Public Administration Discussion Paper 82-4, University of Arizona, 1982.

Chew, S. H. "A Generalization of the Quasilinear Mean with Applications to the Measurement of Income Inequality and Decision Theory Resolving the Allais Paradox." *Econometrica* 51 (1983), pp. 1065-1092.

Chew, S. H., and MacCrimmon, K. R. "Alpha-Nu Choice Theory: A Generalization of Expected Utility Theory." Faculty of Commerce and Business Administration Working Paper 669, University of British Columbia, 1979.

Chipman, J. S. "The Foundations of Utility." *Econometrica* 28 (1960), pp. 193-224.

de Finetti, B. "La prévision ses lois logiques, ses sources subjectives." *Annals de l'Institut Henri Poincaré* 7 (1937), pp. 1-68. Translated by H. E. Kyburg in *Studies in Subjective Probability*, ed. by H. E. Kyburg and H. E. Smokler. New York: Wiley, 1964.

Edwards, W. "The Theory of Decision Making." *Psychological Bulletin* 51 (1954), pp. 380-417.

Ellsberg, D. "Risk, Ambiguity, and the Savage Axioms." *Quarterly Journal of Economics* 75 (1961), pp. 643-669.

Fishburn, P. C. "Preference-Based Definitions of Subjective Probability." *Annals of Mathematical Statistics* 38 (1967), pp. 1605-1617.

Fishburn, P. C. *Utility Theory for Decision Making.* New York: Wiley, 1970.

Fishburn, P. C. "Lexicographic Orders, Utilities, and Decision Rules: A Survey." *Management Science* 20 (1974), pp. 1442-1471.

Fishburn, P. C. "Subjective Expected Utility: A Review of Normative Theories." *Theory and Decision* 13 (1981), pp. 139-199.

Fishburn, P. C. *The Foundations of Expected Utility.* Dordrecht, Holland: Reidel, 1982. a.

Fishburn, P. C. "Nontransitive Measurable Utility." *Journal of Mathematical Psychology* 26 (1982), pp. 31-67. b.

Fishburn, P. C. "Transitive Measurable Utility." *Journal of Economic Theory* 31 (1983), pp. 293-317. a.

Fishburn, P. C. "Ellsberg Revisited: A New Look at Comparative Probability." *Annals of Statistics* 11 (1983), pp. 1047-1059. b.

Fishburn, P. C. "Dominance in SSB Utility Theory." *Journal of Economic Theory* 34 (1984), pp. 130-148. a.

Fishburn, P. C. "Probabilistic Social Choice Based on Simple Voting Comparisons." *Review of Economic Studies* 51 (1984), pp. 683-692. b.

Fishburn, P. C. "SSB Utility Theory and Decision-Making under Uncertainty." *Mathematical Social Sciences* 8 (1984), pp. 253-285. c.

Fishburn, P. C. "Nontransitive Preference Theory and the Preference Reversal Phenomenon." *International Review of Economics and Business* 32 (1985), pp. 39-50.

Fishburn, P. C. "Uncertainty Aversion and Separated Effects in Decision Making under Uncertainty." Unpublished manuscript (1986).

Friedman, M., and Savage, L. J. "The Utility Analysis of Choices Involving Risk." *Journal of Political Economy* 56 (1948), pp. 279-304.

Gilboa, I. "Expected Utility with Purely Subjective Non-Additive Probabilities." Working Paper 6-85, Foerder Institute for Economic Research, Tel-Aviv University, 1985.

Hausner, M. "Multidimensional Utilities." In *Decision Processes*, ed. by R. M. Thrall, C. H. Coombs, and R. L. Davis. New York: Wiley, 1954, pp. 167-180.

Herstein, I. N., and Milnor, J. "An Axiomatic Approach to Measurable Utility." *Econometrica* 21 (1953), pp. 291-297.

Kahneman, D., and Tversky, A. "Prospect Theory: An Analysis of Decision Under Risk." *Econometrica* 47 (1979), pp. 263-291.

Libby, R., and Fishburn, P. C. "Behavioral Models of Risk Taking in Business Decisions: A Survey and Evaluation." *Journal of Accounting Research* 15 (1977), pp. 272-292.

Loomes, G., and Sugden, R. "Regret Theory: An Alternative Theory of Rational Choice Under Uncertainty." *Economic Journal* 92 (1982), pp. 805-824.

Loomes, G., and Sugden, R. "A Rationale for Preference Reversal." *American Economic Review* 73 (1983), pp. 428-432.

Luce, R. D., and Narens, L. "Classification of Concatenation Measurement Structures According to Scale Type." *Journal of Mathematical Psychology* 29 (1985), pp. 1-72.

Luce, R. D., and Raiffa, H. *Games and Decisions*. New York: Wiley, 1957.

MacCrimmon, K. R. "Descriptive and Normative Implications of the Decision-Theory Postulates." In *Risk and Uncertainty*, ed. by K. Borch and J. Mossin. New York: Macmillan, 1968, pp. 3-32.

MacCrimmon, K. R., and Larsson, S. "Utility Theory: Axioms versus 'Paradoxes'." In *Expected Utility Hypotheses and the Allais Paradox*, ed. by M. Allais and O. Hagen. Dordrecht, Holland: Reidel, 1979, pp. 333-409.

Machina, M. J. "'Expected Utility' Analysis Without the Independence Axiom." *Econometrica* 50 (1982), pp. 277-323. a.

Machina, M. J. "A Stronger Characterization of Declining Risk Aversion." *Econometrica* 50 (1982), pp. 1069-1079. b.

May, K. O. "Intransitivity, Utility, and the Aggregation of Preference Patterns." *Econometrica* 22 (1954), pp. 1-13.

Morrison, D. G. "On the Consistency of Preferences in Allais' Paradox." *Behavioral Science* 12 (1967), pp. 373-383.

Mosteller, F., and Nogee, P. "An Experimental Measure of Utility." *Journal of Political Economy* 59 (1951), pp. 371-404.

Payne, J. W. "Alternative Approaches to Decision Making Under Risk: Moments versus Risk Dimensions." *Psychological Bulletin* 80 (1973), pp. 439-453.

Pratt, J. W. "Risk Aversion in the Small and in the Large." *Econometrica* 32 (1964), pp. 122-136.

Pratt, J. W., Raiffa, H., and Schlaifer, R. "The Foundations of Decision Under Uncertainty: An Elementary Exposition." *Journal of the American Statistical Association* 59 (1964), pp. 353-375.

Preston, M. G., and Baratta, P. "An Experimental Study of the Auction-Value of an Uncertain Outcome." *American Journal of Psychology* 61 (1948), pp. 183-193.

Ramsey, F. P. "Truth and Probability." In *The Foundations of Mathematics and Other Logical Essays*, by F. P. Ramsey. New York: Harcourt, Brace, 1931. Reprinted in *Studies in Subjective Probability*, ed. by H. E. Kyburg and H. E. Smokler. New York: Wiley, 1964, pp. 61-92.

Savage, L. J. *The Foundations of Statistics*. New York: Wiley, 1954. Second revised edition, Dover, 1972.

Schmeidler, D. "Subjective Probability and Expected Utility Without Additivity." Preprint #84, The Institute for Mathematics and its Applications, University of Minnesota, 1984.

Slovic, P. "The Relative Influence of Probabilities and Payoffs upon Perceived Risk of a Gamble." *Psychonomic Science* 9 (1967), pp. 223-224.

Slovic, P., and Lichtenstein, S. "Preference Reversals: A Broader Perspective." *American Economic Review* 73 (1983), pp. 596-605.

Tversky, A. "Intransitivity of Preferences." *Psychological Review* 76 (1969), pp. 31-48.

von Neumann, J., and Morgenstern, O. *Theory of Games and Economic Behavior*. Princeton: Princeton University Press, 1944. Second edition, 1947; third edition, 1953.

Whitmore, G. A., and Findlay, M. C. (eds.). *Stochastic Dominance*. Lexington, Massachusetts: D. C. Heath, 1978.

PARTIAL STRUCTURES OF PREFERENCE

Jean-Paul Doignon
Université Libre de Bruxelles
c.p. 216
Bd du Triomphe
1050 Bruxelles - Belgium

Abstract. Interval orders and semiorders are models of preference structures involving a discrimination threshold. Recently two kinds of generalizations were described: one leads to the corresponding partial structures, the other covers the case of multiple levels of preference. Here the two extensions are combined. Numerical representations of the ensuing structures are derived from a general result on directed weighted multiple graphs.

1. Interval orders and semiorders.

Suppose that we want to encode the preferences of an individual with respect to some given set of actions or objects. For the present time, we consider that among two objects a and b, either one is prefered to the other, or they are indifferent, or they are incomparable; in particular no strength of preference is taken into account. The corresponding mathematical formulation is as follows; the objects form a set X, that we will assume finite, and the preferences are collected into a (binary) relation P on X. Indifferent pairs form the relation I on X. In many cases, P will be asymmetric and I will be *reflexive* and *symmetric*. (*For relation terminology*, we generally follow Roberts, 1979; however, we denote by RS the product of the relations R and S.) We are interested in particular models of triples (X,P,I) that enjoy nice properties. Such a structure is said to be *complete* when the relation $P \cup I$ is complete (strongly complete in Roberts, 1979), that is $x(P \cup I)y$ or $y(P \cup I)x$ for all x, y in X; thus no pair of objects are incomparable. Otherwise it is a *partial* structure.

This work is partially supported by NSF grant IST84-18860 to J.-Cl. Falmagne at New York University.

The easiest model is that of a *weak order*. It is described by the following (numerical) representation: there exists a real-valued mapping f on X such that:

$$xPy \Leftrightarrow f(x) > f(y),$$
$$xIy \Leftrightarrow f(x) = f(y).$$

This is known to be equivalent to : P is transitive, $P \cap I = \emptyset$ (the empty set), I is reflexive, symmetric and transitive, and $P \cup I$ is complete. The transitiveness of the indifference was questioned by psychologists (see e.g. Roberts, 1979, for historical examples and references). This led Luce (1956) to modify the weak order model as follows. When the subject compares two objects x and y, he may judge these as equivalent because their associated *utility values* f(x) and f(y) are to close each to the other; in other words, he will discriminate between the objects only when their utilities will fall enough apart. Luce formalized this by considering a *threshold value* . This can be taken as dependent on the object, or as having a constant value. Relations having the resulting representations were characterized respectively by Scott and Suppes (1958), and Fishburn (1970); we recall their results.

PROPOSITION 1. Let P and I be relations on the same finite set X. There exist a real-valued function f on X and a non-negative real number r such that

(1) $xPy \Leftrightarrow f(x) > f(y) + r$, and

(2) $xIy \Leftrightarrow |f(x) - f(y)| \leq r$,

if and only if

(3) $aPb, cPd \Rightarrow aPd$ or cPb,

(4) $aPb, bPd \Rightarrow aPc$ or cPd,

(5) $P \cap I = \emptyset$,

(6) I is reflexive and symmetric, and

(7) $P \cup I$ is complete.

PROPOSITION 2. Let P and I be relations on the same finite set X. There exist real-valued functions f and t on X such that

(1) $t(x) \geq 0$,

(2) $xPy \Leftrightarrow f(x) > f(y) + t(y)$, and

(3) $xIy \Leftrightarrow -t(x) \leq f(x) - f(y) \leq t(y)$

if and only if

(4) $aPb, cPd \Rightarrow aPd$ or cPb,

(5) $P \cap I = \emptyset$,

(6) I is reflexive and symmetric, and

(7) $P \cup I$ is complete.

Pairs of relations satisfying the first proposition are called *semiorders*, those satisfying the second proposition *interval orders*. In the original formulation of these propositions, only the relation P was used; since $I = (X \times X) - (P \cup P^{-1})$, the present statements are easily derived.

In both types of relations, intransitiveness of I can hold. This was the motivation for introducing the models in the study of preference relations. In fact, it appears now that interval orders constitute a particular case of another type of relations, namely the so-called Guttman scales (see e.g. Guttman, 1944, or Ducamp and Falmagne, 1969; for more recent references, see Doignon, Monjardet, Roubens, and Vincke, 1986). Moreover, interval orders were yet studied by Wiener (1914).

When the representations of interval orders and semiorders are stated in terms of P and I, they have extensions to partial structures. These extensions are respectively due to Roy (1980), and Roubens and Vincke (1984). (The presentation given here is slightly different; compare with Doignon, Ducamp and Falmagne, 1987.) It is enlighting to first reformulate parts of Propositions 1 and 2 (see Roubens and Vincke, 1985). By a *cycle* of a relation R, we mean any set of pairs of the form

$$x_1x_2,\ x_2x_3,\ \dots,\ x_px_1 \in R,$$

where $p \geq 1$ (thus a loop is a cycle). An *acyclic* relation is a relation having no cycle. A cycle is *simple* if it never uses twice the same pair x_kx_{k+1} (here and later on, the subindices are to be taken modulo the length of the cycle).

LEMMA 1. Let P and I be relations on the same finite set X, such that conditions (5), (6), and (7) in Proposition 1 are satisfied. Then the conjunction of conditions (3) and (4) in Proposition 1 is equivalent to:

(1) in any cycle of the relation $P \cup I$, there are more pairs from I than from P.

Proof. Since by conditions (5) and (6) xIy implies (not yPx), conditions (3) and (4) have as direct consequences

(3') $PIP \subset P$,

(4') $PPI \subset P$,

from which easily follows the present assertion (1). Reciprocally, assume aPb, cPd, and (not aPd). Then by conditions (7) and (6) $d(P \cup I)a$ holds, and, by our assumption (1), it follows that neither bPc

nor bIc can hold. Thus cPb is true, and we have established condition (3) in Proposition 1. Now assume aPb, bPd, and (not aPc). Thus $c(P \cup I)a$, and we cannot have neither dPc nor dIc. This implies cPd, and (4) is established. □

LEMMA 2. _Let_ P _and_ I _be relations on the same finite set_ X _such that conditions_ (5), (6) _and_ (7) _in Proposition_ 2 _are satisfied. Then the condition_ (4) _in Proposition_ 2 _is equivalent to_:

(1) _the relation_ PI is _acyclic_.

Proof. As in the preceding proof, we have $PIP \subset P$, and the acyclicity of PI follows. The reciprocal part is left to the reader. □

We now turn to the promised generalizations of Propositions 1 and 2.

PROPOSITION 3. _Let_ P _and_ I _be relations on the same finite set_ X _with_ I _reflexive. There exist a real-valued function_ f _on_ X _and a non-negative real number_ r _such that_

(1) $xPy \Rightarrow f(x) > f(y) + r$, _and_

(2) $xIy \Rightarrow f(x) - f(y) \leq r$,

if and only if

(3) _in any cycle of the relation_ $P \cup I^{-1}$, _there are more pairs taken in_ I^{-1} _than in_ P.

PROPOSITION 4. _Let_ P _and_ I _be relations on the same finite set_ X, _with_ I _reflexive. There exist real-valued functions_ f _and_ t _on_ X _such that_

(1) $t(x) \geq 0$,

(2) $xPy \Rightarrow f(x) > f(y) + t(y)$, _and_

(3) $xIy \Rightarrow f(x) - f(y) \leq t(y)$,

if and only if

(4) _the relation_ PI^{-1} _is acyclic_.

That Propositions 1 and 2 respectively follow from Propositions 3 and 4 is easily seen. For instance, assume conditions (3) to (7) in Proposition 1 are true. Thanks to Lemma 1, we may apply Proposition 3 and derive the existence of mappings f and t. On the other hand, exactly one of xPy, yPx, and xIy holds for any elements x, y. This entails that the implications (1) and (2) in Proposition 3 must be equivalences. Using the symmetry of I, one obtains conditions (1) and (2) in Proposition 1.

A common generalization of Propositions 3 and 4 will be stated and proved in section 4. All our proofs will be based on an easy extension of a classical result in graph theory. For the reader's convenience, we show in the next section how to establish Propositions 3 and 4 using this result.

2. A result in graph theory.

The following proposition extends a classical theorem on weighted directed graphs. The theorem obtains when $E_2 = E'_2 = E_3 = E'_3 = \ldots = E_n = E'_n = \emptyset$, and in fact could be used to establish the proposition. We prefer to give a proof which is independent, although inspired, from a proof of the classical theorem.

Let us first fix some terminology. By a *(weighted directed oddly-multiple) graph*, we mean a finite set X of *vertices*, provided with subsets $E_0, E_1, E'_1, E_2, E'_2, \ldots, E_n, E'_n$ of $X \times X$ (formed by *edges*), and a real-valued mapping w on $E \equiv E_0 \cup E_1 \cup E'_1 \cup E_2 \cup E'_2 \cup \ldots \cup E_n \cup E'_n$. If xy is an edge (we write xy for the pair (x,y)), then $w(xy)$ is the *weight* of that edge. For a graph $(X, E_0, E_1, E'_1, E_2, E'_2, \ldots, E_n, E'_n, w)$, we define a *path* as any set of edges of the form

$$x_1x_2,\ x_2x_3,\ \ldots,\ x_qx_{q+1},$$

where $q \geq 1$, each edge being taken in $E_0, E_1, E'_1, E_2, E'_2, \ldots, E_n$, or E'_n. This path is *simple* if it never takes the same edge in the same $E_0, E_1, E'_1, E_2, E'_2, \ldots, E_n$, or E'_n. It is a <u>cycle</u> when $x_{q+1} = x_1$ (we then consider subindices modulo q).

PROPOSITION 5. <u>The following two assertions are equivalent for any graph</u> $(X, E_0, E_1, E'_1, E_2, E'_2, \ldots, E_n, E'_n, w)$:

(i) <u>there exist real-valued mappings</u> $f, g_1, g_2, \ldots, g_n$ <u>on</u> X <u>such that for</u> $i = 1, 2, \ldots, n$

(1) $xy \in E_0 \Rightarrow f(x) \geq f(y) + w(xy)$,

(2) $xy \in E_i \Rightarrow f(x) \geq g_i(y) + w(xy)$, <u>and</u>

(3) $xy \in E'_i \Rightarrow g_i(x) \geq f(y) + w(xy)$;

(ii) <u>for any cycle</u> $x_1x_2, x_2x_3, \ldots, x_px_1$ <u>such that for</u> $k = 1, 2, \ldots,$

p <u>and</u> $i = 1, 2, \ldots, n$

(4) $x_k x_{k+1}$ <u>is taken in</u> E_i <u>iff</u> $x_{k+1}x_{k+2}$ <u>is taken in</u> E'_i

<u>the following holds</u>:

(5) $\Sigma_k \ w(x_k x_{k+1}) \leq 0$.

Proof. (i) Assume the mappings $f, g_1, g_2, \ldots, g_n$ do exist. Then given a cycle as in (ii), we write for each edge $x_k x_{k+1}$ the corresponding inequality (1), (2), or (3), depending on whether $x_k x_{k+1}$ was taken in E_0, E_i, or E'_i. We then add all these inequalities up. The assumption (4) implies that all values $f(x_k)$ appear on both sides of the resulting inequality. The same remark applies to the values $g_i(x_k)$. Thus the simplified inequality is exactly what we had to prove.

(ii) Assume (ii) is true. In order to define $f(x)$, consider all paths

$$x_1x_2,\ x_2x_3,\ \ldots,\ x_qx_{q+1} \in E$$

with $x = x_1$, x_1x_2 not taken in any E'_i, and for any $k = 1, 2, \ldots, q-1$ and any $j = 1, 2, \ldots, n$:

$x_k x_{k+1}$ is taken in E_j iff $x_{k+1}x_{k+2}$ is taken in E'_j .

The weight of such a path is, by convention, equal to

$$\Sigma_k \ w(x_k x_{k+1}) .$$

As a consequence of (ii)(5), if two edges $x_k x_{k+1}$ and $x_\ell x_{\ell+1}$ with $k < \ell$ of such a path are taken in the same E_h or E'_j and coincide, the shortened path

$$x_1x_2,\ x_2x_3,\ \ldots,\ x_kx_{k+1},\ x_{\ell+1}x_{\ell+2},\ \ldots,\ x_qx_{q+1}$$

has a weight not less than the original path. Thus if we look for the maximum weight of all these paths starting at $x = x_1$, we need only consider those paths without edges repeatedly taken in the same E_h or E'_j; and these paths are finite in number. If there exists some such path starting at x, the maximum weight is thus a real number, and we set $f(x)$ equal to it. If no such path starts at x, we set $f(x)$ equal to zero. It follows immediately

$$xy \in E_0 \quad \Rightarrow \quad f(x) \geq f(y) + w(xy).$$

Now in order to define $g_i(x)$, consider all paths

$$x_1x_2,\ x_2x_3,\ \ldots,\ x_qx_{q+1} \in E$$

with $x = x_1$, $x_1x_2 \in E'_i$, and such that for any $k = 1, 2, \ldots, q-1$ and any $j = 1, 2, \ldots, n$:

$x_k x_{k+1}$ is taken in E_j iff $x_{k+1}x_{k+2}$ is taken in E'_j.

As above, the maximum weight of such paths is a real number. We set $g_i(x)$ equal to this maximum, in case at least one path exists; otherwise, $g_i(x) = 0$. Then one derives from the definitions of f and g_i that the conditions (2) and (3) hold. Hence (i) is proved. □

REMARK. In condition (ii) of Proposition 5, one can substitute "any simple cycle" for "any cycle". The modified statement will sometimes be used in the sequel.

We shall now establish Propositions 3 and 4 using particular cases of Proposition 5. This approach is not the original one; in the case of semiorders, it appears to be due to Roy (as reported by Vincke), and the proof given here for partial semiorders is the same as in Roubens and Vincke (1985).

Proof of Proposition 3. (i) When f and r are given satisfying (1) and (2), there are only a finite number of values of f, and we can find a positive real number ε such that

$$xPy \quad \Rightarrow \quad f(x) \geq f(y) + r + \varepsilon, \qquad \text{and}$$
$$xI^{-1}y \quad \Rightarrow \quad f(x) \geq f(y) - r.$$

Define a graph on X by introducing an edge xy of weight

$$r + \varepsilon \qquad \text{whenever} \qquad xPy,$$
$$-r \qquad \text{whenever} \qquad xI^{-1}y.$$

We use Proposition 5 in the case $E_0 = E$. Since f is a mapping as in condition (1) of that proposition, we know that any cycle of the graph has non-positive weight. If C is a cycle of the relation $P \cup I^{-1}$, and if we denote by $|P|_C$ and by $|I^{-1}|_C$ respectively the number of its pairs taken in P and I^{-1}, we thus have

$$(r + \varepsilon)\ |P|_C \ + \ (-r)\ |I^{-1}|_C \ \leq \ 0,$$

from which follows condition (3) in Proposition 3. Conversely, if (3) is satisfied, we first choose any positive real number r, and then any positive real number ε such that

$$\varepsilon\ |P|_C \ \leq \ r\ (\ |I^{-1}|_C \ - \ |P|_C\ )$$

for any simple cycle C. Defining the same graph as above, this last condition ensures that the weight of any cycle of this graph is non-positive. We then derive from Proposition 5 the existence of the real-valued mapping f satisfying conditions (1) and (2). □

Proof of Proposition 4. Given f and t as in conditions (1), (2), (3), first choose a positive real number ε such that

$$f(x) \geq f(y) + t(y) + \varepsilon$$

whenever xPy. Setting $g(y) = f(y) + t(y)$, we see that conditions (2) and (3) imply

$$xPy \Rightarrow f(x) \geq g(y) + \varepsilon, \text{ and}$$
$$xI^{-1}y \Rightarrow g(x) \geq f(y).$$

Now define on X two edge sets E_1 and E'_1, and a weight mapping w by

$$xy \in E_1 \text{ with weight } \varepsilon \qquad \text{whenever } xPy,$$
$$xy \in E'_1 \text{ with weight } 0 \qquad \text{whenever } xI^{-1}y.$$

Applying Proposition 5 with $E = E_1 \cup E'_1$, we obtain the acyclicity of the relation PI^{-1}. For the converse, one can use the same graph, having taken for ε any positive real number. □

3. Multiple thresholds.

In section 1, we have described semiorders and interval orders, and their partial counterparts. In all these four models, the preferences are treated in a homogeneous manner, since they are encoded in a single relation. There are practical situations in which one must distinguish between several levels of preference (for references to various motivations, see Cozzens and Roberts, 1982, and Doignon, 1986). Therefore Cozzens and Roberts (1982) characterized those pairs of relations P_1 and P_2 on a finite set X for which the following is true: there exist a real-valued mapping f and two non-negative real numbers r_1 and r_2 such that

$$xP_1y \Leftrightarrow f(x) > f(y) + r_1,$$
$$xP_2y \Leftrightarrow f(x) > f(y) + r_2.$$

(see also Roy and Vincke, 1987). Thus each of P_1 and P_2 possesses a representation as in Proposition 1(1). Moreover, the two representations use the same utility function f. An extension of this result to any finite family of relations appear in Doignon (1986). Also, the thresholds need not be constant, that is there could be in the family a third relation Q_1 described by

$$xQ_1y \Leftrightarrow f(x) > f(y) + t_1(y)$$

for some non-negative real-valued function t_1 (as in Proposition 2(2)). (Notations are changed for reasons that will soon become clear.)

We shall reformulate here the representation theorem for families of semiorders and interval orders using the preference levels as well as the indifference relation. This reformulation suggests a new extension of the theorem to partial structures, that we shall derive from Proposition 5 on graphs. We need some notations and terminology.

Suppose that $2(m+n)$ relations $P_1, I_1, P_2, I_2, \ldots, P_m, I_m, Q_1, J_1, Q_2, J_2, \ldots, Q_n, J_n$ are given on the same finite set X. We shall denote by $\mathbf{P}_{m,n}$ the family of all these relations. A *picycle* from $\mathbf{P}_{m,n}$ is any nonempty sequence

$$x_1x_2, x_2x_3, \ldots, x_px_1$$

of pairs taken in

$$P_1 \cup I_1^{-1} \cup P_2 \cup I_2^{-1} \cup \ldots \cup P_m \cup I_m^{-1} \cup Q_1J_1^{-1} \cup Q_2J_2^{-1} \cup \ldots \cup Q_nJ_n^{-1}$$

but not all in $I_1^{-1} \cup I_2^{-1} \cup \ldots I_m^{-1}$ (this slightly generalizes a notion of Fishburn, 1983). A *k-picyclone* is any nonempty union of at most k picycles, or when $k = 0$, any picycle. It is *simple* if it never takes twice the same pair in the same P_i, I_i^{-1} or $Q_jJ_j^{-1}$. For a given picyclone C, we denote by $|P_i|_C$, $|I_i^{-1}|_C$, and $|Q_jJ_j^{-1}|_C$ respectively the number of its pairs that were taken in P_i, I_i^{-1}, $Q_jJ_j^{-1}$ respectively. The picyclone C is *balanced* when $|P_i|_C = |I_i^{-1}|_C$ for $i = 1, 2, \ldots, m$, it is *sheer* when $|P_i|_C = |I_i^{-1}|_C = 0$ for $i = 1, 2, \ldots, m$. Of course, the qualifiers simple, balanced and sheer also apply to picycles.

PROPOSITION 6. Let $\mathbf{P}_{m,n}$ be a family of relations as above. The two following conditions are equivalent:

(i) there exist real-valued mappings $f, t_1, t_2, \ldots, t_n$ on X and non-negative real numbers $r_1, r_2, \ldots, r_m$ such that for $i = 1, 2, \ldots, m$ and $j = 1, 2, \ldots, n$

(1) $t_j(y) \geq 0$,

(2) $xP_iy \Leftrightarrow f(x) > f(y) + r_i$,

(3) $xI_iy \Leftrightarrow |f(x) - f(y)| \leq r_i$,

(4) $xQ_jy \Leftrightarrow f(x) > f(y) + t_j(y)$, and

(5) $xJ_jy \Leftrightarrow -t_j(x) \leq f(x) - f(y) \leq t_j(y)$;

(ii) the following conditions hold for $i = 1, 2, \ldots, m$ and $j = 1, 2, \ldots, n$

(6) no m-picyclone from $\mathbf{P}_{m,n}$ is balanced (in particular,

_no_ m-_picyclone is sheer_),

(7) $P_i \cap I_i = \emptyset$,

(8) I_i _is reflexive and symmetric_,

(9) $Q_j \cap J_j = \emptyset$,

(10) J_j _is reflexive and symmetric_,

(11) $P_i \cup I_i$ _is complete, and_

(12) $Q_j \cup J_j$ _is complete_.

The above result on complete structures is easily derived from the following proposition on partial structures [because (i) as well as (ii) in Proposition 6 implies $I_i = (X \times X) - (P_i \cup P_i^{-1})$ and $J_j = (X \times X) - (Q_j \cup Q_j^{-1})$; also the conditions (ii)(6) in the two propositions are the same for reflexive relations I_i].

PROPOSITION 7. _Let_ $\mathbf{P}_{m,n}$ _be a family of relations as above, with_ I_i _and_ J_j _reflexive for_ $i = 1, 2, \ldots, m$ _and_ $j = 1, 2, \ldots, n$. _The two following conditions are equivalent_:

(i) _there exist real-valued mappings_ $f, t_1, t_2, \ldots, t_n$ _on_ X _and non-negative real numbers_ $r_1, r_2, \ldots, r_m$ _such that for_ $i = 1, 2, \ldots, m$ _and_ $j = 1, 2, \ldots, n$

(1) $t_j(y) \geq 0$,

(2) $xP_iy \quad \Rightarrow \quad f(x) > f(y) + r_i$,

(3) $xI_iy \quad \Rightarrow \quad f(x) - f(y) \leq r_i$,

(4) $xQ_jy \quad \Rightarrow \quad f(x) > f(y) + t_j(y)$, _and_

(5) $xJ_jy \quad \Rightarrow \quad f(x) - f(y) \leq t_j(y)$;

(ii) _for any_ m-_picyclone_ D _from_ $\mathbf{P}_{m,n}$ _there exists some_ $i \in \{1, 2, \ldots, m\}$ _such that_

(6) $|P_i|_D < |I_i^{-1}|_D$.

4. Proof of Proposition 7.

As was done for complete relations in Doignon (1986), we shall derive Proposition 7 from an intermediate result.

PROPOSITION 8. Let $\mathbf{P}_{m,n}$ be a family of relations as in section 3, with J_j reflexive for $j = 1, 2, \ldots, n$, and let $(r_1, r_2, \ldots, r_m)$ be a m-tuple of real numbers. Then the two following conditions are equivalent:

(i) there exist real-valued mappings $f, t_1, t_2, \ldots, t_n$ on X such that for $i = 1, 2, \ldots, m$ and for $j = 1, 2, \ldots, n$

(1) $t_j(y) \geq 0$,

(2) $xP_iy \Rightarrow f(x) > f(y) + r_i$,

(3) $xI_iy \Rightarrow f(x) - f(y) \leq r_i$,

(4) $xQ_jy \Rightarrow f(x) > f(y) + t_j(y)$, and

(5) $xJ_jy \Rightarrow f(x) - f(y) \leq t_j(y)$;

(ii) for any m-picycle C from $\mathbf{P}_{m,n}$

(6) $\Sigma_i \; (|I_i^{-1}|_C - |P_i|_C) \, r_i > 0.$

REMARK. In case all r_i are zero, condition (ii) states that there is no m-picycle at all.

Proof of Proposition 8. (i) Given the mappings $f, t_1, t_2, \ldots, t_n$ as in condition (i), we can find a positive real number ε such that, setting $g_j(y) = f(y) + t_j(y)$, we have

$$\begin{aligned}
xP_iy &\Rightarrow f(x) \geq f(y) + r_i + \varepsilon,\\
xI_i^{-1}y &\Rightarrow f(x) \geq f(y) - r_i,\\
xQ_jy &\Rightarrow f(x) \geq g_j(y) + \varepsilon,\\
xJ_j^{-1}y &\Rightarrow g_j(x) \geq f(y).
\end{aligned}$$

Define a graph $(X, E_0, E_1, E'_1, E_2, E'_2, \ldots, E_n, E'_n, w)$ by introducing an edge

xy in E_0	with	$w(xy) = r_i + \varepsilon$	whenever xP_iy,
xy in E_0	with	$w(xy) = -r_i$	whenever $xI_i^{-1}y$,
xy in E_j	with	$w(xy) = \varepsilon$	whenever xQ_jy,
xy in E'_j	with	$w(xy) = 0$	whenever $xJ_j^{-1}y$.

From Proposition 5, we deduce that any cycle $x_1x_2, x_2x_3, \ldots, x_px_1$ of this graph, such that

x_kx_{k+1} is taken in E_j iff $x_{k+1}x_{k+2}$ is taken in E'_j,

has non-positive weight. This means that for any picycle from $\mathbf{P}_{m,n}$

$$\Sigma_i\ (r_i+\varepsilon)|P_i|_C\ +\ \Sigma_i\ (-r_i)|I_i^{-1}|_C\ +\ \varepsilon\ \Sigma_j\ |Q_jJ_j^{-1}|_C\ \leq\ 0,$$

or

(α) $\Sigma_i\ (|P_i|_C - |I_i^{-1}|_C)\ r_i\ \leq\ -\varepsilon\ (\Sigma_i\ |P_i|_C\ +\ \Sigma_j\ |Q_jJ_j^{-1}|_C).$

This implies (ii), because the factor of ε is not zero by our definition of a picycle.

(ii) Conversely, assume (ii) holds. Choose a positive real number ε such that (α) holds for any simple picycle C. Then introducing the same graph as in the beginning of the proof, one can apply Proposition 5 again, and obtain the desired mappings $f, t_1, t_2, \ldots, t_n$. □

Proof of Proposition 7. (i) Assume condition (i) holds and let D be any picyclone from $\mathbf{P}_{m,n}$. For each constituting picycle C of D, we apply Proposition 8 and obtain the condition (6) of Proposition 8. Summing over all these picycles, we get

$$\Sigma_i\ (\ |I_i^{-1}|_D - |P_i|_D\ )\ r_i\ >\ 0.$$

Condition (ii) of Proposition 7 follows because $r_i \geq 0$ for $i = 1, 2, \ldots, m$.

(ii) Assume condition (6) holds for any m-picyclone D. In order to apply Proposition 8, we need to prove that the system of inequations in the m-tuples of real numbers $(r_1, r_2, \ldots, r_m)$

(β) $\Sigma_i\ (\ |I_i^{-1}|_C - |P_i|_C\ )\ r_i\ >\ 0,$

(one equation for each picycle C from $\mathbf{P}_{m,n}$) has a solution. It is clearly sufficient to consider only the inequations associated to simple picycles. Hence we handle a finite system of inequations. (It can even be a vacuous system in case no picycle exists.) We set $r_1 = 1$, and follow the same arguments as in the proof of Propositions 4 and 7 in Doignon (1986). (See Rockafellar, 1972, for the theory of systems of inequations.) By applying Helly theorem in the space of (m-1)-tuples $(r_2, r_3, \ldots, r_m)$, we need only to consider a system of ℓ inequations as in (β), with $\ell \leq m$. If $C_1, C_2, \ldots, C_\ell$ are the associated picycles, we write $|I_i^{-1}|_k$ and $|P_i|_k$ for the number of pairs of C_k that were taken in I_i^{-1} and P_i respectively. Thus we have to show the existence of a common solution $(r_2, r_3, \ldots, r_m)$ to

$$\Sigma_{i>1}\ (\ |I_i^{-1}|_k - |P_i|_k\ )\ r_i\ \ >\ \ -(\ |I_1^{-1}|_k - |P_1|_k\ )\ 1,$$

for $k = 1, 2, \ldots, \ell$. This is equivalent to the following assertion: if $\lambda_1, \lambda_2, \ldots, \lambda_\ell$ are non-negative real numbers, not all zero, such that (γ) $\qquad \Sigma_k \quad \lambda_k \ (\ |I_i^{-1}|_k - |P_i|_k \ ) \quad = \quad 0$

for $i = 2, 3, \ldots, m$, then the following also holds

(δ) $\qquad \Sigma_k \quad \lambda_k \ (\ |I_1^{-1}|_k - |P_1|_k \ ) \quad > \quad 0.$

Now because all the $|I_i^{-1}|_k - |P_i|_k$ are integers, we need only consider rational λ_k, and thus also only natural ones. Let D be the m-picyclone that is the union of the picycles obtained by traversing λ_k times the picycle C_k. Then (γ) states $|I_i^{-1}|_D = |P_i|_D$ for $i = 2, 3, \ldots, m$. Thus by our assumption, we must have $|P_1|_D < |I_1^{-1}|_D$, which gives (δ).

Hence we know that Proposition 8 may be used. We deduce the existence of real-valued mappings f and $t_1, t_2, \ldots, t_n$ as in the condition (i) of the Proposition 7 we are proving. Finally, $r_i \geq 0$ for $i = 1, 2, \ldots, m$ follow from the reflexivity of I_i. □

5. Conclusion and two additional remarks.

All the numerical representations of semiorders and interval orders, of their partial counterparts, and of the most general families of such preference relations, have been deduced from a single theorem on graphs.

The partial structures were related here to a change in the representations of complete structures. There seems to be a better notion of partial semiorders and interval orders based on a dimensionality concept; the reader is referred to Doignon, Ducamp, and Falmagne (1987) for this notion.

All the relations we have been considering possess nice tableau descriptions; see Doignon, Monjardet, Roubens, and Vincke (1986).

References

COZZENS, M.B. and ROBERTS, F.S. Double semiorders and double indifference graphs. *SIAM Journal on Algebraic and Discrete Methods*, 1982, **3**, 566-582.

DOIGNON, J.-P. Threshold representations of multiple semiorders. *SIAM Journal on Algebraic and Discrete Methods*, 1986, **7**, to appear.

DOIGNON, J.-P., DUCAMP, A., and FALMAGNE, J.-Cl. On the separation of two relations by a biorder or a semiorder. *Mathematical Social Sciences*, 1987, **13**, to appear.

DOIGNON, J.-P., MONJARDET, B., ROUBENS, M., and VINCKE, Ph. Biorder families, valued relations and preference modelling. *Journal of Mathematical Psychology,* 1986, **30**, 435-480.

DUCAMP, A., and FALMAGNE, J.-Cl. Composite Measurement. *Journal of Mathematical Psychology,* 1969, **6**, 359-390.

FISHBURN, P.C. Intransitive indifference with unequal indifference intervals. *Journal of Mathematical Psychology,* 1970, **7**, 144-149.

FISHBURN, P.C. Threshold-bounded interval orders and a theory of picycles. *SIAM Journal on Algebraic and Discrete Methods,* 1983, **4**, 290-305.

GUTTMAN, L. A basis for scaling quantitative data. *American Sociological Review,* 1944, **9**, 139-150.

LUCE, R.D. Semiorders and a theory of utility discrimination. *Econometrica,* 1956, **24**, 178-191.

ROBERTS, F.S. *Measurement theory* . Encyclopedia of Mathematics and its Applications, vol.**7**. Reading, MA : Addison-Wesley, 1979.

ROCKAFELLAR, R.T., *Convex Analysis* . Princeton, NJ: Princeton University Press, 1972.

ROUBENS, M. and VINCKE, Ph. A definition of partial interval orders. In *Trends in Mathematical Psychology,* eds. E.Degreef and J.Van Buggenhaut. Amsterdam : North-Holland, 1984 (pp. 309-315).

ROUBENS, M. and VINCKE, Ph. *Preference Modelling.* Lecture Notes in Economics and mathematical Systems, 250. Berlin : Springer-Verlag, 1985.

ROY, B. Préférence, indifférence, incomparabilité. *Documents du LAMSADE* n°9, Université de Paris-Dauphine, 1980.

ROY, B., and VINCKE, Ph. Pseudo-orders : definition, properties and numerical representation. *Mathematical Social Sciences,* 1987, **14**, to appear.

SCOTT, D. and SUPPES, P. Foundational aspects of theories of measurement. *Journal of Symbolic Logic,* 1958, **23**, 113-128.

WIENER, N. Contribution to the theory of relative position. *Proceedings of the Cambridge Philosophical Society,* 1914, **17**, 441-449.

A GENERALISATION OF PROBABILISTIC CONSISTENCY : LINEARITY CONDITIONS FOR VALUED PREFERENCE RELATIONS

Bernard MONJARDET
Université Paris V and Centre d'Analyse et de Mathématique Sociales
54, bd Raspail 75 270 Paris Cédex 06 - France

ABSTRACT.

We show how the theory of "probabilistic consistency" developped in the framework of pair comparison methods with forced choice can be extended to arbitrary valued preference relations. Especially we generalize classical "stochastic transitivity" conditions securing the "linearity" of valued relations and we study the implications between such conditions.

1 - Introduction

In this paper we intend to show how the "probabilistic consistency" theory (see references below), developped in the framework of paired comparisons method with "forced choice" can be extended to arbitrary valued (or "fuzzy") relations. Especially we generalize classical "stochastic transitivity conditions" securing the "linearity" of a valued preference relation and we study the implications between such conditions.

We begin by recalling the four most classical relational models used to formalize individual preference. We shall use the "asymmetrical" version of these models (rather than the "complete" version), with the following notations : $X = \{x,y,z,...\}$ is a finite set whose elements are called "objects" (they can be alternatives, candidates, motions, social states, etc...). A preference relation on X is modelled by a binary relation P on X. We write $(x,y) \in P$ or $x\,Py$ if the two objects x and y are related by P, and write $(x,y) \notin P$ or xP^cy otherwise ; we write xIy if and only if xP^cy and yP^cx, and xP^dy if and only if yP^cx. We can interpret xPy as a strict preference of x to y, xIy as an indifference between x and y. For binary relations P and Q on X, PQ is the usual relative product, that is $x\,PQy$ if and only if there is some $z \in X$ such that xPz and zQy.

For each type of model in the following list we give a relational definition and an equivalent characterization based on a real-valued representation (we omit the quantifications like "for each x, y in X").

M1 LINEAR ORDER.

(a) P is transitive (xPy and yPz imply xPz), asymmetric (xPy implies yP^cx), and weakly connected ($x \neq y$ implies xPy or yPx).

(b) There is a real-valued mapping f on X such that xPy iff $f(x) > f(y)$ and $x = y$ iff $f(x) = f(y)$.

M2 WEAK ORDER.

(a) P is antisymmetric and negatively transitive (xP^cy and yP^cz imply xP^cz).

(b) There is a real-valued mapping f on X such that xPy iff $f(x) > f(y)$.

M3 SEMIORDER

(a) P is irreflexive (xP^cx for all x), $PIP \subseteq P$ and $P^2 P^d \subseteq P$.

(b) There is a real-valued mapping f on X such that xPy iff $f(x) > f(y)+1$.

M4 INTERVAL ORDER.

(a) P is irreflexive and $PIP \subseteq P$.

(b) There are real-valued mappings f and g on X such that $f(x) \leq g(x)$ and xPy iff $f(x) > g(y)$.

Notice that in all these models P is a strict partial order, i.e. an irreflexive and transitive relation ; moreover, if P is a weak order - respectively a linear order - I is an equivalence relation - respectively the equality relation. Remark also that if one sets $g(x) = f(x) + \sigma(x)$; one gets a classical characterization of interval order, the positive function $\sigma(x)$ being the "threshold discrimination" function. More details and comments on these well known models can be found, for instance, in Fishburn (1972), Roberts (1979), Barthélemy, Flament and Monjardet (1982), or Roubens and Vincke (1985).

Here we introduce a fifth model, that is no more generally a partial order, but that will play a significant role in the sequel.

M5 BIORDER.

(a) $PP^dP \subseteq P$

(b) There are real-valued mappings f and g on X such that xPy iff $f(x)>g(y)$.

Notice that a biorder can be neither irreflexive nor reflexive ; but an irreflexive biorder is an interval order (see characterization (b)). So this model generalizes the four first models. There is another very simple and useful characterization of a biorder : it is a relation such it is adjacency matrix ($a_{xy} = 1$ iff xRy, $a_{xy} = 0$ iff xR^cy) can take a "step-type" form (see figure 1). In such a representation the lines and columns of the matrix are indexed by two linear orders, not necessarily identical ; indeed the adjacency matrix of an irreflexive relation can take such a step-type form with the same linear order for lines and columns iff this relation is a semiorder. The importance of the notion of biorder has been brought to light by several authors these last years ; see for instance, Monjardet (1978), Cogis (1982), Doignon, Ducamp and Falmagne (1984) and Doignon, Monjardet, Roubens and Vincke (1986), the first and last of these papers containing also historical comments and a lot of references ; notice that in the two first papers, biorders are called Ferrers relations.

	c	e	b	d	a
c	1	1	1	1	1
e	0	0	1	1	1
a	0	0	0	1	1
d	0	0	0	0	0
b	0	0	0	0	0

Figure 1

In all our five preference models a subject prefers - or does not prefer - x to y. Now in certain situations this assumption of "yes or no" preference is too strong and one needs a less "crisp" model. In the recent years, applications of fuzzy set theory to collective decision making has led to some interesting works on these lines, with "fuzzy preferences" modellized by mappings from X^2 into [0,1] (see, especially Nurmi 1981, Ovchinnikov 1981, Tanino 1984). But, as noticed by this last author, mathematical psychologists have far before introduced such models, called for instance valued or probabilistic relations, in order to deal with the often "observed "instability" of preference : at one time a subject may say he prefers x to y and at another near time y to x. Nevertheless if the subject is "probabilistically consistent", his preference can be explained by a model based on numerical representation of compared objects. The general idea of such models is that the more different are the "utilities" u(x) and u(y) of the two objects, the more different are the observed frequences with which x (respectively y) is chosen against y (respectively x). The theory of probabilistic consistency (see, for instance, Luce and Suppes 1965, Roberts 1979) gives "observable" consistency conditions for the existence of such utility models. In section 2 we shall review some results of this theory and especially some classical "stochastic transitivity" conditions securing the existence of utility models. All these results have been obtained for "probabilistic" valued relations, i.e. mappings v from X^2 into [0,1], satisfying v(x,y) + v(y,x) = 1. We shall show in section 3 how we can generalize these results to arbitrary valued relations. In our conclusion we shall point out further generalizations not tackled here. With a few exceptions we shall not give proofs of the stated results. First a lot of these results can be found with their proofs in Doignon, Monjardet, Roubens and Vincke (1986) ; secondly most of the other results have proofs straightforwardly generalized from classical results.

2 - Stochastic transitivity conditions in the theory of probabilistic consistency.

Figure 2 below shows individual preference data obtained from a "forced choice" pair comparison method. A subject has been asked several times to give a definite preference between objects (no indifference or incomparability answer allowed), and an array gathers the proportion of times he prefered object x to object y. For instance, he prefered a to b fifty five per cent.

	a	b	c	d	e
a	.5	.55	.5	.34	.55
b	.45	.5	.22	.20	.5
c	.5	.78	.5	.47	.78
d	.66	.8	.53	.5	.8
e	.45	.5	.22	.20	.5

2a

	d	c	a	b	e
d	.5	.53	.66	.8	.8
c	.47	.5	.5	.78	.78
a	.34	.5	.5	.55	.55
b	.2	.22	.45	.5	.5
e	.2	.22	.45	.5	.5

2b

Figure 2

In order to describe the properties of such data, we introduce some definitions and notations. A *valued (binary) relation* on the set X is a map v from the set X^2 of all ordered pairs of X into the set [0,1] ; v(x,y) denotes the image by v of the ordered pair (x,y). A *probabilistic* valued relation is a valued relation with v(x,y) + v(y,x) = 1 for all x,y. We define the scores $s^+(x)$, $s^-(x)$ and s(x) of x by :

$$s^+(x) = \sum_{y \in X} v(x,y) \qquad s^-(x) = \sum_{y \in X} v(y,x) \qquad s(x) = s^+(x) - s^-(x)$$

and the associated *scores relations* $S^+ = S^+(v)$, $S^- = S^-(v)$, $S = S(v)$ by

$xS^+y \Leftrightarrow s^+(x) > s^+(y)$ $\quad xS^-y \Leftrightarrow s^-(x) < s^-(y)$ $\quad xSy \Leftrightarrow s(x) > s(y)$.

Hence these relations are complete preorders (a preorder being a reflexive and transitive relation).

If v is a probabilistic (valued) relation, we have

$s^+(x)+s^-(x) = v \qquad s(x) = v - 2s^-(x) = 2s^+(x) - v$

and the three scores preorders are identical.

The example above (figure 2) is a probabilistic relation, for which $s^+(a)=1.89$, $s^+(b)=s^+(e)=1.37$, $s^+(c) = 2.25$, $s^+(d) = 2.49$. So, the score preorder is d>c>a>b~e.

We now define the *right-trace* $T^r = T^r(v)$, *left-trace* $T^l = T^l(v)$ and *trace* $T = T(v)$ by

xT^ry iff for every $z \in X$, $v(x,z) > v(y,z)$

xT^ly iff for every $z \in X$, $v(z,x) < v(z,y)$

xTy iff for every $z \in X$, $v(x,z) > v(y,z)$ and $v(z,x) < v(z,y)$

Hence, $T = T^r \cap T^l$, and the different traces of v are-not necessarily complete-preorders. We denote the equivalences associated with these preorders by E^r, E^l and E. So, for instance :

xE^ry iff for every z in X $v(x,z) = v(y,z)$.

We obviously have :

$T^r \subseteq S^+$, $T^l \subseteq S^-$, $T \subseteq S$.

When v is probabilistic, we have $T^r = T^l = T$; so there is an unique trace preorder. In our example, one can check that $s^+(x)>s^+(y)$ implies $v(x,z)>v(y,z)$ for every Z, so that one has S = T. This is a special but significant case, and we are going to give several other characterizations of it.

First it is easy to see that when v is probabilistic, S = T, if and only if v satisfies the following *strong linearity* (called also *weak independance*) condition :

for all x,y,z,t∈X v(x,z) › v(y,z) implies v(x,t) ≥ v(y,t).

A second characterization uses the form that can be given to the array presenting such data. We shall use the abstract notion of "tableau". A *tableau* for a valued relation v on X is a pair of linear orders L_1,L_2 on X. We denote this tableau by (v,L_1,L_2) and we can visualize it by an array A_{ij},

with $1 \le i,j \le |X|$, and $A_{ij} = v(x,y)$ iff x is the ith element of X with respect to L_1 and y the jth element of X with respect to L_2.

A tableau (v,L_1,L_2) is *coherent* iff $L_1=L_2$; such a tableau will be denoted by (v,L) where $L = L_1 = L_2$.

Figure 2 shows two arrays representing two coherent tableau of the *same* valued relation (v , a›b›c›d›e) in Figure 2a, and (v , d›c›a›b›e) in Figure 2b.

A tableau (v,L_1,L_2) is *L_1 monotone* iff, for all x,y∈X

$xL_1y \Rightarrow \forall z \in X, v(x,z) \geq v(y,z)$.

A tableau (v,L_1,L_2) is *L_2 monotone* iff, for all x, y ∈ X

$xL_2y \Rightarrow \forall z \in X, v(z,x) \leq v(z,y)$.

A tableau (v,L_1,L_2) is *monotone* iff it is L_1 monotone and L_2 monotone.

So the entries in a column (line) of the array A_{ij} visualizing a L_1 monotone (L_2 monotone) tableau are non decreasing from bottom (left) to top (right).

When v is probabilistic, the coherent tableau $(v, L_1 = L_2)$ is L_1 monotone iff it is L_2 monotone, thus monotone.

All the above definitions can be used for a binary relation R ; a tableau is then denoted (R,L_1,L_2). One notices that a coherent tableau (R,L) is monotone iff $LRL \subseteq R$ or iff the corresponding array is step-type. Then the characterization of semiorders stated in section 1 becomes : an irreflexive relation is a semiorder iff it has a monotone coherent tableau.

In our example, the valued relation has been given by a no monotone coherent tableau (Figure 2a), but it has a monotone coherent tableau (Figure 2b). Indeed, fo probabilistic relations the property to have a monotone coherent tableau is equivalent t the above strong linearity condition. It is not difficult to see these conditions are als equivalent to the following property of monotone scalability : a probabilistic relation v i *monotonically scalable* iff there exists two mappings $u : X \to \mathbb{R}$, F :

$u(X) \times u(X) \xrightarrow{F} [0,1]$ such that for all x,y in X, $v(x,y) = F[u(x),u(y)]$, with F non decreasing i its first argument ($a < b$ implies $F(a,.) \leq F(b,.)$) and non increasing in its second argument.

Finally we define the "cut-relations" (also called "threshold relations") associated wit the valued relation v : given $\lambda \in [0,1]$, the λ-cut of v is the relation R_λ defined by

$R_\lambda = \{ (x,y) \in X^2 : v(x,y) \geq \lambda \}$

Let us assume that $v(X^2) = \{0 \leq \lambda_1 < ... \lambda_i ... < \lambda_m \leq 1\}$.

Then, the λ_i-cuts form a chain (a nested family) of binary relations that we call th chain $\mathfrak{C} = \mathfrak{C}(v)$ associated with v ; we denote it by

$\mathfrak{C}: X^2 = R_{\lambda_1} \supset .... R_{\lambda_i} .... \supset R_{\lambda_m} \supset \emptyset$

Figure 3 shows tableau of two λ-cuts of our example. Since these tableau ar monotone and coherent and that $R_{.53}$ and $R_{.8}$ are irreflexive, these λ-cuts are semiorders

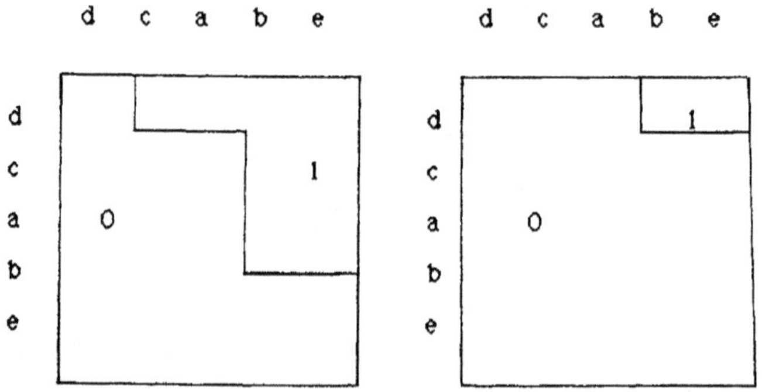

$R_{.53}$ $R_{.8}$

Figure 3

Indeed one can check that in our example each R_λ, with $\lambda > 1/2$, is a semiorder ; so $\{R_\lambda ; \lambda > 1/2\}$ defines a chain of semiorders. Moreover, one can also check that all these semiorders have a monotone coherent tableau (v,L) with the same linear order L = d > c > a > b > e. We shall say that they form an *homogeneous chain of semiorders*. This notion has been introduced by Roberts (1971) with a different - but equivalent - definition (based on a notion of compatibility between weak orders and semiorders ; see also Monjardet 1984). In order to have more convenient notations, we shall assume that the chain $\{R_\lambda, \lambda > 1/2\}$ contains p relations and we will denote it by : $P_1 \supset \ldots P_i \ldots \supset P_p \supset \emptyset$; notice that all these relations are irreflexive.

All remarks made on our example are contained in the following theorem that - except condition (4) introduced in Monjardet (1984) - summarizes results of Luce (1958), Roberts (1971) and Fishburn (1973).

Theorem.

Let v be a probabilistic relation ; the following conditions are equivalent :

(1) T is complete.

(2) T = S.

(3) v is strongly linear (weak independance condition).

(4) There exists a monotone coherent tableau (v;L) for v.

(5) v is monotonically scalable.

(6) $\{R_\lambda, \lambda > 1/2\} = (P_1 \supset \ldots P_i \ldots \supset P_p\}$ is an homogeneous chain of semiorders.

(7) There exist real-valued mappings f, $\sigma_1, \ldots \sigma_i, \ldots \sigma_p$ on X such that

$0 \leq \sigma_1(x) \leq \ldots \sigma_i(x) \ldots \leq \sigma_p(x)$.

$xP_iy \Leftrightarrow f(x) > f(y) + \sigma_i(y)$

$f(x) + \sigma_i(x) \geq f(y) + \sigma_i(y) \Leftrightarrow f(x) \geq f(y)$.

This theorem shows how "observable properties" like conditions (3) or (6) secure the existence of "explicative models" like (5) or (7) ; moreover a condition like (1) shows that such properties are easily testable.

N.B. An equivalent way to state condition I used by authors like Fishburn or Roubens and Vincke (1984) is to say that the relation T^d (where xT^dy iff yT^cx) is asymmetric, i.e. is a weak order.

Now we list some classical conditions weaker or stronger than the conditions of the theorem and we point out some equivalences and implications between them. We deal mainly with conditions that can be called "stochastic transitivity" conditions (in a broad sense). It will be easier to use abbreviations for their name (we omit the quantifications such that "for all x,y,z,t in X").

Independance : I

$v(x,z) \geq v(y,z) \Leftrightarrow v(x,t) \geq v(y,t)$.

Substituability : S

$v(x,y) \geq 1/2 \Leftrightarrow v(x,t) \geq v(y,t)$.

Strict strong stochastic transitivity : SSST.

$\text{Min}\,[v(x,y),v(y,z)] \geq 1/2 \Rightarrow v(x,z) \geq \text{Max}\,[v(x,y),v(y,z)]$

with strict inequality in the hypothese implies strict inequality in the conclusion.

Strong stochastic transitivity : SST.

$\text{Min}\,[v(x,y),v(y,z)] \geq 1/2 \Rightarrow v(x,z) \geq \text{Max}\,[v(x,y),v(y,z)]$

Strong linearity (or weak independance) : SL

$v(x,z) > v(y,z) \Rightarrow v(x,t) \geq v(y,t)$.

K stochastic transitivity : KST.

$v(x,z) > \text{Max}\,[v(y,z),\ 1/2] \Rightarrow \text{Max}[v(x,t),1/2] \geq v(y,t)]$.

Interval stochastic transitivity : IST.

$\text{Max}\,[v(x,y),v(z,t)] \geq \text{Min}\ [v(x,t),\ v(y,t)]$.

We use also the simple scalability condition : SS défined like the above montone scability condition, with the difference that mapping F is strictly increasing in its first argument and strictly decreasing in its second argument.

Then we can state the following results due to various authors (see references in Roberts, 1979) :

$I \Leftrightarrow S \Leftrightarrow SSST \Leftrightarrow SS \Rightarrow SST \Leftrightarrow T = R_{1/2} \Leftrightarrow T = S = R_{1/2} \Leftrightarrow SL \Rightarrow T = S$

$\Leftrightarrow MS \Rightarrow KST \Rightarrow IST$.

Moreover if, $v(x,y) = 1/2$ implies $v(x,t) = v(y,t)$ for every t, conditions SST and SL are equivalent. In our example, we have $T = S \subset R_{1/2}$; as a matter of fact $v(c,a) = 1/2$ but $v(c,b)$ different from $v(a,b)$.

Notice that the λ-cut $R_{1/2}$ is nothing else that the "majoritary relation $M = M(v)$ associated with v : $xMy \Leftrightarrow v(x,y) \geq v(y,x) \Leftrightarrow v(x,y) \geq 1/2$.

To be sure, as in the theorem above one could state other equivalent conditions based on λ-cuts or representation properties (for a lot of such conditions, see Fishburn 1973).

3 - Generalized stochastic transitivity conditions for valued relations.

In this section v is an arbitrary valued (binary) relation. Especially, $v(x,x)$ is not necessarily constant (or constant and equal to 1/2) ; we set up

$$\beta = \min_{x \in X} v(x,x).$$

We illustrate some of the notions already defined in section 2 for such a relation with the example given Figure 4a.

	a	b	c	d	e
a	.6	.5	.4	.6	.4
b	.1	.5	.2	.2	.3
c	.6	.8	.9	.7	.8
d	.4	.5	.3	.5	.4
c	.6	.6	.4	.7	.5

4a

	c	e	a	d	b
c	.9	.8	.6	.7	.8
e	.4	.5	.6	.7	.6
a	.4	.4	.6	.6	.5
d	.3	.4	.4	.5	.5
b	.2	.3	.1	.2	.5

4b

Figure 4

For the above valued relation, we have $T^{r} = S^{+} = R_{\beta} = c > e > a > d > b$, whereas $T^{\ell} = \{e > b, a > d\} \subset S^{-} = c > a \sim e \sim d > b$; $s(a) = -.2$ $s(b) = -1.6$, $s(c) = 1.6$; $s(d) = -.6$, $s(e) = .4$; so $T = \{e > b, a > d\} \subset S = c > e > a > d > b$.

Now we define some generalized stochastic transitivity conditions.

β Right Substitutability, βRS :

$v(x,y) \geq \beta \Leftrightarrow v(x,t) \geq v(y,t)$.

Right Independance, RI :

$v(x,z) \geq v(y,z) \Leftrightarrow v(x,t) \geq v(y,t)$.

β Right Strict Strong Stochastic Transitivity, βRSSST :

$\text{Min}\ [v(x,y), v(z,y)] \geq \beta \Rightarrow v(z,x) \geq v(y,x)$

$\text{Min}\ [v(x,y), v(y,z)] \geq \beta \Rightarrow v(x,z) \geq v(y,z)$

with strict inequalities in both hypotheses implies strict inequalities in the conclusions.

β Right Strong Stochastic Transitivity, βRSST :

$\text{Min}\ [v(x,y),v(z,y)] \geq \beta \Rightarrow v(z,x) \geq v(y,x)$

$\text{Min}\ [v(x,y),v(y,z)] \geq \beta \Rightarrow v(x,z) \geq v(y,z)$.

Right Linearity, RL :

$v(x,z) > v(y,z) \Rightarrow v(x,t) \geq v(y,t)$.

μ Right Linearity, μRL :

$v(x,z) > \text{Max}\ [v(y,z),\mu)] \Rightarrow \text{Max}\ [v(x,t),\mu] \geq v(y,t)$.

Biorder Stochastic Transitivity, BST :

$\text{Max}\ [v(x,t), v(z,y)] \geq \text{Min}\ [v(x,y), v(z,t)]$.

μ Biorder Stochastic Transitivity, μBST :

$\text{Max}\ [v(x,t), v(z,y),\mu] \geq \text{Min}\ [v(x,y), v(z,t)]$.

Let us also define generalized conditions of scalability.

We say that v is *right simply*-respectively *right monotonically- scalable* iff there exists two mappings $u : X \to \mathbb{R}$, $F : u(X) \times u(X) \xrightarrow{F} [0,1]$ such that for all x,y in X, $v(x,y) = F[u(x)\ u(y)]$, with F strictly increasing - respectively non decreasing - in its first argument ; we denote these two conditions respectively by RSS and RMS.

First we are going to state equivalences and implications always true between the above conditions and some other ones, for instance conditions on traces or λ-cuts. Then we shall consider the case of valued relations satisfying specific properties.

Since $xT^r y$ implies $v(x,y) \geq v(y,y) \geq \beta$, we always have $T^r \subseteq R_\beta$. If condition βRS is satisfied we have $R_\beta \subseteq T^r$, so $R_\beta = T^r$; then, if $x(T^r)^c y$, i.e. there exists t such that v(y,t) › v(x,t), one has $v(y,x) \geq \beta$, thus yT^rx ; so T^r is complete ; finally if v(x,z) = v(y,z) we have $xR_\beta y$ and $yR_\beta x$, thus xE^ry (i.e. v(x,t) = v(y,t) for every t). So if we consider the following condition :

(E_r) $v(x,z) = v(y,z) \Rightarrow v(x,t) = v(y,t)$

we have just shown that condition βRS implies that $T^r = R_\beta$ is complete and (E_r) is satisfied. As the converse is easily proved, one obtains :

βRS $\Leftrightarrow$ $T^r = R_\beta$ is complete and v satisfies (E_r).

Concerning the right independance condition, one easily proves :

RI $\Leftrightarrow$ T^r is complete and v satisfies (E_r).

Condition βRSSST will be only considered later, because it implies additional properties for v. Concerning condition βRSST, we just notice the obvious fact that $R_\beta = T^r$ implies it ; so βRS $\Rightarrow$ RSST.

We come now to the right linearity condition, a condition generalizing the strong linearity condition of section 2. Indeed we can state a result generalizing the theorem of this section. Beforehand we generalize the notion of homogeneous chain of semiorders used in this theorem.

A chain of biorders $(R_1 \supset .... R_i \supset ... R_m)$ is called a *right-homogeneous chain of biorders* iff there exist linear orders $L_1, L^1_2, ..., L^m_2$ on X such that for i = 1,2,...m (L_1, L^i_2, R_i) is a monotone tableau for R_i (equivalently, the corresponding array is step type).

Theorem. (Doignon, Monjardet, Roubens, Vincke, 1986).

Let v be a valued relation. The following conditions are equivalent :

1) T^r is complete.

2) $T^r = S^+$.

3) v is right-linear.

4) There exists a L_1-monotone tableau (v, L_1, L_2) for v.

(5) v is right monotonically scalable.

(6) The chain $\mathcal{C} : X^2 = R_{\lambda_1} \supset \ldots R_{\lambda_i} \ldots \supset R_{\lambda_m} \supset \emptyset$ is a right homogeneous chains of biorders.

(7) There exists real valued mappings g, $g_1, \ldots g_i, \ldots g_m$ on X such that

$g_1 \leq \ldots \leq g_i \ldots \leq g_m$ and $x R_{\lambda_i} y \Leftrightarrow f(x) > g_i(y)$.

(8) v is μ right linear for every μ in [0,1].

N.B. Like for the corresponding theorem of section 2, it would be possible to stat condition (1) by saying that the dual relation of T^r ($x(T^r)^d y$ iff there exists z such tha $v(x,z) > v(y,z)$) is asymmetric.

We came now to the condition of μ right linearity. In order to make it more explici we set up $v^\mu(x,y) = \text{Max}\,[v(x,y),\mu]$, for all x,y. Since we have

$xT^r(v^\mu)y \Leftrightarrow$ for all z, $\text{Max}[v(x,z),\mu)] \geq v(y,z)$

one sees that μRL means that v^μ is right-linear. So we can use the above theorem t obtain equivalent conditions, for instance the condition that the chain $\mathcal{C}(v^\mu) = (X^2 \supset R_\lambda$ $\ldots \supset R_{\lambda_m} \supset \emptyset$ (where $\lambda_{j-1} < \mu < \lambda_j$) is a right homogeneous chain of biorders.

Finally it is easy to see that μBST is equivalent to say that the chain defined by th R_λ, $\lambda > \mu$ is a chain of biorders. We have also :

BST $\Leftrightarrow$ μBST, for every μ in [0,1]

μRL $\Rightarrow$ μBST

We summarize below some of the equivalences or implications given above; it ca be shown by examples that all the converses of these implications are false.

βRS	$\Rightarrow$	RI	$\Rightarrow$	RL	$\Rightarrow$	BST
$\Updownarrow$		$\Updownarrow$		$\Updownarrow$		
$T^r = R_\beta$ complete		T^r complete		T^r complete		
$+(E_T)$		$+(E_T)$		$\Updownarrow$		
$\Downarrow$				$T^r = S$		
β RSST						

We shall assume now that the valued relation v satisfies additional properties. There are a lot of possible such properties, but here we shall only consider the three following ones :

(C_β) The relation R_β is complete : $v_{xy} < \beta \Rightarrow v_{yx} \geq \beta$.

(C_θ) For every x in X, $v(x,x) = \theta$, and R_θ is complete.

(D_θ) There exists $\theta \in [0,1]$, such that for all $x,y \in X$ $\ v(x,y) \leq \theta$ iff $v(y,x) \geq \theta$.

Notice the implications

$(D_\theta) \quad \Rightarrow \quad (C_\theta) \quad \Rightarrow \quad (C_\beta)$.

To begin with let us assume that v satisfies (C_β). Define a new condition E_β by

$(E_\beta) \quad \mathrm{Min}[v(x,y),v(y,x)] \geq \beta \Leftrightarrow v(x,t) = v(y,t)$.

Then one can prove the equivalences :

β RSST $\Leftrightarrow T^r = R_\beta \Leftrightarrow T^r$ complete and v satisfies (E_β).

So, one obtains

$$\begin{array}{ccccc} & & \text{RI} & & \\ & \nearrow & & \searrow & \\ \beta\text{RS} & & & & \text{RL} \Rightarrow \text{BST} \\ & \searrow & & \nearrow & \\ & & \beta\text{RSST} & & \end{array}$$

In the example given Figure 4, we have $T^r = R_\beta$, so v satisfies βRSST, but v does not satisfy RI because condition (E_r) is not satisfied : indeed we have, for instance, v(a,a) = v(c,a), but v(a,b) $\neq$ v(c,b). It is also easy to find examples with v satisfying RI but not βRSST. Notice that our example satisfying βRSST satisfies also μ βBST : each R_μ is a biorder. In fact, Figure 1 shows $R_{.6}$; notice that it is not an interval order (it is not irreflexive).

Let us assume now that there exists θ with $v(x,x) = \theta$ for every x in X and R_θ complete. Then conditions θRS and RI become equivalent : indeed, we always have $T^r \subseteq R_\theta$, and if RI is satisfied, $xR_\theta y$, i.e. $v(x,y) \geq \theta = v(y,y)$ implies xT^ry ; so $T^r = R_\theta$ and RI implies θRS.

The diagram of implications became a chain with four (not equivalent) conditions.

θ RS	$\Leftrightarrow$	RI	$\Rightarrow$	θRSST	$\Rightarrow$	RL	$\Rightarrow$	BST
$\Updownarrow$		$\Updownarrow$		$\Updownarrow$		$\Updownarrow$		
$T^r=R_\theta$ complete		T^r complete		$T^r=R_\theta$ complete		T^r complete		
+		+						
(E_r)		(E_r)		$\Updownarrow$		$\Updownarrow$		
				T^r complete		$T^r = S$		
				$+(E_\theta)$				

Notice that if a valued relation with $v(x,x) = \theta$ for every x satisfies BST, then for $\lambda > \theta$, the corresponding cut R_λ is an irreflexive biorder i.e. an interval order ; moreover for $\lambda \leq \theta$, $(R_\lambda)^d$ the dual relation of R_λ is also an interval order. Then in this case our biorder stochastic transitivity condition could be renamed the interval stochastic transitivity condition ; indeed in the more special case of probabilistic relations this last name and the abbreviation IST have been used by Fishburn (1973). This explains also why a right linear valued relation with $v(x,x) = \theta$ for every x has been called a right linear interval valued relation in Doignon, Monjardet, Roubens and Vincke (1986).

Finally let us assume condition (D_θ) : there exists θ such that $v(x,y) \geq \theta$ iff $v(y,x) \leq \theta$. Then the condition θ-RSSST may be satisfied ; but one can prove that it is equivalent to RI (and θRS). So one obtains yet a chain of four non equivalent implications. Notice also that in this case, one has

$$\theta RL \Rightarrow BST$$

and that the condition E_θ can be written

$$v_{xy} = \theta \Rightarrow v_{xt} = v_{yt}$$

All the above results can be now applied to the probabilistic relations of section 2, since such relations satisfy (D_θ), with $\theta = 1/2$. If then one assume $E_{1/2}$ i.e. $v_{xy} = 1/2$

implies $v_{xt} = v_{yt,}$ one obtains the equivalence between the right strong stochastic stochastic transitivity condition and the various conditions expressing the right linearity of v, i.e. a "right generalization" of the main Robert's theorem (1971). Remark also that in the context of probabilistic relations, condition 1/2 RL is called KST by Fishburn (1973). All the generalized transitivity stochastic conditions used up to now - except BST - have been "right" conditions. It is clear that we could define equivalent "left" conditions and obtain the corresponding same results. For instance v is left-linear (v,z,x) < v(z,y) implies v(t,x) $\leq$ v(t,y)) iff the left trace T^{ℓ} is complete. Moreover one can combine the right and left conditions in order to obtain other special classes of valued relations. For instance v is called linear iff it is right and left linear. In this case, T^{ℓ} and T^{r} are complete weak orders, but they may be different ; if they are equal one says that v is *strongly linear* (or linear in Monjardet, 1984). One can find a lot of characterizations of such linear relations in Doignon, Monjardet, Roubens and Vincke (1986).

Finally let us notice that some of our conditions use the relation R_{β}, with β =min v(x,x). By setting up γ = max v(x,x), and $xQ_{\gamma}y$ iff v(y,x) $\leq \gamma$, one could repeat for Q_{γ} the developments made with R_{β}, for instance characterizing the cases when Q_{γ} equals T^{r},T^{ℓ} or T respectively.

4 - Conclusion.

We think have made clear in section 2 how results of the theory of the probabilistic consistency can be generalized to arbitrary valued relations. The basic notion is that of (right or left) linear relation, a notion that appears in Luce (1958, see also Roubens and Vincke 1983, Monjardet, 1984), and generalizes the notion of biorder. When a valued relation is, for instance, right-linear, one can represent its values in an array, whose the entries in a column are non decreasing from bottom to top ; one can also interpret these values from numerical utilities functions ; moreover it is not difficult to recognise such a case by using characterizations based on trace : for instance, the right trace must equal the score relation S^{+}. The other valued relations studied here are - generally - special cases of linear relations, thus satisfy further properties.

We want now sketch other possible generalizations. First we have always worked here with [0,1] as set V of values for the valued relation v. But it would be possible to take other sets V, such that subsets of $\mathbb{R}$ with least and greatest elements. Especially the notion of probabilistic valued relation can be generalized into the notion of ipsodual (valued) relation, i.e. relation v satisfying for all x, y $v(x,y) = h\ v(y,x)$, where h is an involutive antiisomorphism on V : for every $v \in V$, $h^2(\lambda) = \lambda$, and for all λ, $\lambda' \in V$ $\lambda > \lambda'$ iff $h(\lambda) < h(\lambda')$.

Another way of generalization is to notice that several of the valued relations studied here can be defined by conditions on the chains of λ cuts associated with them. Roberts (1971) suggested to remove this chain condition, and so to consider families of binary relations. Indeed one can define homogeneous families of biorders and obtain generalizations of results stated here. These two kinds of generalizations are developped in Doignon, Monjardet, Roubens and Vincke (1986). Finally a third kind of generalization deals with the extension of some results to "partial" preferences, modellized by not complete (or asymmetrical) relations ; see Roubens and Vincke (1985) and Doignon (1987).

5 - **References**.

BARTHELEMY, J.P., FLAMENT, C. and MONJARDET, B., Ordered sets and Social Sciences, in *Rival, I. ed., Ordered sets*, D. Reidel, 1982, 721-758.

COGIS, O., Ferrers digraphs and threshold graphs, *Discrete Mathematics*, 1982, 38, 33-46, (1982).

DOIGNON, J.P., Generalizations of interval orders, in *Eds., Degreef, E. and van Buggenhaut, J., Trends in Mathematical Psychology*, North Holland, Amsterdam, 1984, 209-217, (1984).

DOIGNON, J.P., Partial structure of preference, in *Eds Kacprzyk J. and Roubens M., Non Conventional Preference Relations in Decision Making*, Springer Verlag, (1987).

DOIGNON, J.P., MONJARDET, B., ROUBENS, M. and VINCKE, Ph., Biorders families, valued relations and preference modelling, *Journal of Mathematical Psychology*, 30, 435-480, (1986).

FISHBURN, P.C., *Mathematics of decision theory*, Mouton, Paris, (1972).

FISHBURN, P.C., Binary choice probabilities : on the varieties of stochastic transitivity,

LUCE, R.D., Semiorders and a theory of utility discrimination, *Econometrica*, 24, 178-191, (1956).

LUCE, R.D., A probabilistic theory of utility, *Econometrica*, 26, 193-224, (1958).

LUCE, R.D. and SUPPES, P., Preference, utility and subjective probability, in *Eds., Luce, R.D. Bush, R.R. and Galanter, E., Handbook of Mathematical Psychology*, Wiley, New-York, 1965, Vol.3, pp. 249-410.

MONJARDET, B., Axiomatiques et propriétés des quasi-ordres, *Mathématiques et Sciences humaines*, 63, 51-82, (1978).

MONJARDET, B., Probabilistic consistency, homogeneous families of relations and linear λ-relations, in *Eds., Degreef, E. and van Buggenhaut J., Trends in Mathematical Psychology*, North Holland, Amsterdam, 1984, 271-281.

NURMI, H., Approaches to collective decision making with fuzzy preferences relations, *Fuzzy sets and systems*, 6, 249-259, (1981).

OVCHINNIKOV, S., Structure of fuzzy binary relations, *Fuzzy Sets and Systems*, 6, 169-195, (1981).

ROBERTS, F.S., Homogeneous families of semiorders and the theory of probabilistic consistency, *Journal of Mathematical Psychology*, 8, 248-263, (1971).

ROBERTS, F.S., *Measurement theory*, Encyclopedia of Mathematics and its Applications, Vol.7, Addison Wesley, Reading, M.A., (1979).

ROUBENS, M., and VINCKE, Ph., Linear fuzzy graphs, *Fuzzy Sets and Systems*, 10, 79-86, (1983).

ROUBENS, M. and VINCKE, Ph., On families of semiorders and interval orders imbedded in a valued structure of preference : a survey, *Information Sciences*, 34, 187-198, (1984).

ROUBENS, M. and VINCKE, Ph., *Preference Modelling*, Lecture Notes in Economics and Mathematical Systems, Springer-Verlag, n°250, (1985).

TANINO, T., Fuzzy preferences orderings in group decision making, *Fuzzy Sets and Systems*, 12, 117-131, (1984).

FUZZY PREFERENCE RELATIONS IN GROUP DECISION MAKING

Tetsuzo Tanino
Department of Mechanical Engineering II
Tohoku University, Sendai 980, Japan

ABSTRACT

This paper surveys how fuzzy preference relations are utilized in group decision making. First, several fundamental properties of fuzzy preference relations are reviewed. Secondly, some procedures for deriving a solution (group choice) from individual fuzzy preference relations are discussed. They can be divided into two classes: direct approach and indirect approach. Finally, a systems analytic approach which aims to generate a practically meaningful group fuzzy preference relation which reflects differences or diversity of individual preferences is discussed.

1. Introduction

In the field of decision making, fuzzy theory is very helpful in dealing with fuzziness of human judgment quantitatively, and a number of useful results have been obtained (see, for example, Dubois and Prade [7] and Zimmermann [19]). Some applications of fuzzy theory to group decision making have been made by Blin and Whinston [5], Blin [4], Fung and Fu [8], Bezdek et al. [2,3], Kuz'min and Ovchinnikov [13,14], Nurmi [17], Dimitrov [6], Kim [12], Tanino [18], Kacprzyk [9-11] and some others.

The purpose of this paper is to discuss how fuzzy preference relations are used in group decision making. First, in Section 2, the concept of fuzzy preference relations is introduced and their fundamental properties such as transitivity, measures of fuzziness, and relationships with utility values are discussed. Since nonfuzzy preference relations and utility values are included in the family of fuzzy preference relations, individual preferences are supposed to be represented by fuzzy preference relations. Section 3 is devoted to methods for obtaining a solution (an alternative or a set of alternatives chosen by the group). Two approaches - direct and indirect -

are discussed. In the direct approach, a solution is derived directly from a set of individual fuzzy preference relations, and in the indirect approach, a solution is obtained through a group fuzzy preference relation aggregated from individual fuzzy preference relations. In Section 4, group decision making is regarded as a dynamic process leading to a final decision. Systems analytic procedures which generate practically meaningful group fuzzy preference relations reflecting diversity of individual preferences are explained.

2. Fuzzy Preference Relations

In this section we review the concept of fuzzy preference relations.

2.1 Fuzzy preference relations

A fuzzy binary relation R on a set X is a fuzzy set on the product set X × X, that is, it is characterized by a membership function μ_R from X × X into the interval [0,1]. Throughout this paper, X is assumed to be a finite set of alternatives $x_1, x_2, \dots, x_n$. In this case we can define an n×n matrix whose (i,j) element is given by

$$r_{ij} = \mu_R(x_i, x_j), \qquad i,j=1,\dots,n \tag{2.1}$$

from the membership function μ_R. Conversely an arbitrary n×n matrix with elements in the interval [0,1] defines a fuzzy binary relation on X. Thus, in the following, we identify the fuzzy binary relation R on the set X with the n×n matrix $R = (r_{ij})$ with $0 \leqq r_{ij} \leqq 1$ (i,j=1,...,n). In an ordinary (nonfuzzy) binary relation R, every $r_{ij} = 0$ or 1.

If R is a preference relation, its elements are usually interpreted as follows : $r_{ij} = 1$ indicates the maximum degree of preference of x_i over x_j and each value of r_{ij} in the open interval (0.5,1) indicates a definite preference of x_i to x_j with the intensity of preference corresponding to the value of r_{ij} (a higher value means a stronger intensity). $r_{ij} = 0.5$ indicates the indifference between x_i and x_j. We may also say that $r_{ij} > 0.5$ represents an uncertain preference of x_i over x_j and so x_i is definitely (certainly) preferred to x_j if $r_{ij} = 1$. Thus, fuzzy preference relations can be used as mathematical models of preferences and intensity of preferences.

Since fuzzy theory in itself has aspects quite similar to probability theory, fuzzy preference relations considered in the following naturally have some analogies in concepts with the traditional theory of probabilistic choice (for example, Luce and Suppes [15]). However, fuzzy preference relations have practically meaningful interpretation and provide interesting results especially in group decision making, which are main points in this paper.

If the value of r_{ij} has the meaning described above, it is proper to assume that R is reciprocal in the following sense:

$$r_{ij} + r_{ji} = 1 \qquad \text{for } i,j=1,\dots,n. \tag{2.2}$$

From this equality and the practical meaning of r_{ij}, we put

$$r_{ij} = 0.5 \qquad \text{for any } i=1,\dots,n$$

in this paper. In some cases, they let $r_{ii} = 0$ so that the set of fuzzy preference relations includes ordinary preference relations for which $r_{ij} = 0$ or 1 for every $i,j=1,\dots,n$.

Moreover, if x_i is preferred to x_j and x_j is preferred to x_k, then x_i should be preferred to x_k with at least the same intensity. Thus R should satisfy the following transitivity:

$$r_{ij} \geqq 0.5,\ r_{jk} \geqq 0.5 \Longrightarrow r_{ik} \geqq \min\,(r_{ij}, r_{jk}) \qquad \text{for any } i,j,k=1,\dots,n. \tag{2.3}$$

This relation is called max-min transitivity (Dubois and Prade [7]) with some restriction (preassumption: $r_{ij} \geqq 0.5$, $r_{jk} \geqq 0.5$). This type of transitivity is also called moderate stochastic transitivity in the probabilistic choice theory (Luce and Suppes [15]). A fuzzy binary relation satisfying reciprocity (2.2) and restricted max-min transitivity (2.3) is called a fuzzy preference relation in this paper. The set of all fuzzy preference relations over the set X is denoted by $\mathcal{F}$, that is,

$$\mathcal{F} = \{R = (r_{ij}) : 0 \leqq r_{ij} \leqq 1,\ \ r_{ij} + r_{ji} = 1,\ \ r_{ij} \geqq 0.5,\ r_{jk} \geqq 0.5 \Longrightarrow r_{ik} \geqq \min\,(r_{ij}, r_{jk}) \quad \forall i,j,k\} \tag{2.4}$$

Let $\mathcal{F}_0$ be the set of all nonfuzzy preference relations, that is,

$$\mathcal{F}_0 = \{R \in \mathcal{F} : r_{ij} = 0,\ 0.5 \text{ or } 1 \quad \text{for } \forall i,j=1,\dots,n\}. \tag{2.5}$$

Of course, $r_{ij} = 1$ indicates that x_i is preferred to x_j (denoted by $x_i \succ x_j$) and $r_{ij} = 0.5$ indicates that x_i is indifferent to x_j (denoted by $x_i \sim x_j$). Max-min transitivity implies the usual transitivity:

$$x_i \succsim x_j,\ \ x_j \succsim x_k \Longrightarrow x_i \succsim x_k \qquad \forall i,j,k. \tag{2.6}$$

$\mathcal{F}_0$ is a class of weak orders on X. We may consider the class of linear orders on X as follows:

$$\mathcal{F}_1 = \{R \in \mathcal{F} : r_{ij} = 0 \text{ or } 1 \quad \text{for } i \neq j\}. \tag{2.7}$$

Of course, $\mathcal{F}_1 \subset \mathcal{F}_0$.

The following proposition shows that every fuzzy preference relation is a convex combination of nonfuzzy preference relations.

Proposition 2.1.

$$\mathcal{F} = \text{co } \mathcal{F}_0 = \text{co } \mathcal{F}_1,$$

where co $\mathcal{F}_i$ denotes the convex hull of $\mathcal{F}_i$ (i.e. the set of all convex combinations of elements in $\mathcal{F}_i$) (i=0,1).

Another type of transitivity, which is often called restricted max-max transitivity [7] (or strong stochastic transitivity [15]), is given by the following:

$$r_{ij} \geqq 0.5,\ r_{jk} \geqq 0.5 \implies r_{ik} \geqq \max (r_{ij}, r_{jk}) \quad \forall i,j,k. \qquad (2.9)$$

It is clear, of course, that restricted max-max transitivity is a stronger concept than restricted max-min transitivity. From the practical point of view, consistent fuzzy preference relations might have to satisfy restricted max-max transitivity.

We must note that under the reciprocity condition, (2.3) and (2.9) are equivalent to

$$r_{ij} \leqq 0.5,\ r_{jk} \leqq 0.5 \implies r_{ik} \leqq \max (r_{ij}, r_{jk}) \quad \forall i,j,k \qquad (2.3')$$

and

$$r_{ij} \leqq 0.5,\ r_{jk} \leqq 0.5 \implies r_{ik} \leqq \min (r_{ij}, r_{jk}) \quad \forall i,j,k \qquad (2.9')$$

respectively.

Moreover we may consider another type of transitivity if we understand $r_{ij} - 0.5$ to be an intensity of preference of x_i over x_j. Namely, a transitivity relation of intensities of preference can be defined as follows:

$$(r_{ij} - 0.5) + (r_{jk} - 0.5) = r_{ik} - 0.5 \quad \forall i,j,k. \qquad (2.10)$$

This relation is called additive transitivity in this paper. Additive transitivity is a stronger concept than restricted max-max transitivity (see Proposition 2.2 below).

In the case where $r_{ij} > 0$ for all i,j=1,...,n and r_{ij}/r_{ji} indicates a ratio of the preference intensity for x_i to that for x_j (that is, x_i is r_{ij}/r_{ji} times as good as x_j), the transitivity relation

$$\frac{r_{ji}}{r_{ij}} \frac{r_{kj}}{r_{jk}} = \frac{r_{ki}}{r_{ik}} \quad \forall i,j,k \qquad (2.11)$$

should be satisfied. Since we have

$$r_{ji}/r_{ij} = (1 - r_{ij})/r_{ij} = 1/r_{ij} - 1$$

under the condition (2.2), the above relation (2.11) can be written as follows:

$$(1/r_{ij} - 1)(1/r_{jk} - 1) = 1/r_{ik} - 1 \qquad \forall i,j,k \tag{2.11'}$$

which is called multiplicative transitivity. Multiplicative transitivity (2.11') also implies restricted max-max transitivity (2.9).

Proposition 2.2. (Tanino [18]) If a fuzzy preference relation satisfies additive transitivity (2.10) or multiplicative transitivity (2.11), then it is max-max transitive with restriction.

(Proof) First, suppose that (2.10) holds and $r_{ij} \geqq 0.5$, $r_{jk} \geqq 0.5$, then

$$r_{ik} - r_{ij} = r_{ij} + r_{jk} - 0.5 - r_{ij} = r_{jk} - 0.5 \geqq 0.$$

Similarly, $r_{ik} - r_{jk} \geqq 0$ can be shown. Thus (2.9) is satisfied. Next, suppose that (2.10) holds and $r_{ij} \geqq 0.5$, $r_{jk} \geqq 0.5$. Then $0 \leqq 1/r_{ij} - 1 \leqq 1$ and $0 \leqq 1/r_{jk} - 1 \leqq 1$. So we have

$$1/r_{ik} - 1 \leqq 1/r_{ij} - 1 \quad \text{and} \quad 1/r_{ik} - 1 \leqq 1/r_{jk} - 1$$

i.e.

$$r_{ik} \leqq \max\,(r_{ij}, r_{jk}).$$

2.2 α-level nonfuzzy preference relations

Given a fuzzy binary relation $R = (r_{ij})$ on X, we can consider a nonfuzzy binary relation $R(\alpha)$ for each scalar $\alpha \in [0,1]$, which is defined by

$$r_{ij}(\alpha) = \begin{cases} 1 & \text{if } r_{ij} \geqq \alpha \\ 0 & \text{if } r_{ij} < \alpha \end{cases} \tag{2.12}$$

As for those relations, the following simple but important result holds.

Proposition 2.3. If R is a fuzzy preference relation, then for any $\alpha \in (0.5,1]$, $R(\alpha)$ defined by (2.12) is a strict partial order in the ordinary sense. Namely it is

(1) irreflexive: $r_{ii}(\alpha) = 0 \quad \forall i,$

(2) transitive: $r_{ij}(\alpha) = 1,\ r_{jk}(\alpha) = 1 \Rightarrow r_{ik}(\alpha) = 1 \quad \forall i,j,k.$

Moreover, if $\alpha = 0.5$, $R(\alpha)$ is a weak order. Namely $R(0.5)$ is

(1) transitive: $r_{ij}(0.5)=1,\ r_{jk}(0.5)=1 \Rightarrow r_{ik}(0.5)=1 \quad \forall i,j,k$

(2) connected: $r_{ij}(0.5) = 1$ or $r_{ji}(0.5) = 1 \quad \forall i,j,$

2.3 Measures of fuzziness for fuzzy binary relations

Given a fuzzy binary relation $R = (r_{ij})$ on X, its average fuzziness and average certainty are defined by

$$F(R) = \frac{\sum_{i=1}^{n} \sum_{j \neq i} r_{ij} r_{ji}}{n(n-1)/2} \tag{2.13}$$

and

$$C(R) = \frac{\sum_{i=1}^{n} \sum_{j \neq i} (r_{ij})^2}{n(n-1)/2} \tag{2.14}$$

respectively (Bezdek et al. [2,3]).

Proposition 2.4. (Bezdek et al. [2]) For any reciprocal fuzzy binary relation R,

(1) $F(R) + C(R) = 1$

(2) $F(R) = 0.5 \Leftrightarrow C(R) = 0.5 \Leftrightarrow R = R_{0.5}$

where $R_{0.5}$ is a fuzzy binary relation whose elements are all 0.5.

(3) $F(R) = 0 \Leftrightarrow C(R) = 1 \Leftrightarrow R \in \mathcal{F}_1$ (i.e. $r_{ij}=0$ or 1 $\forall i \neq j$).

2.4 Utility values and fuzzy preference relations

In a general fuzzy preference relation, the degree of freedom, that is, the number of independent elements is $n(n-1)/2$ because of its reciprocity. If additive transitivity or multiplicative transitivity is satisfied, only $(n-1)$ elements are independent. Hence, in such a case, there may exist a utility function (a set of utility values for the alternatives) which is a difference scale or a ratio scale. In other words, utility values are considered to be reflecting the preference intensity.

First, we consider the case in which a utility function $u(x)$ on the set X is given as a difference scale. We denote by u_i the utility value $u(x_i)$ for the alternative x_i $(i=1,\dots,n)$ and assume that u_i's are normalized so that $\max_i u_i - \min_i u_i \leqq 1$. If we define

$$r_{ij} = \frac{1}{2}(1 + u_i - u_j) \tag{2.15}$$

it is clear that $0 \leqq r_{ij} \leqq 1$ and $r_{ij} + r_{ji} = 1$ for any $i,j=1,\dots,n$. Moreover it can be easily checked that additive transitivity (2.10) holds. Thus we have:

Proposition 2.5. If a set of values $\{u_1,\dots,u_n\}$ with $\max_i u_i - \min_i u_i \leqq 1$ is given, then the fuzzy relation R defined by (2.15) is a fuzzy preference relation satisfying additive transitivity.

Conversely if such a fuzzy preference relation is given, then we can assign utility values to the alternatives with $\max_i u_i - \min_i u_i \leqq$

1 since only (n-1) elements in R are independent. Those utility values are unique up to addition of an arbitrary real number.

In the case where utility values $\{u_1,\dots,u_n\}$ on the set X are given on the basis of a positive ratio scale, we may define R by

$$r_{ij} = \frac{u_i}{u_i + u_j} = \frac{1}{1 + u_j/u_i}, \tag{2.16}$$

This type of fourmula has been investigated in the constant utility model under the existence of a ratio scale of preference (Luce and Suppes [15]). Then R clearly satisfies (2.2): $r_{ij} + r_{ji} = 1$ for $i,j=1,\dots,n$, and from

$$\frac{1}{r_{ij}} - 1 = \frac{r_{ji}}{r_{ij}} = \frac{u_j}{u_i}, \tag{2.17}$$

multiplicative transitivity (2.11') immediately follows. Thus we have the following proposition.

Proposition 2.6. If a set of positive values $\{u_1,\dots,u_n\}$ is given then the fuzzy preference relation R defined by (2.16) is a fuzzy preference relation satisfying multiplicative transitivity.

Conversely if such a fuzzy preference relation is given, then we can assign a positive utility value to each alternative since only (n-1) elements of R are independent. Those utility values are unique up to multiplication by a positive scalar. In this case $r_{ij}/r_{ji} = u_i/u_j$, which indicates the ratio of the preference of x_i to that of x_j.

Thus we may identify utility values with fuzzy preference relations satisfying appropriate transitivity conditions.

3. Group Decision Making Based on Individual Fuzzy Preference Relations

In this section we discuss group decision making in the case where each individual preference is represented by a fuzzy preference relation. Let a group consist of m individuals $p=1,\dots,m$ and the preference of the individual p for the alternatives $\{x_1,\dots,x_n\}$ be represented by a fuzzy preference relation $R^p = (r^p_{ij})$ (n×n matrix). In this section we deal with some methods for choosing (possibly unique) alternatives which are considered to be desirable for the group. As is pointed out by Kacprzyk [9-11], roughly speaking, two approaches are here possible:

(1) direct approach — decide a solution (an alternative or a set of alternatives) directly from $\{R^1,\dots, R^m\}$.

(2) indirect approach — first derive a group fuzzy preference relation R from $\{R^1,\ldots, R^m\}$ and then decide a solution from R.

Moreover, if we regard group decison making as a dynamic process, the group may use practically meaningful group fuzzy preference relation as an information for proceeding the decision making process. Such a systems analytic approach will be dealt with in the next section.

3.1 Direct approach

Fuzzy α-core, α-minimax set and so on are known well as solution concepts directly derived from individual fuzzy preference relations $\{R^1,\ldots, R^m\}$ (Nurmi [17]). They are extended from the concepts in the nonfuzzy case.

1) fuzzy α-core

Suppose that a number $q \leq m$ which implies majority in the group is given. Then, the set defined by

$$C_\alpha = \{x_i \in X : \nexists\, x_j \in X \text{ such that } r^p_{ji} > \alpha \text{ for at least } q \text{ individuals}\} \tag{3.1}$$

for $\alpha \in [0.5,1)$ is called the fuzzy α-core. It is clear that if $\alpha_1 < \alpha_2$, then

$$C_{\alpha_1} \subset C_{\alpha_2} \tag{3.2}$$

Particularly $C_{0.5}$ for $\alpha = 0.5$ is called the core. The fuzzy α-core is a set of alternatives which are not sufficiently (at least to degree α) defeated by the required majority q. A core alternative is an optimal solution, while an alternative belonging to α-core is a satisficing solution.

2) α-minimax set

For $\alpha \in (0,0.5]$, let

$$w_\alpha(x_i,x_j) = \#\{p : r^p_{ij} < \alpha\} = \#\{p : r^p_{ji} \geq 1-\alpha\} \tag{3.3}$$

where #A denotes the number of elements in a set A. The quantity $w_\alpha(x_i,x_j)$ is the number of individuals who prefer x_j over x_i at least to degree $1-\alpha$. Let

$$v_\alpha(x_i) = \max_{j=1,\ldots,n} w_\alpha(x_i,x_j) \tag{3.4}$$

and

$$v^*_\alpha = \min_{i=1,\ldots,n} v_\alpha(x_i) \tag{3.5}$$

Then the α-minimax set is defined by

$$M_\alpha = \{x_i \in X : v_\alpha(x_i) = v^*_\alpha\} . \tag{3.6}$$

Particularly, when $\alpha = 0.5$, $M_{0.5}$ is called the minimax set. The α-minimax set contains alternatives that are less preferred at least to degree α by no more than v_α^* individuals, hence by the least number of individuals.

Extensions of these concepts to the case of group decision making with a fuzzy linguistic majority were given by Kacprzyk ([9-11]).

3) Minimax degree set

Let

$$v_D^p(x_j) = \max_i r_{ij} \qquad j=1,\ldots,n \tag{3.7}$$

and

$$v_D(x_j) = \max_p v_D^p(x_j) \tag{3.8}$$

for $p=1,\ldots,m$. Then, the set

$$Q = \{x_j \in X : v_D(x_j) = \min_j v_D(x_j)\} \tag{3.9}$$

is called the minimax degree set. The minimax degree set consists of the alternatives which minimizes the opposition with respect to the other alternatives from the members of the group.

If the concept of coalitions is introduced in the group, we can define the α-vulnerable set and the least alternative α-level set (Nurmi [17]).

3.2 Indirect approach

In the indirect approach, we first derive a group fuzzy preference relation from the given individual fuzzy preference relations and next determine a solution from the obtained relation. Hence there are two issues in the indirect approach. One is how to aggregate the individual fuzzy preference relations to form a group fuzzy preference relation and the other is how to derive a solution on the basis of a given group fuzzy preference relation.

1) Formation of a group fuzzy preference relation

The simplest way of forming a group fuzzy preference relation from given individual fuzzy preference relations $\{R^1,\ldots, R^m\}$ is to let

$$r_{ij} = \frac{1}{m}\sum_{p=1}^{m} r_{ij}^p \tag{3.10}$$

It is clear that $0 \leq r_{ij} \leq 1$ and $r_{ij} + r_{ji} = 1$ for any $i,j=1,\ldots,n$. The obtained relation, however, does not generally satisfy max-min transitivity, and hence is not a fuzzy preference relation in our sense. This implies that it is difficult to form a consistent group preference relation as is known by Arrow's impossibility theorem ([1]). If we assume that each individual preference is represented by difference scale utility values, then the group fuzzy relation by (3.10) is additively transitive. In fact,

$$r_{ij} = \frac{1}{m} \sum_{p=1}^{m} \frac{1}{2} (1 + u_i^p - u_j^p) = \frac{1}{2} (1 + \frac{1}{m} \sum_{p=1}^{m} u_i^p - \frac{1}{m} \sum_{p=1}^{m} u_j^p) \qquad (3.11)$$

where u_i^p is the utility value of the individual p for the alternative x_i. Eq. (3.11) implies that the group fuzzy preference relation is obtained from the group utility values $\{ \frac{1}{m} \sum_{p=1}^{m} u_i^p \}$. Thus we have the following theorem.

Theorem 3.1. If each R^p (p=1,...,m) is a fuzzy preference relation satisfying additive transitivity, then so is R defined by eq. (3.10).

Remark 3.1. In Nurmi [17], a fuzzy binary relation $A^p = (a_{ij}^p)$ was essentially defined by

$$a_{ij}^p = \begin{cases} 1 & \text{if } r_{ij}^p > 0.5 \\ 0.5 & \text{if } r_{ij}^p = 0.5 \\ 0 & \text{if } r_{ij}^p < 0.5 \end{cases} \qquad (3.12)$$

and $R = (r_{ij})$ was defined by

$$r_{ij} = \frac{1}{m} \sum_{p=1}^{m} a_{ij}^p \, . \qquad (3.13)$$

This definition is the same as (3.10) derived from the individual fuzzy preference relations $\{A^1, \ldots, A^m\}$.

Another type of group fuzzy preference relation is given by

$$r_{ij} = \frac{\prod_{p=1}^{m} r_{ij}^p}{\prod_{p=1}^{m} r_{ij}^p + \prod_{p=1}^{m} r_{ji}^p} \, . \qquad (3.14)$$

The obtained R is not generally a fuzzy preference relation in our sense. Even when R does not satisfy max-min transitivity, it can be used as a fuzzy relation which represents the preference attitude of the group.

2) A solution from a given fuzzy preference relation

Let R be a reciprocal fuzzy binary relation. Max-min transitivity is not necessarily assumed. The first solution concept was given by Nurmi [17]. Let α be a number such that $0.5 < \alpha \leq 1$. An alternative x_i is said to be an α-consensus winner if

$$r_{ij} \geqq \alpha \quad \text{for any } j \neq i \tag{3.15}$$

Namely, x_i is the α-consensus winner if it is preferred to any other alternative sufficiently (at least to degree α).

Theorem 3.2. (Nurmi [17]) The α-consensus winner is unique if it exists. If x_i is the α-consensus winner, then it is also α'-consensus winner for any α' such that $0.5 < \alpha' \leqq \alpha$.

An extension of this concept to the case of linguistic majority was provided by Kacprzyk ([9-11]).

The following concept was also given by Nurmi [17]. Let

$$\bar{r}_j = \max_{i=1,\dots,n} r_{ij} \qquad j=1,\dots,n \tag{3.16}$$

and

$$\bar{r} = \min_{j=1,\dots,n} \bar{r}_j = \min_j \max_i r_{ij}. \tag{3.17}$$

When $\bar{r}_i = \bar{r}$, the alternative x_i is said to be a minimax consensus winner. The minimax consensus winner is the alternative which when confronted with its most serious competitors fare best, i.e., win by the largest score (if $\bar{r} \geqq 0.5$) or lose by the smallest score (if $\bar{r} < 0.5$).

Thoerem 3.3. (Nurmi [17]) The minimax consensus winner always exists, but it is not always unique. If $\bar{r} < 0.5$, then it is also the α-consensus winner for $\alpha = 1-\bar{r}$ and hence is unique.

Another solution concept is defined by considering a distance in the space of fuzzy preference relations. A solution is obtained if we can choose a nonfuzzy preference relation belonging to the class of weak orders $\mathcal{F}_0$ or the class of linear orders $\mathcal{F}_1$ that is the closest to a given fuzzy preference relation.

Since every fuzzy binary relation is represented by an n×n matrix, we may consider any distance in the space of n×n matrices, which is isomorphic to the n×n dimensional Euclidean space. A typical distance used by Bezdek et al. [3] is the l_2-metric defined as follows: For two n×n matrices R and S, let

$$\langle R,S\rangle = \operatorname{tr}(RS^T), \tag{3.18}$$

$$\|R\| = (\langle R,R\rangle)^{1/2} = [\sum_{i=1}^{n} \sum_{j=1}^{n} (r_{ij})^2]^{1/2} \tag{3.19}$$

and

$$d(R,S) = \|R - S\|. \tag{3.20}$$

Another distance used by Kuz'min and Ovchinnikov [14] is the l_1-metric

$$|R| = \sum_{i=1}^{n} \sum_{j=1}^{n} |r_{ij}| \tag{3.21}$$

and

$$d(R,S) = |R - S| = \sum_{i=1}^{n} \sum_{j=1}^{n} |r_{ij} - s_{ij}|. \tag{3.22}$$

Of course we can consider a general l_q-metric:

$$d(R,S) = (\sum_{i=1}^{n} \sum_{j=1}^{n} |r_{ij} - s_{ij}|^q)^{1/q} \quad \text{for } 1 \leqq q < \infty . \tag{3.23}$$

In any case, it is not generally possible to find a unique nonfuzzy preference relation closest to a given fuzzy relation, since neither $\mathcal{F}_0$ nor $\mathcal{F}_1$ is convex.

4. Group Fuzzy Preference Relations for Decision Support

As is seen in Arrow's general impossibility theorem, it is impossible to aggregate several individual preferences into a group preference in a completely rational way. In other words, the group preference aggregated from individual preferences by any method is always fuzzy in the sense that it is based on a certain formal procedure and does not fully reflect conflict or diversity of individual opinions in the group. Therefore, if we consider group decision making as a process, it might be rather meaningful to define a group fuzzy preference relation in which the fuzziness is directly related to the degree of conflict in the group. This section is devoted to such group fuzzy preference relations.

4.1 A group fuzzy preference relation based on individual additively transitive fuzzy preference relations

As an example, let R^p be a fuzzy preference relation satisfying additive transitivity (p=1,...,m) and consider the group fuzzy preference relation defined in Section 3, that is,

$$r_{ij} = \frac{1}{m} \sum_{p=1}^{m} r_{ij}^p \tag{4.1}$$

(See Fig. 1 in case of m=2). This group preference cannot reflect the diversity of opinions in the group. For example, consider the following two cases of individual preferences (m=2, n=2):

i) $R^1 = \begin{bmatrix} .5 & 1 \\ 0 & .5 \end{bmatrix}$, $R^2 = \begin{bmatrix} .5 & 0 \\ 1 & .5 \end{bmatrix}$

ii) $R^1 = \begin{bmatrix} .5 & .5 \\ .5 & .5 \end{bmatrix}$, $R^2 = \begin{bmatrix} .5 & .5 \\ .5 & .5 \end{bmatrix}$

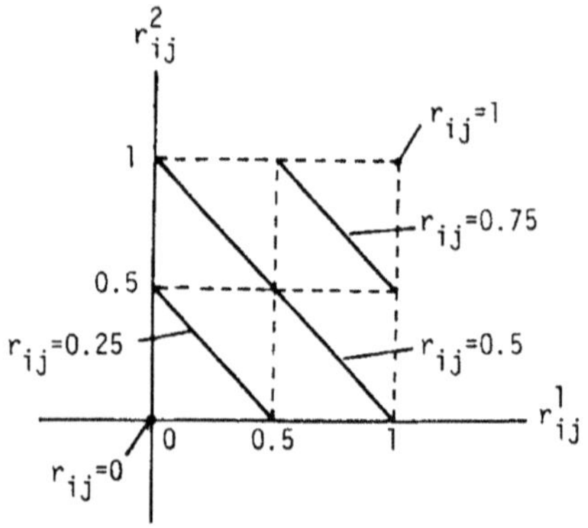

Fig. 1 Group fuzzy preference relation by (4.1)

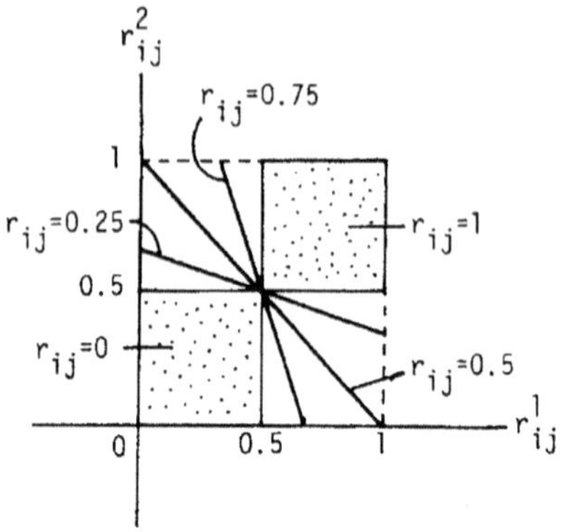

Fig. 2 Group fuzzy preference relation by (4.2)

In both cases, the group fuzzy preference relation defined by (4.1) is

$$R = \begin{bmatrix} .5 & .5 \\ .5 & .5 \end{bmatrix}$$

in spite that the two situations are completely different. Hence the rule (4.1) is not sufficient for understanding the preference situation in the group (for example, diversity of opinions).

Since r^p_{ij} is understood as a measure of how strongly individual p feels about definite preference of x_i over x_j, $r^p_{ij} \geqq 0.5$ for all $p=1,\ldots,m$ and $r^p_{ij} > 0.5$ for some p should imply $r_{ij} = 1$ (Pareto rule). Therefore we may define a group fuzzy preference relation as shown in Fig. 2 in case of m=2. That is, we define

$$r_{ij} = \begin{cases} \dfrac{\sum_{p=1}^{m} \max\,(r^p_{ij}-0.5,\ 0)}{\sum_{p=1}^{m} |r^p_{ij}-0.5|} = \dfrac{1}{2}\,\dfrac{\sum_{p=1}^{m} (r^p_{ij}-0.5)}{\sum_{p=1}^{m} |r^p_{ij}-0.5|} + 0.5 & \text{if } i \neq j \\ 0.5 & \text{if } i=j \end{cases} \tag{4.2}$$

Here we can assume without loss of generality that there are no two alternatives x_i and x_j such that $r^p_{ij} = 0.5$ for all p, since $r^p_{ij} = 0.5$ for all p for $i \neq j$ implies that the group cannot discriminate x_i from x_j at all. It is clear that $0 \leqq r_{ij} \leqq 1$. This fuzzy relation R has desired properties as follows.

Theorem 4.1. (Tanino [18]) If R^p is a fuzzy preference relation satisfying additive transitivity for every $p=1,\ldots,m$, then R defined by (4.2) is a fuzzy preference relation. Moreover, $r_{ij} = 1$ if and only if $r^p_{ij} \geqq 0.5$ for all p and $r^p_{ij} > 0.5$ for some p.

The diversity of preferences may be evaluated by using the measure of fuzziness described in Section 2.

It has already been noted in the previous sections that R^p is additively transitive if and only if it is derived from utility values of a difference scale. Therefore (4.2) can be written by use of utility values. Suppose u^p_i be the utility value of the individual p for the alternative i (p=1,...,m; i=1,...,n) and

$$r^p_{ij} = \frac{1}{2}(1 + u^p_i - u^p_j) \tag{4.3}$$

Then R of (4.2) can be rewritten as

$$r_{ij} = \begin{cases} \dfrac{\sum_{p=1}^{m} \max(u^p_i - u^p_j, 0)}{\sum_{p=1}^{m} |u^p_i - u^p_j|} = \dfrac{1}{2}\dfrac{\sum_{p=1}^{m}(u^p_i - u^p_j)}{\sum_{p=1}^{m}|u^p_i - u^p_j|} + 0.5 & \text{if } i \neq j \\ 0.5 & \text{if } i = j \end{cases} \tag{4.4}$$

Let $\alpha \in (0.5,1]$ and consider the strict partial order $R(\alpha)$ defined from R by (2.12) (note Proposition 2.3). Since $\alpha > 0.5$, we always have $r_{ii}(\alpha) = 0$. For $i \neq j$,

$$r_{ij}(\alpha) = 1 \iff r_{ij} \geqq \alpha$$

$$\iff \frac{\sum \max(u^p_i - u^p_j, 0)}{\sum |u^p_i - u^p_j|} \geqq \alpha$$

$$\iff \sum(u^p_i - u^p_j) - \sum \min(u^p_i - u^p_j, 0)$$

$$- \alpha\{\sum(u^p_i - u^p_j) - 2\sum \min(u^p_i - u^p_j, 0)\} \geqq 0$$

$$\iff (1-\alpha)\sum(u^p_i - u^p_j) + (2\alpha-1)\sum \min(u^p_i - u^p_j, 0) \geqq 0 \tag{4.5}$$

Nakayama, the author and others [16] have introduced several group preference orderings $\succsim_\lambda$ which are based on the additive group utility function and contain a parameter $\lambda \in [0,\infty)$ in order to take into account the diversity of individual preferences as follows:

$$x_i \succsim_\lambda x_j \iff \sum_{p=1}^{m}(u^p_i - u^p_j) + \lambda \sum_{p=1}^{m} \min(u^p_i - u^p_j, 0) \geqq 0 \tag{4.6}$$

(Extended Contributive Rule method — ECR method for short). By comparing (4.6) with (4.5), we can identify these two types of group preference relations — $\succsim_\lambda$ in the ECR method and $R(\alpha)$ from the fuzzy preference relation — through the correspondence $\lambda=(2\alpha-1)/(1-\alpha)$

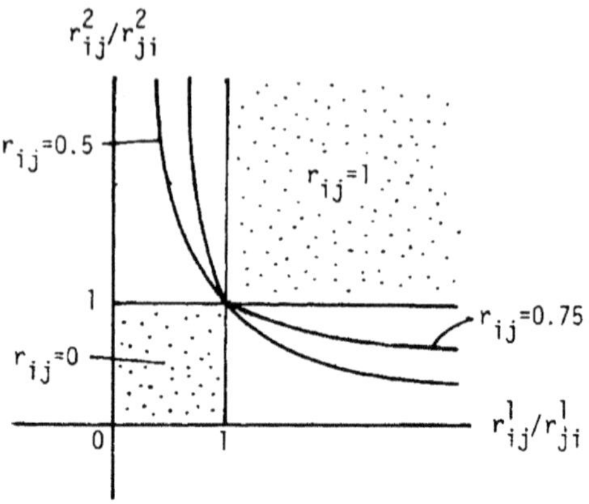

Fig. 3 Group fuzzy preference relation by (4.7)

or $\alpha = (1+\lambda)/(2+\lambda)$. Therefore we can effectively use this group fuzzy preference relation as data for proceeding the group decision making process smoothly, as is intended by the ECR method.

4.2 A group fuzzy preference relation based on individual multiplicatively transitive fuzzy preference relations

Next we shall consider a way of aggregating individual fuzzy preference relations satisfying multiplicative transitivity into a group fuzzy preference. Again we assume without loss of generality that the case $r^p_{ij} = 0.5$ for all p is not possible for $i \neq j$. Also we assume that $0 < r^p_{ij} < 1$ for all $i,j=1,\dots,n$ and $p=1,\dots,m$. In this case we define a group fuzzy preference relation $R = (r_{ij})$ by

$$r_{ij} = \begin{cases} \dfrac{\log \prod_{p=1}^{m} \max\left(\dfrac{r^p_{ij}}{r^p_{ji}}, 1\right)}{\log \prod_{p=1}^{m} \max\left(\dfrac{r^p_{ij}}{r^p_{ji}}, \dfrac{r^p_{ji}}{r^p_{ij}}\right)} = \dfrac{\log \prod_{p=1}^{m} \max\left(\dfrac{1}{r^p_{ji}} - 1, 1\right)}{\log \prod_{p=1}^{m} \max\left(\dfrac{1}{r^p_{ji}} - 1, \dfrac{1}{r^p_{ij}} - 1\right)} & \text{if } i \neq j \\ 0.5 & \text{if } i = j \end{cases} \tag{4.7}$$

(see Fig. 3 in case of m=2). It is clear that $0 \leqq r_{ij} \leqq 1$. The following result holds for this relation R.

<u>Theorem 4.2.</u> (Tanino [18]) If R^p is a fuzzy preference relation satisfying multiplicative transitivity for every $p=1,\dots,m$, then R defined by (4.7) is a fuzzy preference relation. Moreover, $r_{ij} = 1$ if and only if $r^p_{ij} \geqq 0.5$ for any p and $r^p_{ij} > 0.5$ for some p.

As is the case of the fuzzy preference relation given by (4.2), R^p is multiplicatively transitive if and only if it is derived from utility values of a ratio scale. Namely, let

$$r_{ij}^p = \frac{u_i^p}{u_i^p + u_j^p} \qquad i,j=1,\dots,n;\ p=1,\dots,m. \tag{4.8}$$

Then R by (4.7) can be rewritten as

$$r_{ij} = \begin{cases} \dfrac{\log \prod_{p=1}^{m} \max\left(\dfrac{u_i^p}{u_j^p}, 1\right)}{\log \prod_{p=1}^{m} \max\left(\dfrac{u_i^p}{u_j^p}, \dfrac{u_j^p}{u_i^p}\right)} & \text{if } i \neq j \\ 0.5 & \text{if } i = j \end{cases} \tag{4.9}$$

Hence for $\alpha \in (0.5,1]$, the strict partial order $R(\alpha)$ can be derived as follows by simple calculation:

$$r_{ij}(\alpha) = 1 \iff r_{ij} \geqq \alpha$$

$$\iff \log \prod_p \max\left(\frac{u_i^p}{u_j^p}, 1\right) \geqq \alpha \log \prod_p \max\left(\frac{u_i^p}{u_j^p}, \frac{u_j^p}{u_i^p}\right)$$

$$\iff (2\alpha-1)\log \prod_p \min\left(\frac{u_i^p}{u_j^p}, 1\right) + (1-\alpha)\log \prod_p \frac{u_i^p}{u_j^p} \geqq 0$$

Namely, for $i \neq j$

$$r_{ij}(\alpha) = 1 \iff \left[\prod_{p=1}^{m} \frac{u_i^p}{u_j^p}\right]^{1-\alpha} \left[\prod_{p=1}^{m} \min\left(\frac{u_i^p}{u_j^p}, 1\right)\right]^{2\alpha-1} \geqq 1 . \tag{4.10}$$

Thus $R(\alpha)$ is an order which is based on the ordering by the Nash social welfare function and depends on the degree of taking into account opposite opinions to preference of x_i over x_j, represented by $\min(u_i^p/u_j^p, 1)$. Here the order by the Nash social welfare function is as follows:

$$x_i \succsim x_j \iff \prod_{p=1}^{m} \frac{u_i^p}{u_j^p} \geqq 1 \tag{4.11}$$

As $\alpha \to 0.5$, the right-hand side of (4.10) tends to coincide with that of (4.11). While, when $\alpha = 1$, $r_{ij}(\alpha) = 1$ if and only if $u_i^p \geqq u_j^p$ for all p and $u_i^p > u_j^p$ for some p. Therefore we can use this group fuzzy preference relation as data for understanding the decision situation or the preference attitude of the whole group in the decision making on the basis of the Nash social welfare function.

5. Conclusion

It seems to be effective to use fuzzy preference relations in group decision making. Individual preferences are naturally assumed to be represented by fuzzy preference relations which satisfy reciprocity and restricted max-min transitivity, so long as they are consistent. Basic results concerning fuzzy preference relations have been reviewed in Section 2. We may consider several concepts of solutions (group choice) based on the individual fuzzy preference relations. They have been explained in the third section. However, no solution concept is perfect, as can be expected from Arrow's impossibility theorem, even when fuzzy preference relations are used. Therefore, it seems also practical and interesting to aggregate individual preferences into a group fuzzy preference relation in which fuzziness is mainly due to the diversity of preferences in the group. Such an approach discussed in Section 4 is surely useful in constructing a decision support system for group decision making.

References

[1] Arrow, K.J., Social Choice and Individual Values, 2nd ed., Wiley, New York (1963)

[2] Bezdek, J.C., B. Spillman and R. Spillman, "A fuzzy relation space for group decision theory", Fuzzy Sets and Systems 1, 255-268 (1978)

[3] Bezdek, J.C., B. Spillman and R. Spillman, "Fuzzy relation spaces for group decision theory: An application", Fuzzy Sets and Systems 2, 5-14 (1979)

[4] Blin, J.M., "Fuzzy relations in group decision theory", J. Cybernet. 4, 17-22 (1974)

[5] Blin, J.M. and A.P. Whinston, "Fuzzy sets and social choice", J. Cybernet. 3, 28-33 (1973)

[6] Dimitrov, V.N., "Group choice under fuzzy information", Fuzzy Sets and SYstems 9, 25-40 (1983)

[7] Dubois, D. and H. Prade, Fuzzy Sets and Systems : Theory and Applications, Academic Press, New York (1980)

[8] Fung, L.W. and K.S. Fu, "An axiomatic approach to rational decision-making in a fuzzy environment:, in : Zadeh, A.L. et al. Eds., Fuzzy Sets and Their Applications to Cognitive and Decision Processes, Academic Press, New York (1975)

[9] Kacprzyk, J., "Group decision-making with a fuzzy majority via linguistic quantifiers, Part 1 : a consensory-like pooling", Cybernet. and Systems 16, 119-129 (1985)

[10] Kacprzyk, J., "Group decision-making with a fuzzy majority via linguistic quantifiers, Part II: a competitive-like pooling", Cybernet. and Systems 16, 131-144 (1985)

[11] Kacprzyk, J., "group decision making with a fuzzy linguistic majority", Fuzzy Sets and Systems 18, 105-118 (1986)

[12] Kim, J.B., "Fuzzy rational choice functions", Fuzzy Sets and Systems 10, 37-43 (1983)

[13] Kuz'min, V.B. and S.V. Ovchinnikov, "Group decisions I. In arbitrary spaces of fuzzy binary relations", Fuzzy Sets and Systems 4, 53-62 (1980)

[14] Kuz'min, V.B. and S.V. Ovchinnikov, "Design of group decisions II. In spaces of partial order fuzzy relations", Fuzzy Sets and Systems 4, 153-165 (1980)

[15] Luce, R.D. and P. Suppes, "Preferences, utility and subjective probability", in : Luce, R.D. et al. Eds., Handbook of Mathematical Psychology, Vol. III, Wiley, New York (1965)

[16] Nakayama, H., T. Tanino, K. Matsumoto, H. Matsuo, K. Inoue and Y. Sawaragi, "Methodology for group decision making with an application to assessment of residential environment", IEEE Trans. Systems, Man, & Cybernet. 9, 477-485 (1979)

[17] Nurmi, H., "Approaches to collective decision making with fuzzy preference relations", Fuzzy Sets and Systems 6, 249-259 (1981)

[18] Tanino, T., "Fuzzy preference orderings in group decision making", Fuzzy Sets and Systems 12, 117-131 (1984)

[19] Zimmermann, H.J., Fuzzy Set Theory - and Its Applications, Kluwer Academic, Netherlands (1985)

{P, Q, I}- PREFERENCE STRUCTURES

Philippe Vincke
Free University of Brussels
Boulevard du Triomphe, C.P.210, 1050-Bruxelles, Belgium

ABSTRACT

Two criticisms essentially are made about the complete preorder as preference model : the transitivity of indifference and the absence of intermediary relation between indifference and strict preference.
The concepts of semiorder and interval order on one hand, and of "weak preference" on the other hand, try to answer to these criticisms. The purpose of this paper is to study various properties of models which combine both aspects.

1. Introduction

More and more researches have been devoted, these last years, to the study of preference models which are less restrictive than the traditional complete preorder Transitivity of indifference, absence of incomparability, absence of different kinds of preference have been criticized and have led to the concepts of semiorder, interval order, partial relations, pseudo-order, outranking relations, ... ([2], [3] [4]).

This paper is concerned with preference models including three relations : strict preference, weak preference and indifference (the interest of these models and their practical use in algorithms and applications can be found in [2]).
In other words, we assume that an individual who has to compare two alternatives a and b (for a given point of view)
- either strictly prefers a to b (b to a), denoted by a P b (b P a),
- or weakly prefers a to b (b to a), denoted by a Q b (b Q a),
- or is indifferent between a and b, denoted by a I b.

Due to their signification, we also assume that the relations P, Q and I satis "natural properties" of definition 1.

Definition 1 : a {P, Q, I}- structure on a set A is a set of three binary relations P, Q and I, defined on A, and such that :
. $\forall$ a,b $\in$ A : a P b or b P a or a Q b or b Q a or a I b (exclusive or);

. $\forall\, a \in A : a\ I\ a$ (I is reflexive);

$\forall\, a,b \in A : a\ I\ b \Rightarrow b\ I\ a$ (I is symmetric);

$\forall\, a,b \in A : a\ P\ b \Rightarrow b\ \not P\ a$ (P is asymmetric);

$\forall\, a,b \in A : a\ Q\ b \Rightarrow b\ \not Q\ a$ (Q is asymmetric).

and T being binary relations on A, we will denote

$a\ S^{-1}\ b$ iff $b\ S\ a$,

$S \subset T$ iff $a\ S\ b \Rightarrow a\ T\ b,\ \forall\, a,b$,

$a\ S.\ T\ b$ iff $\exists\, c : a\ S\ c$ and $c\ T\ b$,

$a\ S^2\ b$ iff $a\ S.\ S\ b$,

$a\ (S \cup T)\ b$ iff $a\ S\ b$ or $a\ T\ b$ (non exclusive),

$a\ (S \cap T)\ b$ iff $a\ S\ b$ and $a\ T\ b$,

$S = \emptyset$ iff $\nexists\, a,b : a\ S\ b$.

n this paper, A is a finite set. We first study some transitivity properties of a P,Q,I}-structure (section 2) and present in section 3 necessary and sufficient condi- ions to represent such a structure by real functions, generalizing the numerical epresentations of interval orders, semiorders and pseudo-orders. Section 4 presents he motivation of this research and the interpretation of the obtained results. An pen problem is proposed in section 5.

. Transitivity properties of a {P,Q,I}-structure.

efinition 2 : a {P,Q,I}-structure is weakly transitive iff

$$\begin{cases} P.\ P \subset P\ , \\ P.\ Q \subset P\ , \\ Q.\ P \subset P\ , \\ Q.\ Q \subset P \cup Q\ . \end{cases}$$

efinition 3 : a {P,Q,I}-structure is Q^2-transitive iff it is weakly transitive and

$$Q.\ Q \subset P\ .$$

efinition 4 : a {P,Q,I}-structure is P.I-transitive iff it is weakly transitive and

$$P.\ I \subset P \cup Q\ .$$

this condition is equivalent to $I.\ P \subset P \cup Q$ or to $P \cap I^2 = \emptyset$).

efinition 5 : a {P,Q,I}-structure is strongly transitive iff it is Q^2-transitive nd P.I-transitive.

ne following tableau summarizes what is obtained when combining two relations S_1 and $_2$ from the set $\{P, Q, I, Q^{-1}, P^{-1}\}$ under the assumptions of weak transitivity (column), Q^2-transitivity (column 2), P.I-transitivity (column 3) and strong transitivity column 4).

S_1	S_2	$S_1 \cdot S_2$			
		①	②	③	④
P	P	P	P	P	P
P	Q	P	P	P	P
P	I	P U Q U I	P U Q U I	P U Q	P U Q
P	Q^{-1}	P U Q U I	P U Q U I	P U Q U I	P U Q U I
P	P^{-1}	Z	Z	Z	Z
Q	P	P	P	P	P
Q	Q	P U Q	P	P U Q	P
Q	I	P U Q U I	P U Q U I	P U Q U I	P U Q U I
Q	Q^{-1}	Q U I U Q^{-1}	I	Q U I U Q^{-1}	I
Q	P^{-1}	I U Q^{-1} U P^{-1}	I U Q^{-1} U P^{-1}	I U Q^{-1} U P^{-1}	I U Q^{-1} U P^{-1}
I	P	P U Q U I	P U Q U I	P U Q	P U Q
I	Q	P U Q U I	P U Q U I	P U Q U I	P U Q U I
I	I	Z	Z	Q U I U Q^{-1}	Q U I U Q^{-1}

In this tableau, $Z = P \cup Q \cup I \cup Q^{-1} \cup P^{-1}$.

Remark

The strong transitivity is equivalent to the "generalized transitivity" introduced in [5].

3. Numerical representation of a {P,Q,I}-structure.

Definition 6 : a {P,Q,I}-structure is a thresholds-structure iff there exist three functions g, q and p such that, $\forall$ a,b $\in$ A :

$$\begin{cases} a\ P\ b \iff g(a) > g(b) + p(b) , \\ a\ Q\ b \iff g(b) + p(b) > g(a) > g(b) + q(b) , \\ a\ I\ b \iff \begin{cases} g(b) + q(b) > g(a) , \\ g(a) + q(a) > g(b) , \end{cases} \\ 0 < q(a) < p(a) . \end{cases}$$

Definition 7 : a thresholds-structure is

(i) q-coherent,
(ii) p-coherent,
(iii) (p-q)-coherent,
(iv) (q,p,+)-coherent,
(v) (q,p,-)-coherent,
(vi) (q,p)-coherent,
(vii) a pseudo-order,

iff the functions g, q, p can be respectively chosen is such a way that, $\forall$ a,b $\in$ A :

(i) $g(a) > g(b) \Leftrightarrow g(a) + q(a) > g(b) + q(b)$,

(ii) $g(a) > g(b) \Leftrightarrow g(a) + p(a) > g(b) + p(b)$,

(iii) $g(a) + q(a) > g(b) + q(b) \Leftrightarrow g(a) + p(a) > g(b) + p(b)$,

(iv) $g(a) > g(b) + q(b) \Rightarrow g(a) + q(a) > g(b) + p(b)$,

(v) $g(a) + q(a) > g(b) + p(b) \Rightarrow g(a) > g(b) + q(b)$,

(vi) $g(a) > g(b) + q(b) \Leftrightarrow g(a) + q(a) > g(b) + p(b)$,

(vii) $g(a) > g(b) \Leftrightarrow g(a) + q(a) > g(b) + q(b) \Leftrightarrow g(a) + p(a) > g(b) + p(b)$.

Theorem 1 : a {P,Q,I}-structure is a thresholds-structure iff

$$\begin{cases} Q.\ I.\ Q \subset Q \cup P , \\ Q.\ I.\ P \subset P , \\ P.\ I.\ P \subset P , \\ P.\ Q^{-1}.\ P \subset P . \end{cases}$$

Remark : these properties imply weak transitivity.

Proof.

The necessity of the conditions is easy to verify. To prove they are sufficient, let us introduce the relation S_1 such that, $\forall$ a,b $\in$ A :

$$a\ S_1\ b \text{ iff } \exists\ c : a\ P\ c \text{ and } b\ \not P\ c ,$$
$$\text{or} \quad a\ Q\ c \text{ and } c\ (P \cup Q \cup I) b .$$

The conditions of theorem 1 imply that S_1 is a weak order (asymmetric and negatively transitive relation), so that there exists a function g such that

$$a\ S_1\ b \Leftrightarrow g(a) > g(b) .$$

We define then $g(a) + q(a)$ in such a way that

$$\begin{cases} g(a) + q(a) < g(c),\ \forall\ c : c(Q \cup P)a , \\ g(a) + q(a) > g(d),\ \forall\ d : d\ I\ a ; \end{cases}$$

this is always possible because $c(Q \cup P)a$ and $d\ I\ a \Rightarrow c\ S_1\ d \Rightarrow g(c) > g(d)$.

On the other hand, we define $g(a) + p(a)$ in such a way that

$$\begin{cases} g(a) + p(a) < g(c),\ \forall\ c : c\ P\ a , \\ g(a) + p(a) > g(d),\ \forall\ d : d\ \not P\ a ; \end{cases}$$

this is always possible because $c\ P\ a$ and $d\ \not P\ a \Rightarrow c\ S_1\ d \Rightarrow g(c) > g(d)$.

The functions g, q and p verify the desired properties.

Theorem 2 : a thresholds-structure is q-coherent iff

$$\begin{cases} (P \cup Q)^2 \cap I^2 = \emptyset , \\ P^2 \cap I.\ Q = \emptyset , \\ Q.\ P \cap I.\ Q = \emptyset . \end{cases}$$

Proof.

The necessity of the conditions is easy to verify. To prove they are sufficient, let us introduce the relation S_2 such that, $\forall$ a,b $\in$ A :

$$a\ S_2\ b \text{ iff } a\ S_1\ b \text{ (see the proof of theorem 1)}$$
$$\text{or } a \not S_1\ b\ ,\ b \not S_1\ a \text{ and } a\ I.\ (Q \cup P)b\ .$$

The reader can verify that if $\{P,Q,I\}$ is a thresholds-structure, then S_2 is a weak order, so that there exists a function g such that

$$a\ S_2\ b \iff g(a) > g(b)\ .$$

The functions g+q and g+p are defined as in the proof of theorem 1.
To verify the q-coherency, let us first consider $g(a) > g(b)$, i.e. a S_2 b.
If $\exists$ c : a P c and b $\not P$ c, then the conditions of theorem 4.2 imply that $\nexists$ d : d(Q $\cup$ P)a and d I b ; in other words $\nexists$ d : $g(b) + q(b) > g(d) > g(a) + q(a)$, so that q can be chosen in such a way that $g(a) + q(a) > g(b) + q(b)$.
If $\exists$ c : a Q c and c (P $\cup$ Q $\cup$ I)b, then the conditions of theorem 4.2. imply that $\nexists$ d : d(Q $\cup$ P)a and d I b, and we can conclude as in the previous case.
If $\exists$ c : a I c and c(Q $\cup$ P)b, then $g(a) + q(a) > g(c) > g(b) + q(b)$.
Let us now consider $g(a) = g(b)$, i.e. a $\not S_2$ b and b $\not S_2$ a, so that $\nexists$ c : a I c and c(Q $\cup$ P)b and $\nexists$ d : b I d and d(Q $\cup$ P)a; we can then choose q such that $g(a) + q(a) = g(b) + q(b)$.

Theorem 3 : a thresholds-structure is p-coherent iff

$$\begin{cases} P^2 \cap (I \cup Q)^2 = \emptyset\ , \\ P.\ Q \cap I^2 = \emptyset\ , \\ P.\ Q \cap Q.\ I = \emptyset\ . \end{cases}$$

Proof : the proof is similar to that of theorem 2, the relation S_2 being replaced by S_3 such that, $\forall$ a,b :

$$a\ S_3\ b \text{ iff } a\ S_1\ b \text{ (see the proof of theorem 1)}$$
$$\text{or } a \not S_1\ b,\ b \not S_1\ a \text{ and } \exists\ c : c \not P\ a \text{ and } c\ P\ b\ .$$

Theorem 4 : a thresholds-structure is (p-q)-coherent iff

$$P.\ I.\ Q \subset P\ .$$

Proof : corollary of the result obtained in [3], pages 76 and 78, about the homogeneous families of interval orders.

Theorem 5 : a thresholds-structure is (q,p,+)-coherent iff it is Q^2-transitive.

Proof

The necessity of the condition is easy to verify. To prove it is sufficient, let us consider the functions g, q and p as defined in the proof of theorem 1.

f $g(a) > g(b) + q(b)$, then $a(Q \cup P)b$.
f $a P b$, we immediately have $g(a) + q(a) > g(a) > g(b) + p(b)$.
f $a Q b$, then the Q^2-transitivity implies that $\nexists c : c Q a$ and $c \not P b$; in other words, $\nexists c : g(a) + q(a) < g(c) < g(b) + p(b)$, and we can choose q and p in such a way that $g(a) + q(a) > g(b) + p(b)$.

heorem 6 : a thresholds-structure is (q,p,-)-coherent iff it is P.I-transitive.

roof
he necessity of the condition is easy to verify. To prove it is sufficient, let us onsider the functions g,q and p as defined in the proof of theorem 1.
f $g(a) < g(b) + q(b)$, then $b (P \cup Q \cup I)a$.
f $b(P \cup Q)a$, we immediately have $g(b) + p(b) > g(b) > g(a) + q(a)$.
f $b I a$, then the P.I-transitivity implies that $\nexists c : a I c$ and $c P b$; in other ords, $\nexists c : g(a) + q(a) > g(c) > g(b) + p(b)$ and we can choose q and p in such a way hat $q(a) + q(a) < g(b) + p(b)$.

heorem 7 : a thresholds-structure is (q,p)-coherent iff it is strongly transitive.

roof : corollary of theorems 5 and 6 and of definition 5.

heorem 8 : a thresholds-structure is a pseudo-order iff it is q-coherent, p-coherent nd (p-q)-coherent.

roof : the union of the conditions of theorems 1 to 4 coincide with the usual condi-ions defining a pseudo-order (see for example [4] and [6]).

heorem 9 : a strongly transitive {P,Q,I}-structure is a thresholds structure iff

$$\begin{cases} Q.\ I.\ Q \subset Q \cup P\ , \\ P.\ Q^{-1}.\ P \subset P\ . \end{cases}$$

roof : strong transitivity implies $P.\ Q \subset P$, $Q.\ I.\ P \subset P$ and $P.\ I.\ P \subset P$, so that we ust have the two conditions of theorem 9 to satisfy all the conditions of theorem .1.

heorem 10 : a strongly transitive thresholds-structure is q-coherent iff $P \cap I.\ Q = \emptyset$.

oof : We have to verify that a strongly transitive thresholds-structure satisfies e two first conditions of theorem 2.
e first condition is a consequence of $(P \cup Q)^2 \subset P$ and $I^2 \cap P = \emptyset$.
e second condition is due to the fact that $I.P.P \subset (P \cup Q).P \subset P$.

eorem 11 : a strongly transitive thresholds-structure is p-coherent iff

$$\begin{cases} P^2 \cap Q^2 = \emptyset , \\ P.\, Q \cap Q.\, I = \emptyset . \end{cases}$$

Proof : from $I.P.P \subset P$, we obtain $P^2 \cap I^2 = \emptyset$, $P^2 \cap I.Q = \emptyset$ and $P^2 \cap Q.I = \emptyset$; if we add $P^2 \cap Q^2 = \emptyset$, we obtain the first condition of theorem 3.
The second condition of theorem 3 is a consequence of $I.P.Q \subset (Q \cup P).\, Q \subset P$.

Theorem 12 : a strongly transitive thresholds-structure is always (p-q)-coherent an (q,p)-coherent.

Proof : the condition of theorem 4 is satisfied as $P.I.Q \subset (Q \cup P).\, Q \subset P$; the (q,p coherence is a consequence of theorem 7.

Theorem 13 : a strongly transitive thresholds-structure is a pseudo-order iff

$$\begin{cases} Q.\, P \cap I.\, Q = \emptyset , \\ P.\, Q \cap Q.\, I = \emptyset , \\ P^2 \cap Q^2 = \emptyset . \end{cases}$$

Such a structure will be called a strongly transitive pseudo-order.

Proof : consequence of theorems 8, 10, 11, 12.

Theorem 14 : a thresholds-structure is a strongly transitive pseudo-order iff it is

$$\begin{cases} \text{q-coherent,} \\ \text{p-coherent,} \\ \text{(p-q)-coherent,} \\ \text{(q,p)-coherent,} \end{cases}$$

iff it is a thresholds-structure such that $p = 2\, q = \text{constant}$.

Proof : the first part of the theorem is a corollary of theorems 7 and 8; the secon is proved in [6].

4. Comments

In the case where the relation Q is absent, two fundamental structures exist which allow intransitivity of indifference : the interval order and the semiorder. The two following results are well-known :

R1. $\{P,I\}$ is an interval order iff

$P.I.P. \subset P$,

iff there exist two functions g and p such that, $\forall\, a,b \in A$:

$$\begin{cases} a\ P\ b \iff g(a) > g(b) + p(b) , \\ a\ I\ b \iff \begin{cases} g(a) + p(a) > g(b) , \\ g(b) + p(b) > g(a) . \end{cases} \end{cases}$$

R2. {P,I} is a semiorder iff

$$\begin{cases} P.I.P \subset P, \\ P^2 \cap I^2 = \emptyset, \end{cases}$$

iff there exist two functions g and p such that, $\forall$ a,b $\in$ A :

$$\begin{cases} a\ P\ b \iff g(a) > g(b) + p(b), \\ a\ I\ b \iff \begin{cases} g(a) + p(a) > g(b), \\ g(b) + p(b) > g(a), \end{cases} \\ g(a) > g(b) \Rightarrow g(a) + p(a) > g(b) + p(b), \end{cases}$$

iff there exist a function g and a constant p such that :

$$\begin{cases} a\ P\ b \iff g(a) > g(b) + p, \\ a\ I\ b \iff |g(a) - g(b)| < p. \end{cases}$$

Considering three relations I, Q and P, we can introduce the two following strucures, each with two relations :

{P, Q U I U Q^{-1}} (weak preference is assimilated to indifference)

{P U Q, I} (weak preference is assimilated to strict preference).

n the other hand, the natural extension of the numerical representation of an interal order to the three relations case, consists in trying to find three functions g, and p such that

$$(I) \begin{cases} a\ P\ b \iff g(a) > g(b) + p(b), \\ a\ Q\ b \iff g(b) + p(b) > g(a) > g(b) + q(b), \\ a\ I\ b \iff \begin{cases} g(b) + q(b) > g(a), \\ g(a) + q(a) > g(b), \end{cases} \\ 0 < q(a) < p(a). \end{cases}$$

his motivates the introduction of definition 6.

his numerical representation, together with R1, imply that {P, Q U I U Q^{-1}} and P U Q, I} are interval orders.

eciprocally, if {P, Q U I U Q^{-1}} and {P U Q, I} are interval orders, R1 implies that here exist g_1, g_2, q and p such that

$$\begin{cases} a\ P\ b \iff g_1(a) > g_1(b) + p(b), \\ a\ (Q \cup I \cup Q^{-1})b \iff \begin{cases} g_1(b) + p(b) > g_1(a), \\ g_1(a) + p(a) > g_1(b), \end{cases} \end{cases}$$

nd

$$\begin{cases} a\ (P \cup Q)b \iff g_2(a) > g_2(b) + q(b), \\ a\ I\ b \iff \begin{cases} g_2(b) + q(b) > g_2(a), \\ g_2(a) + q(a) > g_2(b), \end{cases} \end{cases}$$

ut this is not sufficient to obtain representation (I).

eorem 1 shows that one condition has to be added :

$Q.I.P \subset P$.

If $\{P \cup Q, I\}$ is an interval order, one obtains a semiorder if the following condition is added (see R2) :

$$(P \cup Q)^2 \cap I^2 = \emptyset \ .$$

In this case R2 shows that the functions g_2 and q satisfy the q-coherency. However, in order to obtain q-coherency in representation (I), it is necessary to add two other conditions, as proved in theorem 2.

Theorem 3 is similar to theorem 2 for the case where $\{P, Q \cup I \cup Q^{-1}\}$ is a semiorder.

Theorem 4 gives a necessary and sufficient condition to have the numerical representation (I) with the particularity that g+p is an increasing function of g+q, what is called (p-q)-coherency.

Theorems 5 to 7 show that Q^2-transitivity, P.I-transitivity and strong transitivity respectively coincide qith (q, p, +)-coherency, (q,p,-)-coherency and (q,p)-coherency, for a thresholds-structure.

If a $\{P,Q,I\}$-structure is q-coherent and p-coherent, then $\{P \cup Q, I\}$ and $\{P, Q \cup I \cup Q^{-1}\}$ are semiorders but (p-q)-coherency is not necessarily satisfied. Adding this property leads to the concept of pseudo-order ([4]), also called homogeneous family of two semiorders ([3]) : this is the subject of theorem 8.

Theorem 9 precises what must be added to the strong transitivity to have numerical representation (I), and the next theorems give the conditions which must be satisfied by a strongly transitive thresholds-structure in order to obtain the different types of coherency.

The strongest structure which is obtained is the strongly transitive pseudo-order, which satisfies all the coherence properties and which can be represented by a function g and two constant q and p, such that p = 2q.

The interested reader will find in [4] and [6] the characterization of pseudo-orders with two constant thresholds and in [1] a generalization to structures with more than two thresholds.

All the results presented here can obviously be interpreted as various representations of preference-structures by intervals of the real line : to each element $a \in A$, one associates the intervals (g(a), g(a) + q(a)) and (g(a), g(a) + p(a)).

5. An open problem

It is also possible to represent a $\{P,Q,I\}$-structure by a "single-threshold model" as follows :

$$\begin{cases} a\ P\ b \text{ iff } g(a) > g(b) + \sigma(b)\ , \\ a\ Q\ b \text{ iff } g(a) + \sigma(a) > g(b) + \sigma(b) > g(a) > g(b)\ , \\ a\ I\ b \text{ iff } \begin{cases} g(b) + \sigma(b) > g(a) + \sigma(a) > g(a) > g(b)\ , \\ \qquad \text{or} \\ g(a) + \sigma(a) > g(b) + \sigma(b) > g(b) > g(a)\ . \end{cases} \end{cases}$$

This structure naturally appears when one compares intervals as illustrated here below

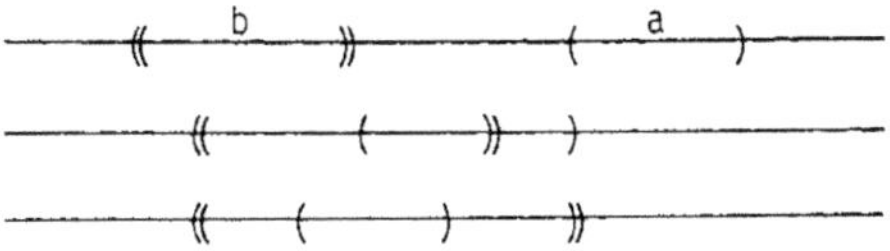

a P b

a Q b

a I b

To our knowledge, necessary and sufficient conditions to have this structure are not known. The interested reader can verify that the following properties are necessary and try to find if something has to be added in order to obtain sufficient conditions.

$$\begin{cases} .\ \{P \cup Q, I\} \text{ is a partial order of dimension 2}\ , \\ .\ \{P, \hat{I}\} \text{ is an interval order, where } \hat{I} = Q \cup I \cup Q^{-1}\ , \\ .\ \{P, Q, I\} \text{ is weakly transitive}\ , \\ .\ P.\ \hat{I} \cap \hat{I}.\ P \subset P \cup Q\ , \\ .\ (P.\ \hat{I} \cap I)^2 \cap Q = \emptyset\ , \\ .\ (\hat{I}.\ P \cap I)^2 \cap Q = \emptyset\ . \end{cases}$$

References

[1] Doignon, J.-P. : "The threshold representations of multiple semiorders", SIAM Journal on Algebraic and Discrete Mathematics, to appear.

[2] Roy, B. : Méthodologie Multicritère d'Aide à la Décision, Economica, 1985.

[3] Roubens, M. and Vincke, Ph. : Preference Modelling, Lecture Notes in Economics and Mathematical Systems, Springer Verlag, Nr 250, 1985.

[4] Roy, B. and Vincke, Ph. : "Pseudo-orders : definition, properties and numerical representation", International Journal of Mathematical Social Sciences, to appear.

[5] Valadares Tavares, L. : "Proposition d'un système relationnel de préférences et développement d'une méthode interactive utilisant le modèle TRIDENT", communication presented at the 22nd meeting of the European Working Group on "L'Aide à la Décision Multicritère", Chania (CRETE), 1985.

[6] Vincke, Ph. : "Vrais, quasi, pseudo et précritères dans un ensemble fini : propriétés et algorithmes", Cahiers du LAMSADE, n°27, 1980.

IDENTIFYING NONINFERIOR DECISION ALTERNATIVES BASED ON FUZZY BINARY RELATIONS

Sergei V. OVCHINNIKOV
Mathematics Department
San Francisco State University
San Francisco, CA 94132, U.S.A.

Vladimir M. OZERNOY
Department of Management Sciences
California State University, Hayward
Hayward, CA 94542, U.S.A.

ABSTRACT

After the introduction of a fuzzy noninferiority relation, fuzzy relations of preference, strict preference, indifference, and incomparability are specified and their properties are investigated. A definition is given for a fuzzy noninferior subset and basic characteristics are established for that subset. An algorithm is given to identify a fuzzy set of noninferior alternatives for decision-making where a certain number of noninferior alternatives must be selected for more detailed study.

1. Introduction

The purpose of the analysis in many decision-making problems is to determine the "best" alternative. A complete rank-order of the set of feasible alternatives is unnecessary in such problems, where analysis begins with the identification of all nondominant alternatives. After that, the most preferred of these nondominated alternatives is selected. Other decision-making problems involve the selection for more detailed study of a relatively small number of preferred decision alternatives. In these cases, the preferred alternatives are chosen from among top rank-ordered alternatives or from among nondominated alternatives. Methods developed for both of these types of problems use additional information about the decision maker's preferences. Kirkwood and Sarin [4] derive conditions to determine whether two multicriteria alternatives can be ranked given only partial information about the weighted-additive evaluation function. Kirkwood and Sarin also develop an algorithm which partially rank-orders the set of alternatives based on pairwise ranking information. Ozernoy and Gaft [7] demonstrate a multiple step procedure which allows at least partial identification and elimination of dominated alternatives by obtaining a sequence of different types of preference information from the decision maker at each step of the procedure.

Zionts [15] notes that it may not always be desirable to reject all dominated alternatives. There are cases where a dominated alternative is so close in the criteria space to a nondominated alternative that the decision maker's choice might be based on a secondary criterion not used in the analysis. Furthermore, there are cases where any attempt to precisely quantify alternatives would yield an exaggerated idea of the precision with which alternatives could be evaluated. In these cases it would be inappropriate to exclude dominated alternatives from further analysis.

Several techniques have been suggested for the identification of nondominated alternatives. Gaft and Ozernoy [3] develop an algorithm which identifies nondominated alternatives regardless of the specific way in which binary relations are introduced defining such concepts as "more preferred alternative" or "set of nondominated alternatives". This algorithm uses the concept of incomparability of alternatives. Here we are introducing a new approach for identifying nondominated decision alternatives, which is based on the use of a fuzzy noninferiority relation that enables us to determine a fuzzy noninferior subset of a finite set. The degree to which an element is noninferior in the finite set is the value of the membership function. A procedure for the selection of noninferior elements is developed and, considering this finite set as the set of feasible decision alternatives in a decision-making problem, it is proven that the 1-cut of a noninferior subset is a nonempty set of unfuzzy undominated alternatives in the set of feasible alternatives. This reestablishes Orlovsky's main result [5].

In this article we have established an approach which allows one to identify different numbers of noninferior decision alternatives based on different values of α in constructing an α-cut of noninferior subset. The significance of this is that by change of value of α one can identify a required number of noninferio alternatives (or a number close to the required one) for more detaile study.

The article is organized in the following manner:

Section 2 introduces a fuzzy noninferiority relation and it properties. The fuzzy binary relations of strict preference indifference, incomparability, and preference are defined based o this fuzzy noninferiority relation. A theorem is proved whic establishes some compatibility properties for these relations. It i also shown that the inverse image of a crisp nondominance relatio under fuzzy correspondence is a fuzzy noninferiority relation. This i of particular interest in the area of fuzzy multicriteria decisio making.

Section 3 defines a fuzzy noninferior subset. Here it is show that two noninferior elements are either incomparable or equivalent The basic characteristic properties of a fuzzy noninferior subset ar specified. These are fuzzy analogs of respective properties of cris choice functions.

Section 4 presents an algorithm for constructing an α-cut of noninferior subset and identifying noninferior elements.

2. Fuzzy noninferiority relation

Let Q be a fuzzy binary relation on a finite set A. This relatio is defined by its membership function $Q(x,y)$, which maps a direc product $A \times A$ into the unit interval $[0,1]$. We regard this relation a an noninferiority relation: the value $Q(x,y)$ represents the degree t which element x is not inferior to y.

This interpretation imposes certain restrictions on Q, which w introduce as properties of this relation. First of all, Q is reflexive fuzzy binary relation, i.e.

$$Q(x,x) = 1, \quad \text{for all } x \in A,$$

meaning that any element in A is certainly not inferior to itself. Th second property is completeness (strong linearity in [5]) which i defined as follows:

$$Q(x,y) \vee Q(y,x) = 1, \quad \text{for all } x,y \in A,$$

(We define, as usual, $a \vee b = \max(a,b)$ and $a \wedge b = \min(a,b)$.)
This property guarantees that, for any two given elements in A certainly at least one of them is not inferior to another one.

There are many ways to define an antisymmetric part of a fuzzy binary relations [5, 6, 8]. In this paper we adopt the following definition [5]:

$$P(x,y) = (Q(x,y) - Q(y,x)) \vee 0, \qquad \text{for all } x,y \in A,$$

which corresponds to the crisp definition given by $P = Q \setminus Q^{-1}$. This relation is regarded as a <u>strict preference</u> associated with the noninferiority relation Q. As usual, such a relation is supposed to be a <u>transitive</u> fuzzy binary relation, i.e.

(PP) $\qquad P(x,y) \wedge P(y,z) \leq P(x,z), \qquad \text{for all } x,y,z \in A.$

Note, that, by completeness of Q, P is a fuzzy complement of Q^{-1}, i.e.

$$P(x,y) = 1 - Q(y,x), \quad \text{for all } x,y \in A.$$

In the crisp case, reflexive, complete binary relations with transitive antisymmetric parts are called <u>quasi-transitive</u> relations [10]. We use the same name for fuzzy binary relations satisfying all the introduced properties and, following [10], denote transitivity property of strict preference by (PP). Therefore, by definition, a fuzzy quasi-transitive relation is a reflexive complete fuzzy binary relation satisfying the (PP) property. It is easy to verify that a reflexive fuzzy binary relation Q is a fuzzy quasi-transitive relation if and only if the following property is satisfied

(QT) $\qquad Q(x,y) \vee Q(y,z) \geq Q(x,z),$

for all $x,y,z \in A$.

A symmetric part S of fuzzy binary relation Q is defined by

$$S(x,y) = Q(x,y) \quad Q(y,x), \quad \text{for all } x,y \quad A.$$

the value $S(x,y)$ is considered to be a degree to which elements x and y are incomparable or indifferent.

In order to separate incomparability and indifference subrelations of S we define an <u>indifference</u> relation I as a crisp equivalence relation contained in S. Then $I(x,y)$ is a function with range $\{0,1\}$, such that

(1) $I(x,x) = 1,$

(2) $I(x,y) = I(y,x),$

(3) $I(x,y) \wedge I(y,z) \leq I(y,z),$

(4) $I(x,y) \leq S(x,y),$

for all $x,y,z \in A$. We denote the transitivity property (3) of the indifference relation by (II).

An <u>incomparability</u> relation N is defined by its membership function as follows

$$N(x,y) = S(x,y) - I(x,y), \quad \text{for all } x,y \in A.$$

It is easy to verify that N is an antireflexive and symmetric fuzzy binary relation, i.e. $N(x,x) = 0$ and $N(x,y) = N(y,x)$, for all $x,y \in A$. We also have the decomposition $S = N \cup I$, such that $N \cap I = \emptyset$.

Since an indifference relation I is not defined by means of the relation Q, certain <u>compatibility</u> conditions must be imposed on I in order to guarantee properties similar to crisp ones (see [2]). We employ the following compatibility conditions:

(QI) $$Q(x,y) \wedge I(y,z) \leq Q(x,z),$$

(IQ) $$I(x,y) \wedge Q(y,z) \leq Q(x,z),$$

for all $x,y,z \in A$, which are similar to the conditions used in [10].

A fuzzy <u>preference</u> relation R is defined as the union $P \cup I$ of a strict preference P and indifference relation R, i.e.

$$R(x,y) = P(x,y) \vee I(x,y), \quad \text{for all } x,y \in A.$$

Further, in this paper, we assume that the noninferiority relation Q and indifference relation I satisfy properties (QT), (II), (QI) and (IQ). (Note, that, in many important special cases, I is an identity relation; then conditions (II), (QI), and (IQ) are trivially satisfied.)

The following theorem establishes some compatibility properties of the strict preference relation P, the preference relation R, the indifference relation I, and the incomparability relation N (cf. [3] and [10]). First, we prove a useful lemma.

<u>Lemma 2.1.</u> $I(y,z) = 1$ implies $Q(x,y) = Q(x,z)$ and $Q(y,x) = Q(z,x)$.

<u>Proof</u>. By (QI), we have

$$Q(x,y) = Q(x,y) \wedge I(y,z) \leq Q(x,z), \text{ and}$$

$$Q(x,z) = Q(x,z) \wedge I(z,y) \leq Q(x,y).$$

Hence, $Q(x,y) = Q(x,z)$. Similarly, by (IQ), $Q(y,x) = Q(z,x)$. ■

<u>Theorem 2.1.</u> Conditions (PP), (II), (QI) and (IQ) together imply

(PI) $$P(x,y) \wedge I(y,z) \leq P(x,z),$$

(IP) $\qquad I(x,y) \wedge P(y,z) \leq P(x,z),$

(NI) $\qquad N(x,y) \wedge I(y,z) \leq N(x,z),$

(IN) $\qquad I(x,y) \wedge N(y,z) \leq N(x,z),$

(RR) $\qquad R(x,y) \wedge R(y,z) \leq R(x,z),$

for all $x,y,z \in A$.

<u>Proof.</u> (PI) Obvious, if $I(y,z) = 0$. Otherwise, by Lemma 2.1, $P(x,y) = (Q(x,y) - Q(y,z)) \vee 0 = (Q(x,z) - Q(z,x)) \vee 0 = P(x,z)$.

(IP) Similar to (PI).

(NI) Obvious, if $I(y,z) = 0$ or $N(x,y) = 0$. Otherwise, $I(y,z) = 1$ and $I(x,y) = 0$. Therefore, by transitivity of I, $I(z,x) = 0$. By Lemma 2.1, we have

$$N(x,y) = S(x,y) - I(x,y) = Q(x,y) \wedge Q(y,x) =$$
$$Q(x,z) \quad Q(z,x) = S(x,z) - I(x,z) = N(x,z).$$

(IN) Similar to (NI).

(RR) $R(x,y) \wedge R(y,z) = (P(x,y) \vee I(x,y)) \wedge (P(y,z) \vee I(y,z)) =$ $(P(x,y) \wedge P(y,z)) \vee (P(x,y) \wedge I(y,z)) \vee (I(x,y) \wedge P(y,z)) \vee (I(x,y) \wedge I(y,z))$ $\leq R(x,z)$, by (PP), (PI), (IP), and (II).

Note, that (RR) is, simply, a transitivity property of a preference relation R.

There exists a particularly interesting mechanism generating fuzzy quasi-transitive relations. Namely, it turns out that an inverse image of a crisp quasi-transitive relation under fuzzy correspondence is a fuzzy quasi-transitive relation. Let A and B be finite sets. A <u>fuzzy correspondence</u> $F: A \to B$ [6] is a fuzzy subset of the direct product A B and defined by its membership function $F(x,u)$, x A, u B. We assume that, for any given x A, an <u>image</u> $F(x)$ of x under F is a normal fuzzy subset of B, i.e. the 1-cut $F_1(x)$ is a nonempty subset of B.

Let $\underline{Q}$ be a crisp quasi-transitive relation on B, i.e. $\underline{Q}$ is a reflexive, complete binary relation with transitive antisymmetric part $\underline{P} = \overline{\underline{Q}}^{-1}$. By definition, an <u>inverse image</u> $Q = F^{-1} \circ \underline{Q} \circ F$ of $\underline{Q}$ under a fuzzy correspondence F is given by its membership function as follows:

$$Q(x,y) = \bigvee_{u,v} F(x,u) \wedge \underline{Q}(u,v) \wedge F(y,v) = \bigvee_{u\underline{Q}v} F(x,u) \wedge F(y,v).$$

<u>Lemma 2.2.</u> The inverse image Q of a crisp quasi-transitive relation $\underline{Q}$ on B under fuzzy mapping F is a reflexive and complete fuzzy binary relation on A.

<u>Proof.</u> 1) $Q(x,x) = \bigvee_{u\underline{Q}v} F(x,u) \wedge F(x,v) \leq \bigvee_{u} F(x,u) = 1,$

since $\underline{Q}$ is a reflexive binary relation and $F(x)$ is a normal fuzzy subset.

2) Let $u_o \in F_1(x)$ and $v_o \in F_1(y)$. We have $Q(x,y) \vee Q(y,x) =$

$$[\bigvee_{u,v} F(x,u) \wedge \underline{Q}(u,v) \wedge F(y,v)] \vee [\bigvee_{s,t} F(y,s) \wedge \underline{Q}(s,t) \wedge F(x,t)] \geq$$

$$[F(x,u_o) \wedge \underline{Q}(u_o,v_o) \wedge F(y,v_o)] \vee [F(y,v_o) \wedge \underline{Q}(v_o,u_o) \wedge F(x,u_o)] =$$

$\underline{Q}(u_o,v_o) \vee \underline{Q}(v_o,u_o) = 1$, since $\underline{Q}$ is a complete binary relation. ■

Theorem 2.2. The inverse image of a crisp quasi-transitive binary relation $\underline{Q}$ under fuzzy correspondence F is a fuzzy quasi-transitive relation Q.

Proof. By Lemma 2.2, it suffices to prove that Q satisfies the (QT) property

$$[\bigvee_{u\underline{Q}v} F(y,u) \wedge F(x,v)] \vee [\bigvee_{p\underline{Q}q} F(z,p) \wedge F(y,q)] \geq \bigvee_{s\underline{Q}t} F(z,s) \wedge F(x,t).$$

or that, for any given s and t such that $s\underline{Q}t$, there are u and q such that $u\underline{Q}t$, $s\underline{Q}q$, and

$$[F(y,u) \wedge F(x,t)] \vee [F(z,s) \wedge F(y,q)] \geq F(z,s) \wedge F(x,t).$$

Let us prove, first, that there are u_o and q_o such that $u_o\underline{Q}t$, $s\underline{Q}q_o$, and $F(y,u_o) \vee F(y,q_o) = 1$. Suppose that $F(y,u)<1$ and $F(y,q)<1$ for all u and q such that $u\underline{Q}t$ and $s\underline{Q}q$. Then, for any $w \in F_1(y)$, $w\underline{Q}t$ and $s\underline{Q}w$ are both false, which implies both $t\underline{P}w$ and $w\underline{P}s$. Therefore, $t\underline{P}s$, which contradicts $s\underline{Q}t$.

We have now $[F(y,u_o) \wedge F(x,t)] \vee [F(z,s) \wedge F(y,q_o)] =$

$$[F(y,u_o) \vee F(z,s)] \wedge [F(y,u_o) \vee F(y,q_o)] \wedge [F(x,t) \vee F(z,s)] \wedge [F(x,t) \vee F(y,q_o)] \geq$$

$F(z,s) \wedge [F(x,t) \vee F(z,s)] \wedge F(x,t) = F(z,s) \wedge F(x,t)$, Q.E.D. ■

It follows from Theorem 2.2 that a strict preference P associated with Q is a fuzzy partial order. This result can be strengthened in the following way. An irreflexive fuzzy binary relation P is said to be a fuzzy interval order if it satisfies condition

(IO) $\quad P(x,y) \wedge P(u,v) \leq P(x,v) \vee P(u,y)$

This condition generalizes the crisp notion of interval order (see [2]). Obviously, (IO) implies transitivity of P. It is easy to verify that Q associated with P satisfies exactly the same condition (IO); we use the same name for Q. The following theorem (cf. [9]) is proven by essentially the same argument as Theorem 2.2

Theorem 2.3. The inverse image of a crisp quasi-transitive binary relation $\underline{Q}$ under fuzzy correspondence F is a fuzzy interval order.

In practice, A is a set of decision alternatives, B is a subset of finite dimensional real space ("criteria" space), and $\underline{Q}$ is a vector non-dominance relation. It is assumed that fuzzy information about alternative a A is given in the form of a normal fuzzy subset F(a) of B representing the value of a linguistic variable. For example, this fuzzy subset might represent the following judgement about alternative a: "alternative a is more or less good with respect to criterion C_1 and fair with respect to criterion C_2". A fuzzy set F(a) is regarded then as a fuzzy image of alternative a A under fuzzy correspondence F between A and B. In accordance with Theorem 2.2, the inverse image Q of $\underline{Q}$ under F is a noninferiority relation on the set of alternatives A. Therefore, fuzzy information about alternatives generates a noninferiority relation by means of the inverse image construction. (Note, that, in the one-dimensional case, the so defined noninferiority relation is the dominance relation R introduced in [12] by means of a different construction.)

3. Fuzzy noninferior subset

Given noninferiority relation Q on a finite set A we define a fuzzy <u>noniferior subset</u> L(A) by means of its membership function L(A)(x) as follows

$$L(A)(x) = \bigwedge_{y \in A} Q(x,y), \quad \text{for} \quad x \in A.$$

The value L(A)(x) is regarded as a degree to which an element x is noninferior in A. Since Q is a complement of P^{-1}, a noninferior subset defined above coincides with the fuzzy set of nondominated elements introduced in [5]. (Note, that, in the particular case when Q is generated as an inverse image of the vector non-dominance relation (see previous section), the so defined noninferior subset can be regarded as a fuzzy Pareto set of nondominated alternatives.)

The following theorem shows that a noninferior subset is, actually, a normal fuzzy subset of A (cf. Theorem 6.4 in [5]).

<u>Theorem 3.1.</u> $\bigvee_{x \in A} L(A)(x) = 1.$

<u>Proof.</u> Suppose that $\bigvee_{x \in A} L(A)(x) < 1$. Then for any $x \in A$ there is $y \in A$ such that $Q(x,y) < 1$. Then, by finiteness of A, there is a cycle $x_0, x_1, \ldots, x_n = x_0$, such that $Q(x_i, x_{i+1}) < 1$, for $0 \leq i \leq n-1$. We have, by the (QT) property, $1 > Q(x_0,x_1) \vee \ldots \vee Q(x_{n-1},x_n) \geq Q(x_0,x_0) = 1$, a contradiction. ■

In accordance with the theorem proved, the 1-cut of a noninferior subset is a nonempty crisp set; the elements of this crisp set can be regarded as nonfuzzy undominated elements in A (cf.[5]).

A noninferior subset $L(A)$ is compatible with the indifferen relation I, as the following theorem demonstrates.

<u>Theorem 3.2.</u> $I(x,y) = 1$ implies $L(A)(x) = L(A)(y)$.

<u>Proof.</u> Follows immediately from Lemma 2.1.

In the crisp case two noninferior elements are eith incomparable or equivalent [3]. It is also true in the framewo developed in this paper, as the next theorem shows.

<u>Theorem 3.3.</u> $L(A)(x) \wedge L(A)(y) \leq N(x,y) \vee I(x,y)$.

<u>Proof.</u> Since $L(A)(u) \leq Q(u,t)$ for all $t \in A$, we have
$L(A)(x) \wedge L(A)(y) \leq Q(x,y) \wedge Q(y,x) = N(x,y) \vee I(x,y)$. ■

Considering a noniferior subset $L(A)$ as a function of A, where is a finite subset of a certain universe set, one can regard $L(A)$ as fuzzy choice function [6]. Then the value $L(A)(x)$ is a degree to whi x is the "best" element in the set A. The next three theore establish basic characteristic properties of the fuzzy choice functi $L(A)$.

<u>Theorem 3.4.</u> $A' \subseteq A$ implies $L(A') \supseteq L(A) \cap A'$.

<u>Proof.</u> For $x \in A'$, we have

$$L(A')(x) = \bigwedge_{t \in A'} Q(x,t) \geq \bigwedge_{t \in A} Q(x,t) = L(A)(x).$$

The property established in the theorem proved is Sen's propert (α) [10]; it is called Heritage property (H) in [1]. ■

<u>Theorem 3.5.</u> $L(A' \cup A") \supseteq L(A') \cap L(A")$.

<u>Proof.</u> For $x \in A' \cap A"$, $L(A')(x) \wedge L(A")(x) =$

$$\bigwedge_{t \in A'} Q(x,t) \wedge \bigwedge_{u \in A"} Q(x,u) = \bigwedge_{y \in A' \cup A"} Q(x,y) = L(A' \cup A")(x).$$

Otherwise, $L(A')(x) \wedge L(A")(x) = 0$.

The proved property is the Concordance property (C) in [1] c property (γ) in [11].

Finally, we establish a property which can be regarded as a fuzz analog of the classical "independence of irrelevant alternatives property. ■

<u>Theorem 3.6.</u> Let A' be a subset of A such that $L(A)(y) < L(A)(x)$ for all $x \in A'$ and $y \in A \setminus A'$. Then $L(A') = L(A) \cap A'$.

<u>Proof.</u> From Theorem 3.4, $L(A') \supseteq L(A) \cap A'$. Suppose that ther is $x \in A'$ such that $L(A')(x) > L(A)(x)$, i.e.

$$\bigwedge_{t\in A'} Q(x,t) > \bigwedge_{t\in A} Q(x,t).$$

It means that there exists a $y\in A\backslash A'$ such that for all $u\in A'$

$$Q(x,y) < Q(x,u). \qquad (*)$$

Since $L(A)(y) < L(A)(x)$, there is a y_1 such that $Q(y,y_1)<L(A)(x)$. If $y_1\in A'$, there is a y_2 such that $Q(y_1,y_2)<L(A)(x)$, and so on. Since A is a finite set and there is no cycle with the property $Q(y_i,y_{i+1})<1$ (see the proof of Theorem 3.1), we construct a sequence $y_0=y,y_1,\dots,y_n$ such that $y_i \in A\backslash A'$ for $i < n$, $y_n\in A'$, and $Q(y_i,y_{i+1}) < L(A)(x)$ for $0\leq i\leq n-1$. By the (QT) property, for all $t\in A$

$$Q(y,y_n) \leq \bigvee_i Q(y_i,y_{i+1}) < L(A)(x) \leq Q(x,t).$$

In particular, $Q(y,y_n)<Q(x,y_n)$, which implies, together with (*), $Q(x,y)\vee Q(y,y_n) < Q(x,y_n)$ - a contradiction with the (QT) property. ■

Recall that $L(A)(x)$ is considered to be a degree to which an element x is the "best" in A. Let us suppose that a threshold α is given such that elements x with $L(A)(x) < \alpha$ are deleted from consideration (irrelevant alternatives). Then Theorem 3.6 states that the (fuzzy) "best" elements in the remainder set A′ are exactly the same as in the given set A. Actually, A′ is an α-cut of fuzzy set L(A). An algorithm constructing the α-cuts of a noninferior subset L(A) is presented in the next section.

In the conclusion of this section, we establish necessary and sufficient conditions on fuzzy binary relation Q to generate normal noninferior subsets. We say that a fuzzy binary relation P is an <u>acyclic</u> relation if, for any finite sequence $x_0,\dots,x_n$, $P(x_i,x_{i+1}) > 0$, for all $0\leq i\leq n-1$, implies $P(x_n,x_0) = 0$.

<u>Theorem 3.7.</u> Let Q be a fuzzy binary relation. A noninferior subset L(A) defined by its membership function

$$L(A)(x) = \bigwedge_{y\in A} Q(x,y)$$

is a normal fuzzy subset for any finite set A if and only if Q is a reflexive complete fuzzy binary relation with acyclic antisymmetric part P.

<u>Proof.</u> Sufficiency is proved, essentially, by repeating the argument used in the proof of Theorem 3.1.

To prove necessity, we note, first, that, for any element x, $1 = L(\{x\})(x) = Q(x,x)$ which implies reflexivity of Q. Second, we have, for $A=\{x,y\}$, $1 = L(A)(x) \vee L(A)(y) = (Q(x,x)\wedge Q(x,y))\vee (Q(y,x)\wedge Q(y,y)) = Q(x,y)\vee Q(y,x)$ which proves completeness of Q.

Finally, let $A = x_0,\dots,x_n$ and $P(x_i,x_{i+1})>0$ for all $0 \leq i \leq n-1$. Therefore, $Q(x_{i+1},x_i)<1$ for all $0 \leq i \leq n-1$. Hence, $L(A)(x_i)<1$ for all $0 \leq i \leq n-1$. Since $L(A)$ is a normal fuzzy set, $L(A)(x_n) = 1$, which implies $Q(x_n,x_0) = 1$. Therefore, $P(x_n,x_0) = 0$, i.e., P is an acyclic fuzzy binary relation.

■

4. The algorithm

By definition, an α-cut of a fuzzy set $L(A)$ is a crisp set $L_\alpha(A) = \left\{x \in A\colon L(A)(x) \geq \alpha\right\}$. Since $L(A)(x) = \bigwedge_{y \in A} Q(x,y)$,

we have

$$L_\alpha(A) = \left\{ x \in A\colon (\forall y \in A)\ xQ_\alpha y \right\},$$

where Q_α is an α-cut of fuzzy binary relation Q, i.e. $xQ_\alpha y$ if and only if $Q(x,y) \geq \alpha$.

We introduce a symmetric S_α and an antisymmetric P_α parts of Q as follows:

$$xS_\alpha y \text{ if and only if } xQ_\alpha y \text{ and } yQ_\alpha x,$$

and

$$xP_\alpha y \text{ if and only if } xQ_\alpha y \text{ and not } yQ_\alpha x.$$

Note, that P_α is <u>not</u> an α-cut of fuzzy strict preference P, while S <u>is</u> an α-cut of S.

<u>Lemma 4.1.</u> Q_α is a crisp quasi-transitive binary relation.

<u>Proof.</u> Obviously, Q_α is a reflexive complete binary relation. Let us prove transitivity of P_α. By definition, $xP_\alpha y$ if and only if $Q(y,x) < \alpha$. Suppose that $xP_\alpha y$ and $yP_\alpha z$, or, equivalently, $Q(y,x) < \alpha$, and $Q(z,y) < \alpha$. Then, by the (QT) property, $\alpha > Q(z,y)\ \ Q(y,x) \geq Q(z,x)$. Hence, $xP_\alpha z$.

■

<u>Lemma 4.2.</u> For any $y \in A \setminus L_\alpha(A)$, there is $x \in L_\alpha(A)$ such that $xP_\alpha y$.

<u>Proof.</u> Since $\bigwedge_{t \in A} Q(y,t) = L(A)(y) <$, there exists a y_1 such that $Q(y,y_1) < \alpha$. Hence, $y_1 P_\alpha y$. If $y_1 \notin L_\alpha(A)$, then there exists a y_2 such that $y_2 P_\alpha y_1$, and so on. Since P_α is a partial order and A is a finite set, there is an $x \in L_\alpha(A)$ such that $xP_\alpha y$.

■

Let $B = A \cup \{b\}$, $b \notin A$, so that B has just one more element than A. Then, from Theorem 3.4, $L_\alpha(A) \supseteq L_\alpha(B) \cap A$. Therefore, any element in $L_\alpha(B)$ is either b, or an element of $L_\alpha(A)$. The following theorem establishes important relationships between sets $L_\alpha(B)$ and $L_\alpha(A)$ in terms of relation P_α.

<u>Theorem 4.1.</u> (i) If there is $x \in L_\alpha(A)$ such that $xP_\alpha b$, then $L_\alpha(B) = L_\alpha(A)$;

(ii) otherwise, $L_\alpha(B) = (L_\alpha(A)\setminus Y) \cup \{b\}$, where $Y = \{x \in L_\alpha(A)\colon bP_\alpha x\}$.

<u>Proof.</u> (i) Since $xP_\alpha b$, $bQ_\alpha x$ is false. Therefore, $b \notin L(B)$. Suppose that there is a $t \in L_\alpha(A)$ such that $t \notin L_\alpha(B)$. Then $bP_\alpha t$, which implies, by transitivity of P_α, $xP_\alpha t$. Hence $tQ_\alpha x$ is false, which contradicts $t \in L_\alpha(A)$.

(ii) In this case for all $x \in L_\alpha(A)$ we have $bQ_\alpha x$. Hence, $L_\alpha(A)\setminus Y = \{t \in L_\alpha(A)\colon bS_\alpha t\}$. It suffices to prove that (1) any element of Y does not belong to $L_\alpha(B)$, (2) any element of $L_\alpha(A)\setminus Y$ belongs to $L_\alpha(B)$, and (3) b belongs to $L_\alpha(B)$.

(1) Let $t \in Y$. Then $bP_\alpha t$. Therefore, $tQ_\alpha b$ is false. Hence, t does not belong to $L_\alpha(B)$.

(2) Let $t \in L_\alpha(A)\setminus Y$. Then $tQ_\alpha y$ for all $y \in A$ and $tQ_\alpha b$. Therefore, t belongs to $L_\alpha(B)$.

(3) Since $bQ\,x$ for all $x \in L_\alpha(A)$, it suffices to prove that $bQ_\alpha y$ for all $y \in A\setminus L_\alpha(A)$. Suppose that $yP_\alpha b$ for some $y \in A \setminus L_\alpha(A)$. Then, by Lemma 4.2, there is an $x \in L_\alpha(A)$ such that $xP_\alpha y$. By transitivity of P, $xP_\alpha b$ which contradicts $bQ_\alpha x$. ■

The dichotomy of Theorem 4.1 can be easily expressed in terms of the membership function $Q(x,y)$. Indeed, $xP_\alpha b$ if and only if $Q(b,x) < \alpha$; therefore, the two cases of Theorem 4.1 are 1) $Q(b,x) < \alpha$, and 2) $Q(b,x) \geq \alpha$.

It follows from Theorem 4.1 that, in order to obtain $L_\alpha(B)$ from $L_\alpha(A)$, one needs to compare b with elements of $L_\alpha(A)$ only.

We introduce now an algorithm, based on the results of Theorem 4.1, which effectively constructs $L(A)$. (See also [3] where a similar algorithm is suggested in the crisp case.)

Suppose that $A = \{a_1,\ldots,a_n\}$, and consider a nested family of subsets $A_1 \subset A_2 \subset \ldots \subset A_n = A$, where $A_k = \{a_1,\ldots,a_k\}$. Given set $L_\alpha(A_k) = \{a_k,\ldots,a_k\}$, the following algorithm constructs $L(A_{k+1})$.

<u>Step 1.</u> Initialize the counter i of elements in $L(A_k)$ to 0: $i = 0$.

<u>Step 2.</u> Increment the counter by 1: $i := i+1$.

<u>Step 3.</u> Check if there are more elements in $L_\alpha(A_k)$ to compare with a_{k+1}: if $i<m$ then go to Step 4, otherwise go to Step 7.

<u>Step 4.</u> Check if $a_{k_i}P_\alpha a_{k+1}$: if $Q(a_{k+1},a_{k_i}) < \alpha$ then go to Step 8, otherwise go to Step 5.

<u>Step 5.</u> Check if $a_{k_i}S_\alpha a_{k+1}$: if $Q(a_k,a_{k+1}) \geq \alpha$ then go to Step 2,

otherwise go to Step 6.

Step 6. Delete element a_{k_i} from $L_\alpha(A_k)$ and go to Step 2.

Step 7. Add element a_{k+1} to the remaining elements in $L_\alpha(A_k)$. Stop.

Step 8. $L_\alpha(A_{k+1}) = L_\alpha(A_k)$. Stop.

Obviously, $L_\alpha(A_1) = A_1$. Then the above algorithm is applied recursively to the nested family $A_1 \subset A_2 \subset \ldots \subset A_n = A$ until the α-cut of the noninferior set L(A) is constructed.

The algorithm has several distinctive features. In particular, the algorithm makes it possible to identify

1) noninferior decision alternatives independently of the specific way in which the fuzzy binary relation Q is given;

2) noninferior decisions alternatives when the set of feasible decision alternatives is specified as a list and when feasible alternatives are generated in the course of solving the decision-making problem;

3) a required number of decision alternatives (or a number close to required one) for more detailed study in situations where the elimination of dominated alternatives is inexpedient.

Acknowledgment

This research was sponsored by NSF Grant IST-8403431 and the California State University, Hayward.

References

[1] M.A. Aizerman and A.V. Malishevski, General theory of best variants choice: some aspects, IEEE Transactions on Automation and Control, AC-26 (1981) 1030-1040.

[2] P.C. Fishburn, Interval Orders and Interval Graphs (John Willey & Sons, 1985).

[3] M.G. Gaft and V.M. Ozernoy, Isolation of a set of noninferior solutions and their estimates in decision-making problems with a vector-valued criterion, Automation and Remote Control, 34 (1974) 1787-1795.

[4] C.W. Kirkwood and R.K. Sarin, Ranking with partial information: a method and an application, Operations Research, 33 (1985) 38-48.

[5] S.A. Orlovsky, Decision-making with a fuzzy preference relation, Fuzzy Sets and Systems 1 (1978) 155-167.

[6] S.V. Ovchinnikov, Structure of fuzzy binary relations, Fuzzy Sets and Systems 6 (1981) 169-195.

[7] V.M. Ozernoy and M.G. Gaft, Multicriterion decision problems, in: D.E. Bell, R.L. Keeny, and H. Raifa, Eds., Conflicting Objectives in Decisions (John Wiley, London, 1977) 17-39.

[8] M. Roubens and P. Vincke, Fuzzy preferences in an optimization perspective, (unpublished).

[9] M. Roubens and P. Vincke, Fuzzy possibility graphs and their application to ranking fuzzy numbers, (to appear in Fuzzy Sets and Systems).

[10] A.K. Sen, Collective Choice and Social Welfare (Oliver & Boyd, Edinburg and London, 1970).

[11] A.K. Sen, Choice functions and revealed preference, Review of Economic Studies, 38 (1971) 307-317.

[12] R.M. Tong and P.P. Bonissone, A linguistic approach to decisionmaking with fuzzy sets, IEEE Transactions on Systems, Man, and Cybernetics, SMC-10 (1980) 716-723.

[13] L.A. Zadeh, Optimality and non-scalar valued performance criteria, IEEE Transactions on Automatic Control, AC-8 (1963) 315-316.

[14] L.A. Zadeh, The linguistic approach and its applications to decision analysis, in: Y.C. Ho and S.K. Mitter, Eds., Directions in Large -Scale Systems (Plenum Press, 1976) 339-361.

[15] S. Zionts, Multiple criteria mathematical programming: an overview and several approaches, in: G. Fandel and J. Spronk, Eds., Decision Methods and Applications (Springer Verlag, Berlin, 1985) 85-128.

EFFECTIVE CONVOLUTIONS OF VECTOR PREFERENCE RELATIONS IN DECISION MAKING PROBLEMS

Zhukovin V.E.
Institute of Cybernetics
Academy of Sciences of GSSR
S.Euli 5,380086 Tbilisi,USSR

Key Words: Preference relation, Multicriteria decision making, Nondominated alternatives, Pareto set, Effective convolution, Fuzzy.

1. Introduction

Scientific study of decision making problems are practised on a large scale. It comprises traditional psyco-physiological research such new areas as modern theory of decision making ,development of man machine procedures of decision making, decision support systems, expert systems. In this paper we are interested in formal presentation of decision making problems. It so happened that binary relations and functions of utility turned out to describe problems of decision making with most adequate manner. There is certain relationship between them. Moreover, it was the theory of decision making that began to study some classes of nonconventional binary relations.We shall consider some of them in this paper. Traditionally the problem of decision making is presented by the pare $\langle X,R\rangle$, where X is some finite set of comperetive alternatives (decisions) and $R \subseteq E$ is a binary relation,where $E=X\times X$. In the theory of decision making there used a special class of binary relations making it possible to compare a pare of alternatives over some criterium, e.g. bigger, better,more preferable, heavier, taller etc. Fishburn (11) called these binary relations preference relations. For any relation R we can determine reverse relation R^{-1}, equvalence relation $R^{e}=R\cap R^{-1}$, strict preference relation $R^{s}=R/R^{-1}$ and also a set of maximal (nondominated) alternatives $X_{\Pi}(R)$. The latter is the core of the relation R, but we call it Pareto set by analogy with multicriteria problems of decision making. It is clear that any choice of effective alternative must be realized precisely in Pareto set. If comparison of alternatives is realized on the base of some quantity criterium (scalar function) $K(x):X\to Re$,where $x\in X$,then preference relation is introduced in the following way:

$$R = \{ (x,y) \mid K(x) \geqslant K(y) \} \quad , \text{ or}$$
$$R = \{ (x,y) \mid K(x) \leqslant K(y) \} \quad ,$$

where $(x,y) \in E$.

With the help of binary relation we can present any qualitative criterium, if it is presented in the form of a linguistic variable, e.g. as it is in Zadeh (7,9), or Saaty (6). In the form of binary relation we usually present interrogatory data of decision maker (DM) or experts. Later on we shall need some special properties of preference relations that will be given below, the proof of the theorem being not presented in this paper for the sake of simplicity. Neither do we present the definitions of wellknown properties of binary relations such as: reflexivity, symmetry, assymmetry, transitivity, connectivity etc. believing then to be well-known (11).

Definition 1.1. For the subset X_0 of the set X the property "external stability" holds if for any $y \in X / X_0$ there exists $x \in X_0$ such that $(x,y) \in R^s$.

Theorem 1.1. If the set X is finite and R is transitive, then the Pareto set $X_n(R) \neq \emptyset$ and for it the property "external stability" holds.

Theorem 1.2. If X is finite, and R is acyclic then $X_n(R) \neq \emptyset$.

Theorem 1.3. Given a finite set X of the alternatives with two preference relations R_1 and R_2 defined in this set. If $R_1^s \subseteq R_2^s$ then $X_n(R_2) \subseteq X_n(R_1)$.

Consequence 1.1. Given R_1 and R_2 are connected preference relations and $R_1 \subseteq R_2$ then $X_n(R_1) \subseteq X_n(R_2)$.

These properties of Pareto set are of great interest for decision making problems and will be needed in the sequel. They confirm the judgement that effective alternatives are in Pareto set when it is nonempty. In real situations preference relations are usually formed on the basis of interrogatory of DM (or experts) over an alternative pair set E. Very often the results of comparison of alternative pairs can be described by number $\varphi(x,y)$ which show to what extent the alternative x is preferable to the alternative y, where $(x,y) \in E$. For this case we are going to consider two classes of scalar functions:

$$H = \{ \psi(x,y) \mid \psi(x,y) = -\psi(y,x) \},$$
$$T = \{ \psi(x,y) \mid \psi(x,z) + \psi(z,y) = \psi(x,y) \}. \qquad (I)$$

(x,z), (z,y) and (x,y) are any alternatives pairs in E. The latter is a transitivity condition.

Definition 1.2. The scalar function $\varphi(x,y) \in H$ is called the superiority degree (SD) of decision x over y.

Definition 1.3. The scalar function

$$\Phi(x,y) = \frac{1}{n}\sum_{z\in X}\left[\varphi(x,z) - \varphi(y,z)\right],$$

where $\varphi(x,y) \in H$ and n is a number of competetive alternatives, is called the integral superiority degree (ISD) of decision x over y.

Definition 1.4. The binary relation

$$R(l) = \{(x,y) \mid \psi(x,y) \geqslant l\},\ l \geqslant 0,$$

is a preference relation (PR) of the level l. If $l \neq 0$ then it is assymmetric, with $l = 0$ it is reflexive.

To any such relation there corresponds the Pareto set $X_\Pi(l) \subseteq X$.

The introduced concepts have the following main properties (P):

P1: $\Phi(x,y) \in H$ (always).

P2: If $\varphi(x,y) \in H \cap T$ then $\Phi(x,y) = \varphi(x,y)$.

P3: If $\psi(x,y) \in T$ then $R(l)$ is transitive for any l and, therefore, $X_\Pi(l) \neq \emptyset$ and has the property of "external stability" (theorem 1.1).

P4: If $0 < l_1 < l_2$ then $R(0) \supsetneq R(l_1) \supsetneq R(l_2)$ and, therefore, $X_\Pi(0) \subseteq X_\Pi(l_1) \subseteq X_\Pi(l_2)$ since $R(l)$ is a strict (assymmetric) preference relation for all $l \neq 0$ (theorem 1.3).

P5: If $\varphi(x,y) \in H \cap T$ then $\varphi(x,y) = U_\varphi(x) - U_\varphi(y)$, where $U_\varphi(x) = \sum_{y\in X} \lambda(y)\cdot\varphi(x,y)$ and $\lambda(y) \geqslant 0$, $y \in X$, and $\sum_{y\in X} \lambda(y) = 1$.

$U_\varphi(x)$ is in fact the utility function over x.

P6: For any $\varphi(x,y) \in H$ holds $U_\varphi(x) = U_\Phi(x)$.

These results allow to form in X a structure of inbedded one into another nonempty Pareto sets on the basis of interrogatory of DM or experts. They all have the propertyof"external stability ". When necessary, they allow to order the alternatives in X with the help of the corresponding utility function $U_\varphi(x)$, the presented structure being coordinated with interrogatory data. By changing the value of the level l the decision maker has an opportunity to obtain a set of effective elements of different cardinality from which the final choice would be done. Now consider the class of nonconventional preference relations.

2. Vector preference relations (VPR).

Again consider the problem of decision making in the form $\langle X,R\rangle$. If $R = \{R_1, R_2, \ldots, R_m\}$, where $R_j \subseteq E$, $j = \overline{1,m}$ the usual binary preference relations, then we can deal with multicriteria problem of decision making. In this case R is called vector preference relation (VPR). It is a new nonconventional object for scientific research. It is safe to say that such relations in classical mathematics have not been studied. They were formed inthe modern theory of decision making and they are intended for its problems. In future they may have other applications, e.g., for description of conflict situations such papers have been already published (10). Let's make clear some points. Multicriteria problems of decision making arise in many real situations e.g.:

1. Development of annual plan for a manufacture branch.
2. Project competition.
3. Election of candidate for a vacancy.
4. Distribution of homogenious supply (cement, fuel, water).
5. Balancing between industry and nature etc.

In all these situations alternatives are estimated on many aspects in complex. Its own preference relation corresponds to each aspect, and they are incompatible with each other. It means that in the set of competitive decisions X there are no ideal alternatives, which are not worse than other alternatives over whole VPR. The ideal alternatives are the best alternatives which in classical mathematics are called optimal. In the modern theory of decision making there is no concept of optimality in conventional sense. A compromise decision is usually made. The compromise is usually connected with DM,his aims, reasoning, estimations, the information that he uses (4). Different DM's in the same situation may choose different alternatives and no wonder. That is why decision support systems are usually developed as man-machine (dialogue) procedures of decision making. The formal model of estimation and choice of alternatives is realised by computer. It guarantees absense of contradiction in comparison of decisions and Pareto effectivness of the final choice. All the necessary for the model current information gets into computer by the dialogue with DM or experts. It is his preference structure, defined by the goals, reasoning, criteria. In the case this structure is presented by matrices $(n \times n)$ where n - is a number of alternatives in X. There may be a situation when some matricesare partially not filled up the incomplete information case, which brings to the decision making problem with nonconnected preference relations. The results presented in the paper are for dialogue procedures of decision making. These procedures are used together with other auxiliary procedures, such as

1. Revealation and formation of criteria on the basis of system

approach.

2. Formation of competitive alternative set in the case the latter is not given initially
3. Decrease of material processed by experts
4. The possibility for experts to return to the provious steps (feed back) on decision maker's demand.

Consider VRP R. The relation of Pareto-domination $R_K = \bigcap_{j=1}^{m} R_j$ and the corresponding Pareto set $X_\Pi(R_K) = X_\Pi^K$ are defined. We shall call it the main (basic) Pareto set.

Theorem 2.1. For the given VRP R, if all its components R_j, $j=\overline{1,m}$, are linearly (connected) quasi-orders, then R_K is also a quasi order, but not necessary linear.

If VPR satisfies the conditions of theorem 2.1 then $X_\Pi^K \neq \emptyset$ and has the property of "external stability".

Definition 2.1. Any binary relation $\bar{R} = f(R_1, R_2, \ldots, R_m)$ is a convolution of VPR if $\bar{R} \subseteq \bigcup_{j=1}^{m} R_j$ and $X_\Pi(\bar{R}) \neq \emptyset$.

Definition 2.2. The convolution VPR is effective if $R_K^s \subseteq \bar{R}^s$ wheh $X_\Pi^K \neq \emptyset$.

The latter fact is important since we can study models of decision making with an empty Pareto set. Such problems are quite real, e.g. when R_K is intransitive. From the theorem 2.2 it follows, that for the effective convolutions of VPR $X_\Pi(\bar{R}) \subseteq X_\Pi^K$ holds, when $X_\Pi^K \neq \emptyset$. Using them we ensure the choice effectiveness.

Let's define the following scalar functions:

$$\gamma_j(x,y) = \begin{cases} \rho_j(x,y) & \text{if } (x,y) \in R_j^s, \\ 0 & \text{if } (x,y) \; R_j^e, \\ -\rho_j(x,y) & \text{if } (y,x) \; R_j^s. \end{cases} \qquad (2)$$

Here all R_j, $j=\overline{1,m}$ are connected. Let's introduce the function:

$$q(x,y) = \frac{\sum_{j=1}^{m} \gamma_j(x,y)}{\sum_{j=1}^{m} |\gamma_j(x,y)|} \qquad (3)$$

It is clear that it is superiority degree of the alternative x over the alternative y (definition 1.2).

It has the following properties:

a) $q(x,y) \in R$.

b) $-1 \leq q(x,y) \leq 1$ for all pairs of alternatives in E.

c) If $q(x,y) = 1$ then $(x,y) \in R_K^s$ if $q(x,y) = -1$ then $(y,x) \in R_K^s$.

Let's introduce the preference relation of VPR

$$Q(l) = \{ (x,y) \mid q(x,y) \geqslant l \}, \quad 0 \leq l \leq 1.$$

Theorem 2.2. The convolution of VPR Q(l) is effective for all allowable values l.

The numbers $\mathcal{S}_j(x,y), j=\overline{1,m}$ characterize the level of informa-ion, used by DM in his choice. There are 3 levels:

.) $\mathcal{S}_j(x,y)=1$ for all $j=\overline{1,m}$ (majoritary level).

) $\mathcal{S}_j(x,y)=\lambda_j$ where λ_j are significance coefficients of pre-erence relation R_j. These coefficients must satisfy the following ondition:

$$\lambda=\{\lambda_1,\lambda_2,\dots,\lambda_m\},\ \lambda\in\Lambda,$$

here $\Lambda=\{\lambda \mid \lambda_j \geqslant 0, \sum_{j=1}^{m}\lambda_j=1\}$.

here are special methods for determination of significance coeffi-ients.

) $\mathcal{S}_j(x,y)=\lambda_j\cdot\left[K_j(x)-K_j(y)\right]$, where $K_j(x)$ is a criterium,on the asis of which R_j is formed. We presented an example of one effective convolution of VPR R. We can certainly form some other effective con-olutions. They are of interest, because they diminish the number of lternatives in Pareto set, when there are too many alternatives in it nd it is practically vast for DM.

3. Effective linear convolution of VPR

This convolution is of interest in scientific aspect and often ccurs in real situations. It has many good properties and is used n many decision making problems, e.g. with incomplete information or empty Pareto set.

On the basis of the formula (2) let us introduce the following calar function defined in E:

$$\varphi(x,y;\mathcal{S})=\sum_{j=1}^{m}\gamma_j(x,y), \tag{4}$$

here $\mathcal{S}=\{\mathcal{S}_1,\mathcal{S}_2,\dots,\mathcal{S}_m\}$. It is not difficult to verify that $\varphi(x,y;\mathcal{S})\in H$ and, therefore, it is a superiority degree of de-ision x over decision y.

Definition 3.1. The following preference relation

$$L(\mathcal{S})=\{(x,y) \mid \varphi(x,y;\mathcal{S})\geqslant 1\},\ 1\geqslant 0,$$

ill be called linear convolution of VPR R.

We can introduce the relations: $L^{-1}(\mathcal{S})$, $L^{e}(\mathcal{S})$ and $L^{s}(\mathcal{S})$ nd also a Pareto set in the form $X_\Pi[L(\mathcal{S})]$. Note that $X_\Pi[L(\mathcal{S})]\neq\emptyset$ olds.

Theorem 3.1. Linear convolution of VPR given by the definition .1 is effective in the sense of definition 2.2 for all three levels f information $\mathcal{S}$ used by DM.

It means that $X_{\Pi}\left[L(\rho)\right] \subseteq X_{\Pi}^{K}$,when it is not empty, which ensures the effectiveness of compromise alternative in final choice, if DM uses linear convolution or VPR R. For the second and third levels of information ρ the coefficients $\lambda \in \Lambda$ serve as a free parameter that allows DM to some extent to control the choice. It is important for dialogue procedures of decision making. In multicriteria problems of decision making there is a well-known result, which is the USSR is called Karlin's lemma (2). A similar result occurs in the considered case:

Theorem 3.2. (Karlin's lemma). Let $x_0 \in X_{\Pi}^{K}$. Then there exists such a set of coefficients $\lambda^{\circ} \in \Lambda$ that $x_0 \in X_{\Pi}\left[L(\rho^{\circ})\right]$ takes place for the second and third levels of information used by DM.

In this case $\rho^{o} = \left\{ \rho_j(x,y) = \lambda_j^{o} \right\}_1^m$ for the second level of information and $\rho^{o} = \left\{ \rho_j^{o}(x,y) = \lambda_j^{o} \cdot \left[K_j(x) - K_j(y) \right] \right\}_1^m$ for the third level of information. Thus by changing the values $\lambda \in \Lambda$ DM can essetially choose any alternative from the main Pareto set X_{Π}^{K} as a compromise decision and no other.

Now consider the case, when there is incomplete information. It means that the components of VPR R are nonconnected. Let's introduce the notations $I = \left\{ 1,2,\ldots,m \right\}$. Let us denote the subset of preference relations indeces, over which we failed to compare the pair of alternatives $(x,y) \in E$ by $J(x,y) \subseteq I$. At present we are not interested in the reason of this failure. Let us determine the following values:

$$\Lambda(x,y;\rho) = \sum_{j \in J(x,y)} \rho_j(x,y), \quad \Lambda(x,y;\rho) \geqslant 0 \tag{5}$$

Definition 3.2. Let us call

$$\underline{\varphi}(x,y) = \sum_{j \bar{\in} J(x,y)} \delta_j(x,y) - \Lambda(x,y;\rho),$$

$$\overline{\varphi}(x,y) = \sum_{j \bar{\in} J(x,y)} \delta_j(x,y) + \Lambda(x,y;\rho)$$

the lower and upper superiority degrees correspondingly.

Thus to compare a pair of alternatives $(x,y) \in E$ we have interval estimations instead of point estimations. Besides the above properties of superiority degree, which hold also for newly introduced lower and upper superiority degrees, they have two more additional properties:

a) $\underline{\varphi}(x,y;\rho) = -\overline{\varphi}(y,x;\rho)$,

b) $\underline{\varphi}(x,y;\rho) \equiv \overline{\varphi}(x,y;\rho)$ if $J(x,y) = \emptyset$.

To compare the intervals we used a simple rule that became the basis of the following definition.

Definition 3.3. Let us call the following preference relation:

$$L(\wp;J)=\{(x,y)\mid \underline{\varphi}(x,y;\wp)\geqslant\overline{\varphi}(x,y;\wp)\}$$

a linear convolution of VPR R with incomplete information.

It is a strict (assymmetric) preference relation. The alternative x is strictly preferable to alternative y if the interval $[\underline{\varphi}(x,y;\wp), \overline{\varphi}(x,y;\wp)]$ is on the numerical axis on the right of the interval $[\underline{\varphi}(y,x;\wp), \overline{\varphi}(y,x;\wp)]$. Since the intervals can intersect this is a non connected preference relation. Note also that the corresponding Pareto set $X_\Pi[L(\wp;J)]$ is not empty. If $J(x,y)=\emptyset$ that is there is complete information, then $L(\wp;J)=L(\wp)$ and $X_\Pi[L(\wp;J)]=X_\Pi[L(\wp)]$.

Theorem 3.3. $X_\Pi[L(\wp)]\subseteq X_\Pi[L(\wp;J)]$.

As we see, we cannot speak here about effectiveness of the convolution given by the definition 3.3 in the sense of the definition 2.2. Naturally it is because of the incomplete information. But in its Pareto set there is some subset of effective alternatives.

4. The problems of decision making with empty Pareto set

It is another interesting class of preference relations. For some VPR's it may happen that there is no Pareto set. It can be the case when: 1) R_K is intransitive and $X_\Pi^K=\emptyset$.

2) $R_K=\emptyset$ and then $X_\Pi^K=X$ (e.g. tournament).

In both cases there is nothing to choose from but the choice must be done. It is obvious that in this case it is necessary to use effective convolutions of VPR R in the sense of the definition 2.2.

In this paper this problem is also connected with linear convolution of VPR given by the definition 3.1 namely with the preference relation $L(\wp)$ for any level of information $\wp$ - available for DM at the moment of choice. We think that in both cases we must take $X_\Pi[L(\wp)]$ if there is complete information, and $X_\Pi[L(\wp;J)]$ if there is incomplete information, as an initial Pareto set. The latter can be diminished through introduction of additional restrictions. But we are not going to do this in this paper. After introduction of Pareto set the estimation of choice procedures effectiveness, is acomplished as before. Again note that $X_\Pi[L(\wp)]\neq\emptyset$. The problems of decision making with empty Pareto set are certainly of interest for scientific research and they often occur in real situations. Some other app -

roaches and methods are possiple for studying these problems. But the main idea is that singling out of not empty initial Pareto set on some base seems to be common.

Summary

In this paper we considered a class of nonconventional binary relations for the problems of decision making. These are vector preference relations. For the first time they developed in multicriteria problems of decision making and are meant for their description and study. But the field of their application may be more extensive. For vector preference relation we introduced the concept of effective convolution taking into account problem of decision making with empty Pareto set.

The example of linear convolution illustrated in detail such essential for the paper points as effectiveness, Karlin's lemma, interrelation with the problems of decision making with incomplete information and empty Pareto set. In fact, it is a range of questions and problems, that must be considered in studying any convolution of VPR We did not give examples in the paper. But the presented results are constructive and any user who takes an interest can easily use them in this specific situation. The free parameters l in the convolution Q(l) and the coefficients $\lambda \in \Lambda$ in the linear convolution allow DM to view and compare larger or smaller number of alternatives in Pareto set X^{k}_{n} after his wish. It is an important point in dialogue procedures of decision making. It is important to note also that all the considered in the paper problems and the obtained results take place also for fuzzy multicriteria problems of decision making, formulated and studied by us (4).

REFERENCES

1. L.A.Zadeh, Fuzzy Sets, Inform. and Control, vol.8,1965,338 - 353.
2. S.Karlin, Mathematical methods and theory in games, programming and economics, Pergamon Press, London-Paris 1959.
3. V.E. Zhukovin, The multicriteria decision making with vector fuzzy preference relation, Cybernetics and systems research 2,R.Trappl (ed), Elsevier Science Publishers B.V. (North-Holland),1984,179-18
4. V.E. Zhukovin, Multicriteria decision making models with uncertainty, Publ. Metsniereba, Tbilisi,1983, 104.
5. V.E.Zhukovin, F.V.Burstein, The dialodue procedure of the choice of the best decision with respect to multiple objectives and noncomplete information, Proceedings of Tbilisi University, 224, 3, 1981, 19-32.

6. T.L.Saaty, Exploring the interfase between hierarchies, multiple objectives and fuzzy sets, Fuzzy sets and systems, 1 1978,57-68.
7. L.A.Zadeh, Linguistic Cybernetics, Proc. of the Internat. Sympos. on Syst. Sciences and Cybernetics,Oxford, University, 1972.

8. A.P. Weirzbicki, A Mathematical Basis for Satisticing Decision Making IIASA, Luxemburg, Austria, 1980 80-90.
9. L.A.Zadeh, Optimality and Non-Scalar-Valued Performance Criteria, IEEE Transactions on Autimatic Control, AC-8, 59 1963.
10.Z.Pawlak, On conflicts, Int.J.Man Machine Studies,21,1984,127-134.
11.P.C.Fishburn, Decision and Value Theory, Wiley, New York,1964.
12.Kacprzyk J., Yager K.K, Linguistic quantifiers and belief qualification in fuzzy multicriteria and multistage decision making,Control and Cybernetics Vol. 13, No 3, 1984.

CHOICE FUNCTIONS ASSOCIATED WITH FUZZY PREFERENCE RELATIONS

Zbigniew Świtalski

Central Library
A.Mickiewicz University

61-816 Poznań, Poland

Abstract. In this paper we consider generalized choice functions (g.c.f.) in which the choice set C(A,R) is a fuzzy set depending on a crisp set A and a fuzzy relation R. We define generalized fuzzy sets of C-maximal and C-nondominated elements and prove relations between them. We also relate the procedure of Blin (1974) with some special g.c.f. B=B(A,R).

Keywords: choice function, fuzzy choice set, fuzzy preference relation, generalized implication operator.

1. INTRODUCTION

Fuzzy preference relations seem to be a useful tool in modelling decision processes. Among others, they appear in a very natural way when we want to aggreagate individual crisp preferences into group (collective) ones. (compare, e.g., Blin (1974), Nurmi (1981), Seo and Sakawa (1985)).

When a fuzzy preference relation in a (crisp) set of alternatives X is given, then the problem of finding a set of "best" alternatives may be considered (Orlovsky (1978), Nurmi (1981)). In other words, the problem is to find a good (rational) choice function in X, i.e. to assign to each (crisp) subset A of X and each fuzzy relation R in A a choice set $C(A,R) \subset A$ of best alternatives. Of course, a possible solution(s) of this problem will depend on the criteria of "bestness" we are accepting in the particular real situation. In spite of this, it would be interesting to study different possible choice functions and investigate connections between them.

S.A.Orlovsky (1978) and H.Nurmi (1981) tried to define "good" choices for a fuzzy relation R. J.M.Blin (1974) defined a (crisp) ordering of a set X connected with a fuzzy R.

In our paper we will consider, for a fuzzy R, a generalized fuzzy set of greatest elements G(A,R), a generalized fuzzy set of nondominated elements N(A,R), and a generalized fuzzy set of maximal elements $M_{\rightarrow}(A,R)$ depending on some generalized inplication operator $\rightarrow$).

The set $M_{\rightarrow}(A,R)$ generalizes Orlovsky's fuzzy set of nondominated elements and the crisp choice set $N^{*}(A,R) = \arg\max_{x} N(A,R)(x)$ connecte with the set N(A,R) is equal to Nurmi's set of minimax consensus winners S_M. The set G(A,R) was considered in Ovchinnikov (1985) in a general situation (for a fuzzy A).

We will also define fuzzy sets of C-maximal and C-nondominated elements for some abstract choice function C=C(A,R).

Our main results are the following. In Section 5 we prove some relations between the generalized choice sets (generalizing known facts for the crisp case). In Section 6 we prove a theorem relating the choice sets $G^*(A,R)$ and $M^*_{\rightarrow}(A,R)$ (for the max-min transitive R). In Section 7 we prove a result connecting the method of Blin (1974) with choices generated by some special choice function B=B(A,R).

2. CLASSICAL CHOICE SETS

Let X be a universum. P(X) will denote the family of all (crisp) subsets of X. Let $A \in P(X)$ and $R \in P(X^2)$ be a (crisp) relation in X (i.e. R is a subset of $X^2 = X \times X$).

Define the set of greatest elements for R in A by

$$G(A,R) = \{x \in A: \forall y \in A,\ xRy\} \tag{2.1}$$

We can also define

$$N(A,R) = \{x \in A: \forall y \in A, \neg\, yRx\} \tag{2.2}$$

$$M(A,R) = \{x \in A: \forall y \in A,\ yRx \rightarrow xRy\} \tag{2.3}$$

the set of nondominated elements for R in A and the set of maximal elements for R in A, respectively (cf. Naumov (1985)).

By the upper x-cut of R we will mean a set

$$R^+(x) = \{y \in X: yRx\}$$

and by the lower x-cut of R the set

$$R^-(x) = \{y \in X: xRy\}$$

In terms of the upper and lower x-cuts the above choice sets can be characterized as follows (Naumov (1985)):

$$G(A,R) = A \cap \bigcap_{y \in A} R^+(y) \tag{2.4}$$

$$N(A,R) = A \cap \bigcap_{y \in A} \overline{R^-(y)} \tag{2.5}$$

$$M(A,R) = A \cap \bigcap_{y \in A} (R^+(y) \cup \overline{R^-(y)}) \tag{2.6}$$

where $^-$ denotes the usual complement in P(x).

The following proposition states the monotonicity properties of the operators G and N.

PROPOSITION 1. For any $R,S \in P(x^2)$ we have:

(i) $R|A \subset S|A \rightarrow G(A,R) \subset G(A,S)$

(ii) $R|A \subset S|A \rightarrow N(A,S) \subset N(A,R)$

$R|A$ denotes here the restriction of R to A, i.e. $R|A = R \cap A^2$.

The next proposition connects the sets G(A,R), N(A,R) and M(A,R)

PROPOSITION 2. For any $R \in P(x^2)$ we have:

(i) $N(A,R) = G(A,\overline{R^{-1}})$,

(ii) $M(A,R) = G(A,R \cup \overline{R^{-1}})$.

R^{-1} is here the inverse relation, i.e. $R^{-1} = \{(x,y): yRx\}$.

Relation $R \in \underline{P(X^2)}$ will be called complete if $R \cup R^{-1} = X^2$ (equivalently, $\overline{R^{-1}} \subset R$) and asymmetric if $R \cap R^{-1} = \emptyset$ (equivalently, $R \subset \overline{R^{-1}}$).

The following proposition is an immediate consequence of Propositions 1 and 2.

PROPOSITION 3. For any $R \in P(X^2)$ we have:

(i)	$G(A,R) \subset M(A,R)$		
(ii)	$N(A,R) \subset M(A,R)$		
(iii)	$G(A,R) = M(A,R)$	if R|A is complete in A	
(iv)	$N(A,R) = M(A,R)$	if R|A is asymmetric in A	

Proposition 3 states the following well-known facts:

(i) every greatest element is maximal

(ii) every nondominated element is maximal

(iii) if R is complete, then every maximal element is greatest

(iv) if R is asymmetric, then every maximal element is nondominated

3. OPERATIONS ON FUZZY SETS

By a fuzzy set in X we will mean a function $A: X \rightarrow I$, where $I = [0,1]$ denotes the unit interval. We will identify a (crisp) subset A of X with its characteristic function, i.e. we will write

$$A(x) = \begin{cases} 1 & \text{if} \quad x \in A \\ 0 & \text{if} \quad x \notin A \end{cases}$$

Hence, (crisp) subsets of X may be considered as fuzzy sets in X. The symbol F(x) will denote the family of all fuzzy sets in X. For any

$A, B \in F(x)$ we will write $A \subset B$ if

$$A(x) \leqslant B(x) \ , \quad \forall x \in X$$

The operations of summation (union) and intersection of fuzzy sets will be understood as in Zadeh (1965), i.e.

$$(A \cup B)(x) = A(x) \vee B(x)$$

$$(A \cap B)(x) = A(x) \wedge B(x)$$

where $\vee$ =maximum, $\wedge$ =minimum.

The symbol $\bar{\ }$ will denote some fixed strong negation in I, i.e. a unary operation $\bar{\ }$: $I \to I$ such that $\bar{\bar{a}}=a$, and $\bar{a} \leqslant \bar{b}$ if $a>b$, for all $a,b \in I$.

Using $\bar{\ }$ we can introduce the complementation in $F(X)$ by

$$\bar{A}(x) = \overline{A(x)}$$

It can be easily seen that if $A \in P(x)$, then $\bar{A}$ is the usual complement of A.

By a generalized implication operator we will mean a two-argument operation $\to: I^2 \to I$ such that

(i) $1 \to a = a$

(ii) $a \to 0 = \bar{a}$

(iii) $b \leqslant c \Rightarrow a \to b \leqslant a \to c$

(iv) $b \leqslant c \Rightarrow b \to c \leqslant c \to a$

for all $a,b,c \in I$ (this is a special case of implication operators considered, e.g., by Yager (1981) or Kacprzyk and Yager (1984)).

Operator $\to$ induces a two-argument operation in $F(x)$ by

$$(A \to B)(x) = A(x) \to B(x)$$

for $x \in X$. It is easy to see that if A and B are crisp, then $A \to B = \bar{A} \cup B$.

4. FUZZY CHOICE SETS

By a fuzzy relation in X we will mean an element of the set $F(X^2)$, i.e. a function $R: X^2 \to I$. We define the upper x-cut of R $(x \in X)$ by

$$R^+(x)(y) = R(y,x)$$

where $y \in X$, and the lower x-cut of R by

$$R^-(x)(y) = R(x,y)$$

We will define the fuzzy set of greatest elements for fuzzy R in a crisp A by

$$G(A,R) = A \cap \bigcap_{y \in A} R^{+}(y) \tag{4.1}$$

(cf. Ovchinnikov (1985)). The above formula of course generalizes (2.4).

We can also define the fuzzy sets of nondominated and maximal elements for R using (2.5) and (2.6) or, equivalently, by the formulas

$$N(A,R) = G(A,\overline{R^{-1}}) \tag{4.2}$$

$$M(A,R) = G(A,R \cup \overline{R^{-1}}) \tag{4.3}$$

where R^{-1} is defined by

$$R^{-1}(x,y) = R(y,x), \qquad x,y \in X$$

The fuzzy set $M(A,R)$ can be generalized to the set $M_{\rightarrow}(A,R)$ defined by

$$M_{\rightarrow}(A,R) = G(A,R^{-1} \rightarrow R) \tag{4.4}$$

where $\rightarrow$ is a generalized implication operator (notice that $a \rightarrow b = \bar{a} \vee b$ is a generalized implication operator and hence (4.3) is a special case of (4.4)).

$$G(A,R)(x) = \inf_{y \in A} R(x,y) \tag{4.5}$$

Similarly

$$N(A,R)(x) = \inf_{y \in A} \overline{R(y,x)} \tag{4.6}$$

and

$$M_{\rightarrow}(A,R)(x) = \inf_{y \in A} \{R(y,x) \rightarrow R(x,y)\} \tag{4.7}$$

The number $G(A,R)(x)$ may be understood as a degree of "greatestness of element $x \in A$ with respect to R (in A). Analogously, $N(A,R)(x)$ is a degree of nondomination and $M_{\rightarrow}(A,R)(x)$ a degree of maximality (with respect to $\rightarrow$).

It is easy to see that if $\rightarrow$ is the Łukasiewicz implication operator, i.e.

$$a \rightarrow b = \min\{1-a+b, 1\}$$

then $M_{\rightarrow}(A,R) = \mu^{ND}$, i.e. is Orlovsky's fuzzy set of nondominated alternatives (in A) as defined in Orlovsky (1978). The above fact is implied by the equality

$$M_{\rightarrow}(A,R)(x) = \inf_{y\in A} \min\{1-R(y,x)+R(x,y),1\}$$

$$= 1-\sup_{y\in A} \max\{R(y,x)-R(x,y),0\}$$

5. GENERALIZED CHOICE FUNCTIONS

DEFINITION 1. A generalized choice function (g.c.f.) in X is a mapping

$$C\colon P(X)\times F(X^2) \rightarrow F(X)$$

such that $C(A,R)\subset A$ for all $A\in P(X)$, $R\in F(X^2)$.

The formula (4.1) (also (4.2), (4.3)) defines of course a g.c.f. in X.

Let X be a finite set. The following formulas define g.c.f.'s in X:

$$C_{\sqcap}(A,R)(x) = \bigsqcap_{y\in A} R(x,y)\,, \qquad x\in A \tag{5.1}$$

$$C_{\Sigma}(A,R)(x) = \frac{1}{|A|}\sum_{y\in A} R(x,y), \qquad x\in A \tag{5.2}$$

$$C_{Q}(A,R)(x) = \mu_Q\Big(\frac{1}{|A|}\sum_{y\in A} R(x,y)\Big), \quad x\in A \tag{5.3}$$

where $\sqcap$ is a t-norm in I (considered as an n-argument operation), $|A|$ denotes the cardinality of A, and μ_Q is a nondecreasing function $I\rightarrow I$ connected with some generalized quantifier (in the sense of Kacprzyk and Yager (1984)).

The numbers $C_{\sqcap}(A,R)(x)$, $C_{\Sigma}(A,R)(x)$ and $C_Q(A,R)(x)$ may be viewed as generalized degrees of "greatestness" for R in A. From the point of view of many-valued logic they can be interpreted as truth-values of the statement "$\forall y\in A$, xRy" (or, in the case (5.3), as truth value of the statement "for $Qy\in A$, xRy").

In what follows we will assume that each g.c.f. C has the following isotonicity property:

$$R|A \subset S|A \;\Rightarrow\; C(A,R)\subset C(A,S) \tag{5.4}$$

for all $R,S\in F(X^2)$ and $A\in P(X)$.

Here $R|A = R\cap A^2$, analogously as in the crisp case. The property (5.4) generalizes (i) from Proposition 1 and guarantees that $C(A,R)$ depends only on $R|A$. Observe that g.c.f.'s given by (5.1), (5.2) and (5.3) have property (5.4).

Let C be a g.c.f. in X. We define generalized fuzzy sets of

C-nondominated and C-maximal elements by:

$$N^C(A,R) = C(A,\overline{R^{-1}})$$
$$M_{\rightarrow}^C(A,R) = C(A,R^{-1}\rightarrow R) \quad (5.$$

We will say that a fuzzy relation $R \in F(X^2)$ is complete if $R \cup R^{-1} = X^2$, an asymmetric if $R \cap R^{-1} = \emptyset$.
For a g.c.f. C in X we have the following generalization of Proposition 3:

<u>PROPOSITION 4.</u> For any $R \in F(X^2)$ we have:

(i) $C(A,R) \subset M_{\rightarrow}^C(A,R)$
(ii) $N^C(A,R) \subset M_{\rightarrow}^C(A,R)$
(iii) $C(A,R) = M_{\rightarrow}^C(A,R)$ if $R|A$ is complete in A
(iv) $N^C(A,R) = M^C(A,R)$ if $R|A$ is asymmetric in A

PROOF. From the definitions of $^-$ and $\rightarrow$ it can be easily deduced that for all $a,b \in I$ we have:

(i) $a \leqslant b \rightarrow a$
(ii) $\bar{b} \leqslant b \rightarrow a$
(iii) $a \vee b = 1 \Rightarrow b \rightarrow a = a$
(iv) $a \wedge b = 0 \Rightarrow b \rightarrow a = \bar{b}$

Hence if $R \in F(X^2)$, then:

(i) $R \subset R^{-1} \rightarrow R$
(ii) $\overline{R^{-1}} \subset R^{-1} \rightarrow R$
(iii) $R = R^{-1} \rightarrow R$ if R is complete
(iv) $\overline{R^{-1}} = R^{-1} \rightarrow R$ if R is asymmetric

Thus the definitions of N^C and $M_{\rightarrow}^C$ and (4.4) give the needed result.

6. CRISP CHOICES GENERATED BY FUZZY CHOICE SETS

If C is a g.c.f. in X and $A \in P(x)$, $R \in F(X^2)$, then it is natural to consider the crisp choice set consisting of those $x \in A$ for which the function $C(A,R)(x)$ attains its maximum. Define

$$C^*(A,R) = \operatorname*{argmax}_{x \in A} C(A,R)(x) \quad (6$$

It would be interesting to study connections between the sets $G^*(A,$ $N^*(A,R)$ and $M_{\rightarrow}^*(A,R)$ (or, in a general situation, $C^*(A,R)$, $(N^C)^*(A,R)$ a $(M_{\rightarrow}^C)^*(A,R)$). Notice that the set $N^*(A,R)$ (with the negation operator iven by $\bar{a}=1-a$) was considered by Nurmi (1981) and called there the set f minimax consensus winners (denoted by S_M) and the set $M^*_{\rightarrow}(A,R)$ was he set of maximal nondominated elements in Orlovsky (1978) provided hat $\rightarrow$ is the Łukasiewicz implication.

The following example shows that in general the sets $G^*(A,R)$, $N^*(A,R)$ nd $M^*_{\rightarrow}(A,R)$ may be quite different.

XAMPLE 1. Let $A=\{a_1,a_2,a_3\}$ be a 3-element set and R be given by matrix

$$R = \begin{bmatrix} 0.6 & 0.6 & 0.7 \\ 0.5 & 0.5 & 0.5 \\ 0.8 & 0.5 & 0.5 \end{bmatrix}$$

here $R=\{r_{ij}\}=\{R(a_i,a_j)\}$.

et $^-$ be given by $\bar{a}=1-a$ and $\rightarrow$ by $a\rightarrow b = \min\{1-a+b,1\}$. Then:

$$G(A,R)(a_i) = \inf_j r_{ij}$$

$$N(A,R)(a_i) = \inf_j (1-r_{ji})$$

$$M_{\rightarrow}(A,R)(a_i) = \inf_j \min\{1-r_{ji}+r_{ij},1\}$$

ence, by (5.1), $G^*(A,R)=\{a_1\}$, $N^*(A,R)=\{a_2\}$ and $M^*_{\rightarrow}(A,R)=\{a_3\}$.

Now we will prove a theorem relating the sets $G^*(A,R)$ and $M^*_{\rightarrow}(A,R)$ r R being a max-min transitive fuzzy relation.

Consider the following property of an implication operator in I

$$a \rightarrow b = 1 \iff a \leq b \qquad (6.2)$$

r all $a,b \in I$.

The next lemma generalizes a result of Orlovsky (1978).

MMA 1. Let $\rightarrow$ be an implication operator in I with the property (6.2), - a finite and not empty set, R - a max-min transitive fuzzy relation. en there exists $x \in A$ such that

$$M_{\rightarrow}(A,R)(x) = 1$$

OOF. If R is max-min transitive, then the crisp relation

$$x\hat{R}y \iff R(x,y) > R(y,x)$$

transitive (see Orlovsky (1978)), hence $M(A,\hat{R})$ is not empty. Let $M(A,\hat{R})$. Then, by (2.3)

$$\forall y \in A, \quad R(y,x) > R(x,y) \Rightarrow R(x,y) > R(y,x)$$

Hence

$$\forall y \in A, \quad R(y,x) \leq R(x,y)$$

and by (6.2)

$$\forall y \in A, \quad R(y,x) \to R(x,y) = 1$$

Thus

$$M_{\to}(A,R)(x) = 1$$

THEOREM 1. Let $\to$ be an implication operator with the property (6.2), A - a finite and not empty set, and R - a max-min transitive fuzzy relation. Then

$$M_{\to}^{*}(A,R) \subset G^{*}(A,R)$$

PROOF. By Lemma 1 it suffices to prove that

$$[M_{\to}(A,R)]_1 \subset G^{*}(A,R) \qquad (6.$$

where $[M_{\to}(A,R)]_1$ is the 1-cut of $M_{\to}(A,R)$. If $G(A,R)=\emptyset$, then $G^{*}(A,R)=A$ a the inclusion (6.3) is obviously fulfilled. Let $G(A,R)\neq\emptyset$ and assume th $y \in A \setminus G^{*}(A,R)$. Hence there exists $x \in A$ such that $G(A,R)(y)<G(A,R)(x)$ a by (4.5)

$$\inf_{z \in A} R(y,z) < \inf_{z \in A} R(x,z)$$

Let $u \in A$ be such an element that

$$\inf_{z \in A} R(y,z) < R(y,u) < \inf_{z \in A} R(x,z)$$

Hence

$$R(x,u) > R(y,u) \qquad (6.$$

$$R(x,y) > R(y,u) \qquad (6.$$

From the max-min transitivity of R we obtain

$$R(y,u) \geq R(y,x) \wedge R(x,u) \qquad (6.$$

By (6.4) and (6.6) we have

$$R(y,x) \wedge R(x,u) = R(y,x) \qquad (6.$$

and by (6.5), (6.6) and (6.7)

$$R(x,y) > R(y,x)$$

[H]ence by (6.2)

$$R(x,y) \rightarrow R(y,x) < 1$$

[a]nd by (4.7)

$$M_{\rightarrow}(A,R)(y) < 1$$

[T]hus $y \in A \setminus [M_{\rightarrow}(A,R)]_1$ and this proves (6.3).

[7]. BLIN'S METHOD

In Blin (1974) there was proposed a method of obtaining a linear [o]rdering of the set X when a fuzzy relation in X is given. Now we will [o]btain the ordering of Blin with the help of some special g.c.f., [B]=B(A,R).

Let X be a finite set and $R \in R(X^2)$ a fuzzy relation taking values [i]n the finite lattice $\{0, \frac{1}{n-1}, \frac{2}{n-1}, \ldots, 1\}$. R_α will denote the α-cut [o]f R, i.e.

$$R_\alpha = \{x \in X: R(x,y) \geq \alpha\}$$

[I]f R is crisp, then we will say that R has a cycle in X if there exists [a] sequence $(x_1, x_2, \ldots, x_n)$ of elements from X such that $x_1 R x_2 R \ldots R x_n R x_1$. [I]f R has no cycle in X, then we will say that R is acyclic. Let us [c]onsider the following g.c.f. in X

$$B(A,R)(x) = \min\{\min_{y \in A} \overline{R(y,x)}, \overline{l(A,R)}\} \tag{7.2}$$

[w]here $l(A,R) = \sup\{\alpha: R_\alpha | A \text{ has a cycle}\}$ and let $A_1, A_2, \ldots, A_n$ be subsets [o]f X such that:

$$X = A_1 \cup A_2 \cup \ldots \cup A_n$$

$$A_1 = B^*(X,R)$$

$$A_{i+1} = B^*(X \setminus \bigcup_{k=1}^{i} A_k, R)$$

[D]efine the following crisp relation in X

$$x\tilde{R}y \iff x \in A_{i1} \wedge y \in A_{i2} \wedge i_1 < i_2 \tag{7.3}$$

Let $\mathcal{L}(X,R)$ denotes the set of all (strict) linear orders [e]xtending R, i.e. all irreflexive, transitive and weakly complete (i.e. [x]Ry ∨ yRx, for all x≠y) relations in X being extensions of R.

[L]EMMA 2. Let $R \in F(X^2)$. Then

$$\mathcal{L}(X,R) \neq \emptyset \implies R_\alpha \subset \tilde{R}$$

PROOF. Let $x,y \in X$ and $R(x,y) \geq \alpha$. Find i_1 and i_2 such that $x \in A_{i_1}$, $y \in A_{i_2}$. We will prove (by contradiction) that $i_1 < i_2$. Assume that $i_1 \geq i_2$ and let

$$\tilde{A}_{i_2} = X \setminus \bigcup_{k=1}^{i_2 - 1} A_k$$

We will prove that

$$\forall u \in \tilde{A}_{i_2}, \exists\, v \in \tilde{A}_{i_2} : R(v,u) \geq \alpha \qquad (7.$$

Let $u \in \tilde{A}_{i_2}$. From the assumption that $y \in A_{i_2} = B^*(\tilde{A}_{i_2}, R)$ we obtain that

$$B(\tilde{A}_{i_2}, R)(y) \geq B(\tilde{A}_{i_2}, R)(u)$$

Hence

$$\min\{\min_{z \in \tilde{A}_{i_2}} R(z,y), \bar{l}\} \geq \min\{\min_{z \in \tilde{A}_{i_2}} \overline{R(z,u)}, \bar{l}\}$$

or, equivalently,

$$\max\{\max_{z \in \tilde{A}_{i_2}} R(z,y), l\} \leq \max\{\max_{z \in \tilde{A}_{i_2}} R(z,u), l\}, \qquad (7.$$

where $l = l(\tilde{A}_{i_2}, R) = \sup\{\beta : R_\beta | A_{i_2}$ has a cycle$\}$.

If $R_\beta | A_{i_2}$ has a cycle, then of course $\mathcal{L}(X, R_\beta) = \emptyset$. Hence $\alpha > l$. Moreover, by the assumption that $R(x,y) \geq \alpha$ we have

$$\max\{\max_{z \in \tilde{A}_{i_2}} R(z,y), l\} \geq \max\{R(x,y), l\} \geq \alpha > l \qquad (7.$$

By (7.5) and (7.6) we have

$$\max\{\max_{z \in \tilde{A}_{i_2}} R(z,y), l\} = \max_{z \in \tilde{A}_{i_2}} R(z,y) \qquad (7.$$

and

$$\max\{\max_{z \in \tilde{A}_{i_2}} R(z,u), l\} = \max_{z \in \tilde{A}_{i_2}} R(z,u) \qquad (7.$$

Thus by (7.5)

$$\max_{z \in \tilde{A}_{i_2}} R(z,u) \geq \max_{z \in \tilde{A}_{i_2}} R(z,y) \geq R(x,y) \geq \alpha$$

and by the finiteness of $\tilde{A}_{i_2}$ we can find $v \in \tilde{A}_{i_2}$ such that

$$R(v,u) \geq \alpha$$

So, we proved (7.4). From (7.4) it can be easily deduced that R_α has a cycle in $\tilde{A}_{i_2}$ and so in X. Hence $\mathcal{L}(X,R_\alpha)=\emptyset$ and this contradicts our assumption. Thus the proof is finished.

Assume that for $R \in F(X^2)$ and for some $\alpha>0$ there exists the unique linear extension of R_α, i.e. the following condition is satisfied,

$$\exists\ \alpha > 0, \qquad |\mathcal{L}(x,R_\alpha)| = 1 \tag{7.9}$$

THEOREM 2. If for a fuzzy relation R the condition (7.9) is satisfied, then the relation R defined by (7.3) is the ordering of X in the sense of Blin (1974).

PROOF. Let $\alpha>0$ be a number such that $|\mathcal{L}(X,R_\alpha)| =1$. By Lemma 2 we have

$$\mathcal{L}(X,\tilde{R}) \subset \mathcal{L}(X,R_\alpha)$$

The set $\mathcal{L}(X,\tilde{R})$ is not empty, hence

$$\mathcal{L}(X,\tilde{R}) = \mathcal{L}(X,\tilde{R}) = \{\tilde{R}\}.$$

On the other hand, it is easy to see that R is the ordering in the sense of Blin as the unique linear extension of R_α.

Thus we obtained another method for determining Blin's ordering (in the cases when (7.9) is satisfied) - this method consists in finding maxima of the function given by the formula (7.2).

REFERENCES

J.M.Blin (1974), Fuzzy Relations in Group Decision Theory, Journal of Cybernetics, 4, 17-22.

J.Kacprzyk, R.R.Yager, (1984) Linguistic quantifiers and belief qualification in fuzzy multicriteria and multistage decision making, Control and Cybernetics, 13, 155-173.

G.E.Naumov (1985), Sushchestvovanie optimal'nogo vybora na kompaktnom mnozhestve alternativ, Avtomatika i telemekhanika, 3, 5-27.

H.Nurmi (1981), Approaches to Collective Decision Making with Fuzzy Preference Relations, Fuzzy Sets and Systems, 6, 249-259.

S.A.Orlovsky (1978), Decision-making with a Fuzzy Preference Relation, Fuzzy Sets and Systems, 1, 155-167.

S.V.Orchinnikov (1985), A Stochastic Model of Choice, Stochastica, 9, 135-152.

F.Seo, M.Sakawa (1985), Fuzzy Multiattribute utility Analysis for Collective Choice, IEEE Transactions on Systems, Man and Cybernetics, SMC-15, No 1, 45-53.

R.R.Yager (1984), General multiple-objective decision functions and linguistically quantified statements, Int. J. Man-Machine Studies, 21, 389-400.

L.A.Zadeh (1965), Fuzzy Sets, Information and Control, 8, 338-353.

FUZZY POSSIBILITY GRAPHS AND THEIR APPLICATION TO RANKING FUZZY NUMBERS

Marc Roubens
Faculté Polytechnique de Mons, Belgium

Philippe Vincke
Université Libre de Bruxelles, Belgium

ABSTRACT

A fuzzy interval graph is introduced which extends the well-known crisp interval graph. Based on this fuzzy structure, fuzzy possibility and preference digraphs are specified and their properties are investigated. The transitivity and completeness properties of the preference digraphs induce a non-empty core (unfuzzily non-dominated subset) and suggest a procedure to rank fuzzy numbers.

1. Introduction

Let F be a family of non empty sets. The intersection graph of F is obtained by representing each set of F by a vertex and connecting two vertices by an edge iff the corresponding sets intersect.
The intersection graph of a family J of intervals on the real line is called interval graph and denoted (J,I).
Defining, $\forall\ I_1, I_2 \in J$:

$$I_1\ I^c\ I_2 \text{ iff } I_1 \cap I_2 = \emptyset ,$$

the obtained graph (J,I^c) complement of (J,I) is called comparability graph. Each edge of (J,I^c) can be oriented in such a way that the resulting directed graph is transitive (see Ghouila-Houri (1962), Gilmore and Hoffman (1964), Fulkerson and Gross (1965), Roberts (1976), Golumbic (1980), Roubens and Vincke (1985), Roubens (1985)). We denote this transitive directed graph (J,P) and call it preference digraph. The relation P is an interval order.

The purpose of this paper is to extend these definitions to the families of convex fuzzy subsets of the real line, called shortly fuzzy numbers, and to study the associated fuzzy possibility graphs.

2. Definitions and example

A fuzzy number a is characterized by a function μ_a, associating to each real number a value, between 0 and 1, in such a way that

$$\begin{cases} \bigvee_x \mu_a(x) = 1 , \\ x \leq y \leq z \Rightarrow \mu_a(y) \geq \mu_a(x) \wedge \mu_a(z) \end{cases}$$

(we define as usual $a \vee b = \max(a,b)$ and $a \wedge b = \min(a,b)$.)

The intersection $a \cap b$ of two fuzzy numbers a and b is the fuzzy set defined by

$$\mu_{a \cap b}(x) = \mu_a(x) \wedge \mu_b(x) .$$

The <u>height</u> of $a \cap b$ is the maximum value of $\mu_{a \cap b}$:

$$hgt(a \cap b) = \bigvee_x [\mu_a(x) \wedge \mu_b(x)] .$$

Given a family of fuzzy numbers, the fuzzy interval graph associated to this family is the valued undirected graph whose vertices represent the fuzzy numbers and where each pair of vertices is linked by an edge the value of which is the height of the intersection of the corresponding fuzzy numbers.

For each family of fuzzy numbers A, we also define a <u>fuzzy possibility graph</u> : it is a directed graph whose vertices represent the fuzzy numbers and where the number

$$\mu_S(a,b) = \bigvee_{x \geq y} [\mu_a(x) \wedge \mu_b(y)]$$

is associated to each oriented edge (a,b) and defines the <u>fuzzy possibility relation</u> in A x A.

The following example illustrates these concepts. Let us consider three trapezoidal fuzzy numbers defined as follows.

$$\mu_a(x) = \begin{cases} 0 & x < 8.5 , \\ 1 & 8.5 \leq x \leq 9.5 , \\ 0 & x > 9.5 \end{cases}$$

$$\mu_b(x) = \begin{cases} 0 & x \leq 3 , \\ \text{linear} & 3 \leq x \leq 6 , \\ 1 & 6 \leq x \leq 8 , \\ \text{linear} & 8 \leq x \leq 10 , \\ 0 & x \geq 10 . \end{cases}$$

$$\mu_c(x) = \begin{cases} 0 & x \leq 2 , \\ \text{linear} & 2 \leq x \leq 3 , \\ 1 & 3 \leq x \leq 4 , \\ \text{linear} & 4 \leq x \leq 6 , \\ 0 & x \geq 6 . \end{cases}$$

These fuzzy numbers are shown in fig.1, and the corresponding fuzzy interval and possibility graphs appear in fig.2 and 3.

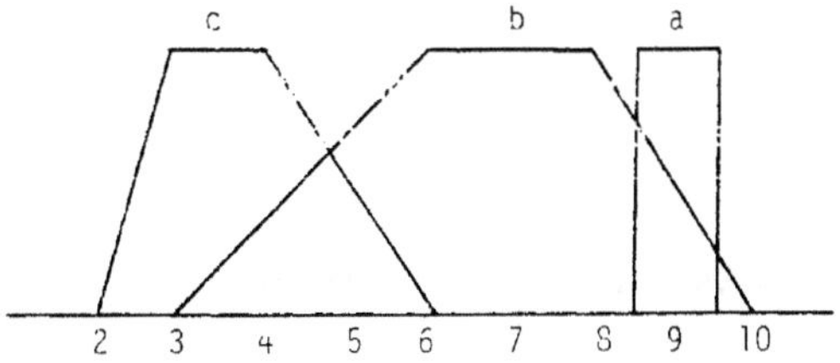

$hgt(a \cap b) = .75$

$hgt(b \cap c) = .60$

$hgt(a \cap c) = 0$

fig.1

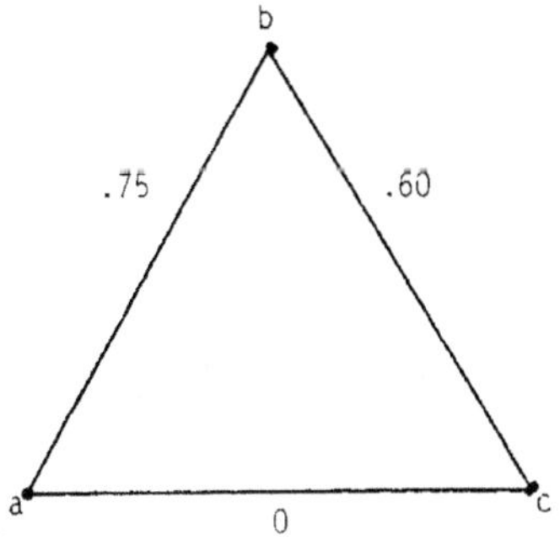

fig.2 : Fuzzy interval graph.

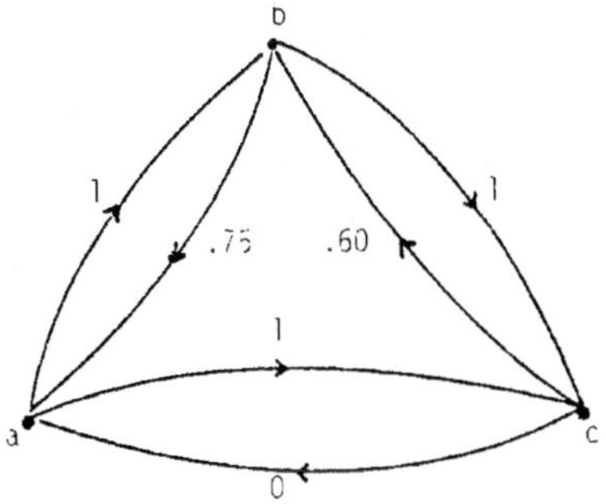

fig.3 : Fuzzy possibility graph.

3. Properties of a fuzzy possibility graph

Theorem : every fuzzy possibility graph has the following properties : $\forall$ a,b,c,d :

(i) $\mu_S(a,a) = 1$ (reflexive graph),

(ii) $\mu_S(a,b) \vee \mu_S(b,a) = 1$ (complete graph)

(iii) $\mu_S(a,b) \wedge \mu_S(b,a) = \text{hgt}(a \cap b)$,

(iv) $\mu_S(a,b) \wedge \mu_S(c,d) \leq \mu_S(a,d) \vee \mu_S(c,b)$ (Ferrers graph) ,

(v) $\mu_S(a,b) \leq \mu_S(a,c) \vee \mu_S(c,b)$ (min-max transitive graph) .

Proof

(i) consequence of $\bigvee_x \mu_a(x) = 1$, $\forall$ a ,

(ii) Let a^+ such that $\begin{cases} \mu_a(a^+) = 1 , \\ \mu_a(x) < 1, \ \forall \ x > a^+ , \end{cases}$

and b^+ such that $\begin{cases} \mu_b(b^+) = 1 , \\ \mu_b(y) < 1, \ \forall \ y > b^+ . \end{cases}$

If $a^+ \geq b^+$; then $\mu_S(a,b) = 1$; if not, $\mu_S(b,a) = 1$.

(iii) First, it is clear, from the definitions, that

$$[\mu_S(a,b) \wedge \mu_S(b,a)] \geq \text{hgt}(a \cap b) .$$

Now, let

$$\text{hgt}(a \cap b) = \mu_a(\hat{x}) \leq \mu_b(\hat{x})$$

and suppose that

$$\mu_S(a,b) \wedge \mu_S(b,a) > \text{hgt}(a \cap b) .$$

This means that $\exists \ x_1, y_1, x_2, y_2$ such that

$$\begin{cases} x_1 > y_1 \text{ and } \mu_a(x_1) \wedge \mu_b(y_1) > \mu_a(\hat{x}) , \\ y_2 > x_2 \text{ and } \mu_b(y_2) \wedge \mu_a(x_2) > \mu_a(\hat{x}) . \end{cases}$$

If $x_1 \leq y_2$, then convexity of μ_b implies

$$\mu_b(x_1) \geq \mu_b(y_1) \wedge \mu_b(y_2) > \mu_a(\hat{x})$$

so that

$$\mu_a(x_1) \wedge \mu_b(x_1) > \text{hgt}(a \cap b) ,$$

a contradiction.

If $y_2 \leq x_1$, then the convexity of μ_a implies

$$\mu_a(y_2) \geq \mu_a(x_2) \wedge \mu_a(x_1) > \mu_a(\hat{x}) ,$$

so that

$$\mu_a(y_2) \wedge \mu_b(y_2) > \text{hgt}(a \cap b) ,$$

a contradiction.

(iv) Let

$$\mu_S(a,b) \wedge \mu_S(c,d) > \mu_S(a,d) \vee \mu_S(c,b) \, . \qquad (1)$$

This implies

$$\mu_S(a,d) \vee \mu_S(c,b) < 1 \, ,$$

so that, thanks to properties (ii) and (iii) :

$$\begin{cases} \forall\, x,t \text{ such that } \mu_a(x) = \mu_d(t) = 1 : x < t \, , \\ \forall\, z,y \text{ such that } \mu_c(z) = \mu_b(y) = 1 : z < y \, , \\ \mu_S(a,d) = \text{hgt } (a \cap d) \, , \\ \mu_S(c,b) = \text{hgt } (c \cap b) \, . \end{cases}$$

Assume first that $\mu_S(a,b) = 1$, so that $\exists\, \hat{x} \geq \hat{y}$ with

$$\mu_a(\hat{x}) = \mu_b(\hat{y}) = 1 \, ;$$

it follows that $\forall$ z,t such that

$$\mu_c(z) = \mu_d(t) = 1 \, ,$$

we must have $t > \hat{x} \geq \hat{y} > z$.

In other words,

$$\begin{cases} \mu_S(d,c) = 1 \, , \\ \mu_S(c,d) = \text{hgt } (c \cap d) \, . \end{cases}$$

Let

$$\text{hgt } (c \cap d) = h = \mu_c(s) \wedge \mu_d(s) \, .$$

If $\mu_a(s) \geq h$, we obtain

$$\text{hgt } (a \cap d) \geq \mu_a(s) \wedge \mu_d(s) \geq h \, ,$$

or

$$\mu_S(a,d) \geq \mu_S(c,d) \, ,$$

which contradicts (1), so that we must have

$$\mu_a(s) < h \, .$$

We prove now that $\hat{x} < s$.

If $\exists\, \bar{t} \leq s : \mu_d(\bar{t}) = 1$, then $\hat{x} < \bar{t} \leq s$.

If not, there exists $\bar{t} > s = \mu_d(\bar{t}) = 1$ and the convexity of μ_d, together with $\bar{t} > \hat{x} \geq s$, would imply

$$\mu_d(\hat{x}) \geq \mu_d(\bar{t}) \wedge \mu_d(s) \geq h \, ,$$

thus

$$\text{hgt}(a \cap d) \geq \mu_a(\hat{x}) \wedge \mu_d(\hat{x}) \geq h = \text{hgt } (c \cap d) \, ,$$

or

$$\mu_S(a,d) \geq \mu_S(c,d) \, ,$$

which contradicts (1).

Now, if we consider $\hat{z}:\mu_c(\hat{z}) = 1$, we obtain $\hat{z} < \hat{y} \leq \hat{x} < s$ and the convexity of μ_c implies

$$\mu_c(\hat{y}) \geq \mu_c(\hat{z}) \wedge \mu_c(s) \geq h ,$$

thus

$$hgt(b \cap c) \geq \mu_b(\hat{y}) \wedge \mu_c(\hat{y}) \geq h = hgt(c \cap d) ,$$

or

$$\mu_S(c,b) \geq \mu_S(c,d) ,$$

which contradicts (1).

So we can conclude that (1) is impossible when $\mu_S(a,b) = 1$ and we can prove in a similar way that (1) is impossible when $\mu_S(c,d) = 1$.

Assume now that $\mu_S(c,d) < 1$. Remember that $\hat{x} < s$ and $\mu_a(s) < h$, and similarly, $s < \hat{y}$ and $\mu_b(s) < h$.

The convexity of μ_a and μ_b implies that

$$\begin{cases} \mu_a(x) < h, \ \forall\, x \geq s , \\ \mu_b(y) < h, \ \forall\, y \leq s , \end{cases}$$

so that

$$hgt(a \cap b) = \bigvee_w [\mu_a(w) \wedge \mu_b(w)] < h = hgt(c \cap d) ,$$

or

$$\mu_S(a,b) < \mu_S(c,d) < 1 .$$

In a similar way, we can prove that $\mu_S(a,b) < 1$ implies

$$\mu_S(c,d) < \mu_S(a,b) < 1 .$$

In other words, it is impossible to have simultaneously the relation (1) togethe with $\mu_S(a,b) < 1$ and $\mu_S(c,d) < 1$.

As (1) is impossible when $\mu_S(a,b) = 1$ or $\mu_S(c,d) = 1$, this completes the proof.

(v) This property is an immediate consequence of (iv), taking $c = d$.

4. Fuzzy preference graphs and cores

Starting with the fuzzy possibility relation S, let us consider

S^- : the converse relation for S, $\mu_{S^-}(a,b) = \mu_S(b,a)$,

S^c : the complementary relation for S, $\mu_{S^c}(a,b) = 1 - \mu_S(a,b)$,

S^d : the dual relation for S, $\mu_{S^d}(a,b) = 1 - \mu_S(b,a)$.

In the crisp situation where S is a binary relation, the strict preference relation $P = S \cap S^d$, the indifference relation $I = S \cap S^-$ and the incomparability relation $R = S^c \cap S^d$.

These concepts can be extended in the fuzzy environment.

The fuzzy preference relation related to S is defined as

$$\mu_P(a,b) = [\mu_S(a,b) \wedge (1 - \mu_S(b,a))]$$

and the fuzzy indifference and incomparability relations respectively as

$$\mu_I(a,b) = \mu_S(a,b) \wedge \mu_S(b,a) ,$$

$$\mu_R(a,b) = 1 - [\mu_S(a,b) \vee \mu_S(b,a)] .$$

If S is a fuzzy possibility relation it turns out that

$$\mu_P(a,b) = \mu_{S^d}(a,b)$$

$$\mu_I(a,b) = hgt(a \cap b) \text{ and } \mu_R(a,b) = 0 .$$

The graph related to the preference relation is called <u>fuzzy preference digraph</u> and corresponds to the oriented comparability graph in the crisp case. The fuzzy interval graph represents the fuzzy indifferences.

Using duality properties it is clear that we obtain the next proposition.

<u>Proposition</u> : every fuzzy preference digraph has the following properties :

$\forall\, a,b,c,d \in A$:

i) $\mu_P(a,a) = 0$ (irreflexive graph)

ii) $\mu_P(a,b) \wedge \mu_P(b,a) = 0$ (antisymmetric graph)

iii) $\mu_P(a,b) \wedge \mu_P(c,d) \leq \mu_P(a,d) \vee \mu_P(c,b)$ (Ferrers graph)

iv) $\mu_P(a,b) \geq \mu_P(a,c) \wedge \mu_P(c,b)$ (max-min transitive graph).

If we call non-domination degree for an element $a \in A$

$$\mu_{ND}(a) = 1 - \bigvee_b \mu_P(b,a) = \bigwedge_b \mu_S(a,b)$$

and if the <u>core</u> of the fuzzy preference digraph is the subset of vertices A_o which are unfuzzily non-dominated, i.e.

$$A_o = \{a : \mu_{ND}(a) = 1\} \quad \text{(see also Orlovski (1978))}$$

the following proposition can be proved.

<u>Proposition</u> : the core of a fuzzy preference digraph is non-empty.

<u>Proof</u> :

If the core is non empty, there exists an element $a^* \in A$ such that $\mu_S(a^*,b) = 1$, for all $b \in A$. Suppose it is not true. Then, for all $a \in A$, there exists at least one b with $\mu_S(a,b) < 1$. Starting with any $a_1 \in A$, we obtain $(a_1, a_2,\ldots,a_n,\ldots)$ with $\mu_S(a_1,a_2) < 1$, $\mu_S(a_2,a_3) < 1$, ..., $\mu_S(a_{n-1}, a_n) < 1$, ... This leads to a cycle $(a_{n_1}, \ldots, a_{n_k}, a_{n_1})$ where each arc presents a value less than 1. Due to the property of min-max transitivity : $\mu_S(a_{n_1}, a_{n_2}) < 1$, $\mu_S(a_{n_2}, a_{n_3}) < 1 \Rightarrow \mu_S(a_{n_1},a_{n_3}) < 1$. Using the same argument repeatively : $\mu_S(a_{n_1}, a_{n_k}) < 1$. The last relation is incompatible with the completeness property and the fact that $\mu_S(a_{n_k}, a_{n_1}) < 1$.

5. Ranking fuzzy numbers

Let us consider n fuzzy numbers a,b, ... A. The ranking of such numbers has been extensively studied (see Roubens (1986) for a short bibliography, Bortolan and Degani (1985) for a review and recent papers by Chen (1985), Ovchinnikov and Migdal (1986)).

Ovchinnikov and Migdal claim that "... the problem of ranking fuzzy sets shoul be a fuzzy ordering. This would provide a natural basis for the linguistic approach to decision-making".

The induced fuzzy relation P is a response to that statement.

If a crisp response is desirable, we propose to compare these numbers using the concept of core. A solution close to that proposal was already given by Buckley (198 Dubois and Prade (1983) and Tong and Bonisonne (1980).

Having defined the fuzzy preference digraph we consider the core A_0 which is no empty. We then obtain a subgraph by considering the vertices of $A \setminus A_0$ which possesses the same properties as A_0. The core of the new subgraph is non empty and is called A The iteration of this procedure leads to the following cores : A_0, A_1, A_2, ...

A possible ranking is given by the crisp total preorder

$$A_0 > A_1 > A_2 > \dots$$

where the elements in each core are considered to be indifferent.

If we consider the example proposed in Roubens (1986) :

$$\mu_a(x) = \begin{cases} 0 & x < 8.5 \\ 1 & 8.5 \leq x \leq 9.5 \\ 0 & x > 9.5 \end{cases}$$

$$\mu_b(x) = \begin{cases} 0 & x < 3 \\ \text{linear} & 3 \leq x \leq 6.5 \\ 1 & 6 < x < 8 \\ \text{linear} & 8.5 \leq x \leq 10 \\ 0 & x > 10 \end{cases} \qquad \mu_c(x) = \begin{cases} 0 & x < 2 \\ \text{linear} & 2 \leq x \leq 3 \\ 1 & 3 < x < 4 \\ \text{linear} & 4 \leq x \leq 6 \\ 0 & x > 6 \end{cases}$$

$$\mu_d(x) = \begin{cases} 0 & x < 3.5 \\ \text{linear} & 3.5 \leq x \leq 4.5 \\ 1 & 4.5 < x < 5.5 \\ \text{linear} & 5.5 \leq x \leq 6.5 \\ 0 & x > 6.5 \end{cases} \qquad \mu_e(x) = \begin{cases} 0 & x < 2.5 \\ \text{linear} & 2.5 \leq x \leq 3.5 \\ 1 & 3.5 < x < 7 \\ \text{linear} & 7 \leq x \leq 8.5 \\ 0 & x > 8.5 \end{cases}$$

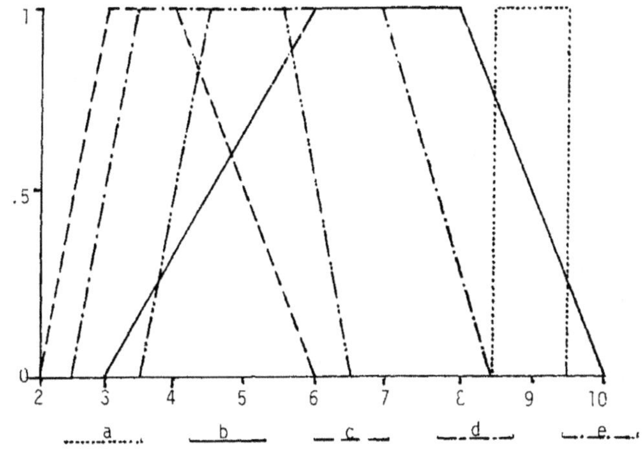

The valued incidence matrix of the corresponding fuzzy possibility digraphs is represented in Table 1.

	a	b	c	d	e
a	1	1	1	1	1
b	.75	1	1	1	1
c	0	.6	1	.833	1
d	0	.875	1	1	1
e	0	1	1	1	1

Table 1

We finally obtain

A_0 = {a}
A_1 = {b,e}
A_2 = {d}
A_3 = {c}

and the crisp preorder : {a} > {b ≈ e} > {d} > {c}

References

[1] G. Bortolan and R. Degani, A review of some methods for ranking fuzzy subsets, Fuzzy Sets and Systems 15, 1-19 (1985)

[2] J.J. Buckley, Ranking alternatives using fuzzy numbers, Fuzzy Sets and Systems 15, 21-31 (1985)

[3] S-H. Chen, Ranking fuzzy numbers with maximizing set and minimizing set, Fuzzy Sets and Systems 17, 113-129 (1985)

[4] D. Dubois and H. Prade, Ranking of fuzzy numbers in the setting of possibility theory, Information Science 30, 183-224 (1983)

[5] D.R. Fulkerson and O.A. Gross, Incidence matrices and interval graphs, Pacific J. of Math. 15, 835-855 (1965)

[6] A. Ghoula-Houri, Caractérisation des graphes non orientés dont on peut orienter les arêtes de manière à obtenir le graphe d'une relation d'ordre, C.R. Acad. Sci. Paris 254, 1370-1371 (1962)

[7] P.C. Gilmore and A.J. Hoffman, A characterization of comparability graphs and interval graphs, Canad. J. Math. 16, 539-548 (1964)

[8] M.C. Golumbic, Algorithmic Graph Theory and Perfect Graphs, Academic Press, New York (1980)

[9] S.A. Orlovsky, Decision-making with a fuzzy preference relation, Fuzzy Sets and Systems 1, 155-167 (1978)

[10] S.V. Ovchinnikov and M. Migdal, On ranking fuzzy sets, Preprint M 86/3, San Francisco St. Univ., CA (1986)

[11] F.S. Roberts, Discrete Mathematical Models, Prentice Hall, New Jersey (1976)

[12] M. Roubens, Comparison of flat fuzzy numbers, in : N. Bandler and A. Kandel (eds), Proceedings of NAFIPS'86, 462-476 (1986)

[13] M. Roubens and Ph. Vincke, Preference modelling, Springer-Verlag, Berlin (1985

[14] R.M. Tong and P.P. Bonissone, A linguistic approach to decision making with fuzzy sets, IEEE Trans. on Systems, Man and Cybernetics, SMC-10, 716-723 (1980)

ON MEASURING CONSENSUS IN THE SETTING OF FUZZY PREFERENCE RELATIONS

Mario Fedrizzi * and Janusz Kacprzyk **

* Institute of Statistics and Operations Research University of Trento, Via Verdi 26, 38100 Trento, Italy

** Systems Research Institute Polish Academy of Sciences, ul. Newelska 6, 01-447 Warsaw, Poland

ABSTRACT. Consensus, traditionally understood as a full and unanimous agreement, is a utopia in virtually all practical cases. A degree of consensus to indicate how far one is from complete agreement does therefore make sense. We present a 'soft' consensus measure which is basically a degree to which, say, "most pairs of individuals agree as to their preferences between almost all relevant options". The point of departure is the set of individual preference relations. A fuzzy-logic-based calculus of linguistically quantified proposition is employed.

KEYWORDS: group decision making, consensus, fuzzy preference relation, fuzzy logic, linguistic quantifier.

1. Introduction

The purpose of group decision making is essentially that of finding some option(s) which is 'best' acceptable by a group of individuals considered as a whole. The individual testimonies are usually expressed as individual preferences over the set of options.

These preferences are often not clear-cut. They can be conveniently represented by fuzzy preference relations. If $S = \{s_1, ..., s_n\}$ is a set of options and $K = \{1, ..., k\}$ is a set of individuals, then a (individual) fuzzy preference relation, of individual k, R_k, is give by its membership function $\mu_{R_k} : S \times S \to [0, 1]$ such that

$$\mu_{R_k}(s_i,s_j) = \begin{cases} 1 & \text{if } s_i \text{ is definitely preferred over } s_j \\ c \in (0.5,\ 1) & \text{if } s_i \text{ is slightly preferred over } s_j \\ 0.5 & \text{if there is no preference} \\ & \text{between } s_i \text{ and } s_j \text{ (i.e., indifference)} \\ d\ \ (0{,}0.5) & \text{if } s_j \text{ is slightly preferred over } s_i \\ 0 & \text{if } s_j \text{ is definitely over } s_i\,. \end{cases} \qquad (1)$$

If card S is small enough (as we assume here) R_k may be represented by a matrix $R_k = r_{ij}^k$, $r_{ij}^k = \mu_{R_k}(s_i, s_j)$; i, j = 1, ..., n; k = 1, ..., m.

R_k is commonly assumed to be reciprocal, i.e. $r_{ij}^k + r_{ij}^k = 1$, and $r_{ii}^k = 0$, for all i, j, k.

Fuzzy preference relations have been successfully used in a large spectrum of decision making problems, notably in group decision making (see, e.g., Bezdek, Spillman and Spillman, 1977, 1978, 1979; Blin, 1974; Blin and Whinston, 1973; Fedrizzi, 1986; Fung and Fu, 1975; Kacprzyk, 1984, 1985b,c; 1986 a,b,c; Kuzmin, 1982; Kuzmin and Ovchinnikov, 1980a, 1980b; Nurmi, 1981).

Consensus is virtually a goal of group decision making. It is usually meant to be a full and unanimous agreement which is, however, not necessarily a clear-cut definition (see, e.g., Farris and Sage, 1975 and the appropriate references in the list of literature).

Consensus as a total and unanimous agreement is obviously an utopia in virtually all practical cases. It does make therefore sense to speak about a degree of, or a distance from consensus.

In the context of fuzzy preference relations this idea has been proposed and advanced mainly by Spillman, Spillman and Bezdek (1977, 1978), and Bezdek, Spillman and Spillman (1978), where a distance from consensus is definded as a difference between some average preference matrix and one of several possible consensus preference matrices; Spillman, Bezdek and Spillman (1979), where a measure of attitudinal similarity between the individuals is introduced as an extension of the classical Tanimoto coefficient; Spillman, Spillman and Bezdek (1980), where a consensus measure based on α-cuts of the respective individual fuzzy preference matrices is derived.

The above consensus measures are "hard" in that they indicate (full) consensus (= 1) only in case of complete agreement, i.e. of all the individuals as to their preferences between all the options. This may often be too rigid and counter-intuitive in practice since we can be fully satisfied, i.e. perceive (full) consensus, when, say, most (almost all, much more than 50%, ...) of the individuals agree as to their preferences between most (almost all, ...) of the (relevant) options. This leads to a new concept of a 'soft' consensus measure proposed in Kacprzyk (1986b) and considered in Kacprzyk and Fedrizzi (1986). To deal with the linguistic quantifiers (e.g., "most") involved in those measures, a fuzzy-logic-based calculus of linguistically quantified propositions (Zadeh, 1983) was employed that had proved to be useful to 'soften' a large spectrum of multiobjective, multistage or group decision making models. (See Kacprzyk, 1985a, 1987 for a rewiev.)

The purpose of this paper is to present the above mention concept of a 'soft' consensus measure (Kacprzyk, 1985c; Kacprzyk and Fedrizzi, 1986) and add some new elements.

In Section 2 we briefly present a calculus of linguistically quantified propositions to be used. In Section 3 we present the derivation of the 'soft' consensus measure proposed. Finally we give some concluding remarks and an extensive list of literature.

Our notation is standard. A fuzzy set A in X, $A \subseteq X$, is represented by, and often informally equated with its membership function $\mu_A : X \rightarrow [0,1]$; $\mu_A(x)$ [0,1] is the grade of membership of x in A. Moreover, $a \wedge b = \min(a, b)$. For further notation, see Kacprzyk (1983).

2. A calculus of linguistically quantified propositions

A linguistically quantified proposition is examplified by "most experts are convinced". In general, it may be written as

QY's are F (2)

where Q is a linguistic quantifier (e.g., most) $Y = \{y\}$ is a set of objects (e.g., experts) and F is a property (e.g., convinced).

Importance B may be introduced into (2) yielding

QBY's are F (3)

e.g., "most (Q) of the important (B) experts (Y's) are convinced (F)".

The problem is basically to find truth (QY's are F) or truth (QBY's are F), respectively, knowing all truth (y_i is F), $y_i \in Y$. This can be done using a fuzzy-logic-based calculus of linguistically quantified propositions (Zadeh, 1983).

First, a linguistic quantifier Q is assumed to be a fuzzy set in [0,1], $Q \subseteq [0,1]$. For instance, Q "most" may be given as

$$\mu_{\text{"most"}}(x) = \begin{cases} 1 & \text{for } x \geq 0.8 \\ 2x - 0.6 & \text{for } 0.3 < x < 0.8 \\ 0 & \text{for } x \leq 0.3 \end{cases} \quad . \tag{4}$$

Throught this paper we will use only the so-called proportional linguistic quantifiers ("most", "almo all", etc.) since they are more appropriate in our context. For the so-called absolute linguistic quantifie (e.g., "about 5") the reasoning is similar.

Particularly important in our context are nondecreasing fuzzy quantifiers defined as

$$x' > x'' \Rightarrow \mu_Q(x') \geq \mu_Q(x'') \qquad \text{for each } x', x'' \in [0, 1] \, . \tag{5}$$

"Most" given by (4) is evidently nondecreasing.

Property F is defined as a fuzzy set in Y, $F \subseteq Y$.

If $Y = \{y_1, ..., y_p\}$, then truth (y_i is F) is based on the (non-fuzzy) cardinalities, ΣCounts, of th respective fuzzy sets (see, e.g., Zadeh, 1979, 1983) and proceeds in the following two steps:

$$r = \Sigma \text{ Count (F)} / \Sigma \text{ Count (Y)} = \frac{1}{p} \sum_{i=1}^{p} \mu_F(y_i) \tag{6}$$

$$\text{truth (QY's are F)} = \mu_Q(r) \quad . \tag{7}$$

Importance is introduced as follows. B = "important" is defined as a fuzzy set in Y, $B \subseteq Y$, such th $\mu_B(y_i) \in [0,1]$ is a degree of importance of y_i: the higher $\mu_B(y_i)$, the more important y_i.

We rewrite "QBY's are F" as "Q(B and F) are B" which leads to the following counterparts of (6) and (7 respectively:

$$r' = \Sigma\text{Count (B and F)} / \Sigma \text{ Count (B)} = \sum_{i=1}^{p} (\mu_B(y_i) \wedge \mu_F(y_i)) / \sum_{i=1}^{p} \mu_B(y_i) \tag{8}$$

("$\wedge$" may be replaced by, e.g., a t-norm; see Kacprzyk, 1986d).

$$\text{truth (QBY's are F)} = \mu_Q(r') \quad . \tag{9}$$

<u>Example 1</u>. Let: Y = "experts" = {A, B, C}; F = "convinced" = 0.1/A + 0.6/B + 0.8/Z; Q = "most" given by (4); B = "important" = 0.2/A + 0.5/B + 0.6/C.

Then, on the one hand, r = 0.5, and truth ("most experts are convinced") = $2 \cdot 0.5 - 0.6$ = C while, on the other hand, r' = 1.2 / 1.3 and truth ("most of the important experts are convinced") = 1.

3. A 'soft' measure of consensus

As mentioned in Section 1, to overcome some "rigidity" in a variety of consensus measures developed in a series of papers by Bezdek, Spillman and Spillman (1977, 1978, 1979), Spillman, Bezdek and Spillman (1979), and Spillman, Spillman and Bezdek (1979, 1980) in which full consensus (= 1) occurs only when "everybody agrees as to everything", some "softer" consensus measures have been proposed in Kacprzyk (1986b) and Kacprzyk and Fedrizzi (1986). Basically, they are equivalent to finding "a degree to which, e.g., most of the individuals agree as to their preferences between, e.g., most pairs of (relevant) options".

For our purposes the derivation of those "soft" measures (degrees) of consensus may be viewed as a hierarchical pooling process shown in Fig. 1 to be interpreted as follows. First, for each pair of individuals we derive a degree of agreement as to their preferences between all the pairs of options, next we pool (aggregate) these degrees to obtain a degree of agreement of each pair of individuals as to their preferences between Q1 (a linguistic quantifier as, e.g., "most") pairs of relevant options, and, finally, we pool these degrees to obtain a degree of agreement of Q2 (a linguistic quantifier as, e.g., "almost all") pairs of individuals as to their preferences between Q1 pairs of options. This is meant to be the degree of consensus sought. Note that, roughly speaking, Q1 = Q2 = "all" for the conventional ("hard") notions of consensus.

We start with the degree of strict agreement between individuals k1 and k2 as to their preference between options s_i and s_j as

$$v_{ij}(k1, k2) = \begin{cases} 1 & \text{if } r_{ij}^{k1} = r_{ij}^{k2} \\ 0 & \text{otherwise} \end{cases} \qquad (10)$$

where k1 = 1, ..., m-1; k2 = k1 + 1, ..., m; i = 1, ..., n-1; j = i + 1, ..., n.

Relevance is assumed to be a fuzzy set defined in the set of options $S = \{s_1, ..., s_n\}$, i.e., $R \subseteq S$, and $\mu_R(s_i) \in [0,1]$ is a degree of relevance of option s_i: from 0 standing for "definitely irrelevant" to 1 standing for "definitely relevant", through all intermediate values.

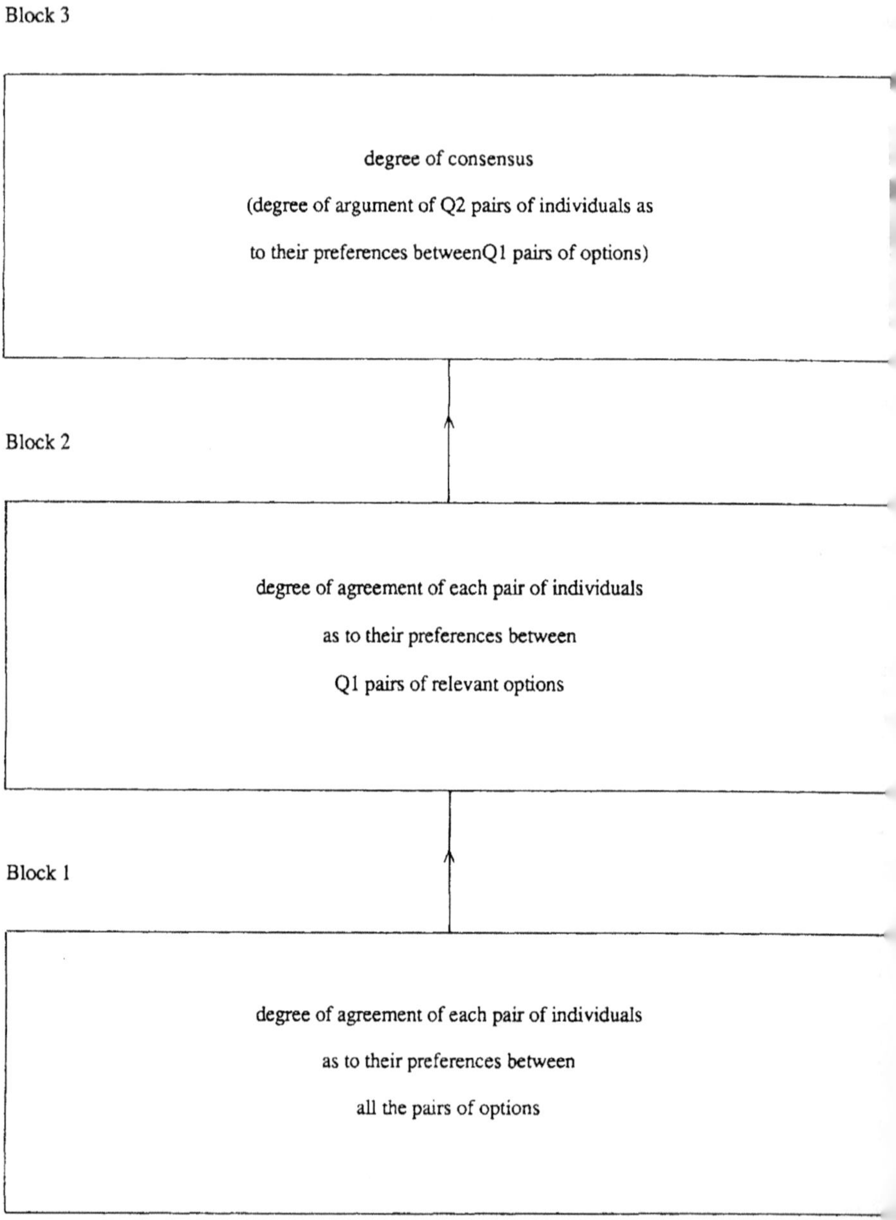

Fig. 1 - Derivation of a degree of consensus as a hierarchical pooling process.

Relevance of a pair of options, say $(s_i, s_j) \in SxS$, can be defined in various ways among which

$$b^R_{ij} = \frac{1}{2}\,(\mu_R(s_i) + \mu_R(s_j)) \tag{11}$$

is certainly the most straightforward. Obviously, $b^R_{ij} = b^R_{ij}$ and b^R_{ii} do not matter, for all i, j, k.

The degree of agreement between individuals k1 and k2 as to their preferences between all the relevant pairs of options is

$$v_R(k1, k2) = \sum_{i=1}^{n-1} \sum_{j=i+1}^{n} (v_{ij}(k1, k2) \wedge b^R_{ij}) \sum_{i=1}^{n-1} \sum_{j=i+1}^{n} b^R_{ij} \ . \tag{12}$$

The degree of agreement between individuals k1 and k2 as to their preferences between Q1 relevant pairs of options is

$$v_{Q1,R}(k1, k2) = \mu_{Q1}(v_R(K1, K2)). \tag{13}$$

In turn, the degree of agreement of all the pairs of individuals as to their preferences between Q1 relevant pairs of options is

$$v_{Q1,R} = \frac{2}{m(m-1)} \sum_{k1=1}^{m-1} \sum_{k2=k1+1}^{m} v_{Q1,R}(k1, k2) \tag{14}$$

and, finally, the degree of agreement of Q2 pairs of individuals as to their preferences between Q1 relevant pairs of options, called the degree of Q1/Q2/R-consensus, is

$$\mathrm{con}_R(Q1, Q2) = \mu_{Q2}(v_{Q1,R}) \ . \tag{15}$$

Since the strict agreement (10) may be too rigid, we can use the degree of sufficient (at least to degree α) agreement of individuals k1 and k2 as to their preferences between options s_i and s_j defined by

$$v^{\alpha}_{ij}(k1, k2) = \begin{cases} 1 & \text{if } |r^{k1}_{ij} - r^{k2}_{ij}| \leq 1 - \alpha < 1 \\ 0 & \text{otherwise} \end{cases} \ . \tag{16}$$

Then, following (12) - (14), we obtain

$$v^{\alpha}_R(k1, k2) = \sum_{i=1}^{n-1} \sum_{j=i+1}^{n} (v^{\alpha}_{ij}(k1, k2) \wedge b^R_{ij}) \,/\, \sum_{i=1}^{n-1} \sum_{j=i+1}^{n} b^R_{ij} \tag{17}$$

$$v^{\alpha}_{Q1,R}(k1, k2) = \mu_{Q1}(v^{\alpha}_R(k1, k2)) \tag{18}$$

$$v^{\alpha}_{Q1,R} = \frac{2}{m(m-1)} \sum_{k1=1}^{m-1} \sum_{k2=k1+1}^{m} v^{\alpha}_{Q1,R}(k1, k2) \tag{19}$$

and, finally, the degree of sufficient (at least to degree α) agreement of Q2 pairs of individuals as to their preferences between Q1 relevant pairs of options, called the degree of α/Q1/Q2/R-consensus is

$$\mathrm{con}^{\alpha}_R(Q1, Q2) = \mu_{Q2}(v^{\alpha}_{Q1,R}) \ . \tag{20}$$

We can also explicitly introduce the strength of agreement into (10) and define the degree of strong agreement of the individuals k1 and k2 as to their preferences between options s_i and s_j, e.g., as

$$v^s_{ij}(k1, k2) = s(\,|\,r^{k1}_{ij} - r^{k2}_{ij}\,|\,) \tag{21}$$

where s: [0,1] → [0,1] is some function representing a degree of strong agreement as, e.g.,

$$s(x) = \begin{cases} 1 & \text{for } x \le 0.05 \\ -10x + 1.5 & \text{for } 0.05 < x < 0.15 \\ 0 & \text{for } x \ge 0.15 \end{cases} \tag{22}$$

such that $x' > x'' \Rightarrow s(x') \ge s(x'')$ and $s(x) = 1$ for some $x \in [0,1]$.

For some other definitions of $v^s_{ij}(k1,k2)$, see Kacprzyk (1986b).

Then, following (12) - (14), and (17) - (19), we obtain

$$v^s_R(k1, k2) = \sum_{i=1}^{n-1} \sum_{j=i+1}^{n} (v^s_{ij}(k1, k2) \wedge b^R_{ij}) \Big/ \sum_{i=1}^{n-1} \sum_{j=i+1}^{n} b^R_{ij} \tag{23}$$

$$v^s_{Q1,R}(k1, K2) = \mu_{Q1}(v^s_R(k1, k2)) \tag{24}$$

$$v^s_{Q1,R} = \frac{2}{m(m-1)} \sum_{k1=1}^{m-1} \sum_{k2=k1+1}^{m} v^s_{Q1,R}(k1, k2) \tag{25}$$

and, finally, the degree of strong agreement of Q2 pairs of individuals as to their preferences between Q1 relevant pairs of options, called the degree of s/Q1/Q2/R-consensus is

$$con^s_R(Q1, Q2) = \mu_{Q2}(v^s_{Q1,R}) \quad . \tag{26}$$

For some properties of the above degrees of consensus, see Kacprzyk and Fedrizzi (1986).

<u>Example 2</u>. Let the individual fuzzy preference relations of individuals k = 1, 2, 3, 4 be, respectively:

$$R^1 = \begin{bmatrix} 0 & 0.4 & 0.7 & 0.1 \\ 0.6 & 0 & 0.8 & 0.2 \\ 0.3 & 0.2 & 0 & 0.7 \\ 0.9 & 0.8 & 0.3 & 0 \end{bmatrix} \qquad R^2 = \begin{bmatrix} 0 & 0.4 & 0.5 & 0 \\ 0.6 & 0 & 0.8 & 0.2 \\ 0.5 & 0.2 & 0 & 0.7 \\ 1 & 0.8 & 0.3 & 0 \end{bmatrix}$$

$$R^3 = \begin{bmatrix} 0 & 0.4 & 0.4 & 0.3 \\ 0.6 & 0 & 0.8 & 0.2 \\ 0.6 & 0.2 & 0 & 0.7 \\ 0.7 & 0.8 & 0.3 & 0 \end{bmatrix} \qquad R^4 = \begin{bmatrix} 0 & 0.4 & 0.7 & 0.1 \\ 0.6 & 0 & 0.7 & 0.1 \\ 0.3 & 0.3 & 0 & 0.7 \\ 0.9 & 0.9 & 0.3 & 0 \end{bmatrix}$$

Q1 = Q2 = "most" be given by (4) and relevance of the particular pairs of options be

$b_R^{12} = 0.5 \quad b_R^{13} = 0.4 \quad b_R^{14} = 0.2 \quad b_R^{23} = 0.6 \quad b_R^{24} = 0.4 \quad b_R^{34} = 0.3$.

Now, due to (12)

$$v_R(1,2) = 0.75 \qquad v_R(1,3) = 0.75 \qquad v_R(1,4) = 0.58$$

$$v_R(2,3) = 0.75 \qquad v_R(2,4) = 0.33 \qquad v_R(3,4) = 0.33$$

(13) implies

$$v_{Q1,R}(1,2) = 0.9 \qquad v_{Q1,R}(1,3) = 0.9 \qquad v_{Q1,R}(1,4) = 0.56$$

$$v_{Q1,R}(2,3) = 0.9 \qquad v_{Q1,R}(2,4) = 0.06 \qquad v_{Q1,R}(3,4) = 0.06$$

and (14) yields

$$v_{Q1,R} = 0.56$$

and, finally, by (15)

$$con_R(Q1,Q2) = 0.52.$$

Second, with $\alpha = 0.9$, from (17)

$$v_R^{0.9}(1,2) = 0.75 \qquad v_R^{0.9}(1,3) = 0.75 \qquad v_R^{0.9}(1,4) = 1$$

$$v_R^{0.9}(2,3) = 0.66 \qquad v_R^{0.9}(2,4) = 0.58 \qquad v_R^{0.9}(3,4) = 0.5$$

and (18) implies

$$v_{Q1,R}^{0.9}(1,2) = 0.9 \qquad v_{Q1,R}^{0.9}(1,3) = 0.9 \qquad v_{Q1,R}^{0.9}(1,4) = 1$$

$$v_{Q1,R}^{0.9}(2,3) = 0.72 \qquad v_{Q1,R}^{0.9}(2,4) = 0.56 \qquad v_{Q1,R}^{0.9}(3,4) = 0.4$$

and (19) yields

$$v_{Q1,R}^{0.9} = 0.75$$

and, finally, by (20)

$$con_R^{0.9}(Q1, Q2) = 0.9 \quad .$$

Third, from (23)

$$v_R^s(1,2) = 0.86 \qquad v_R^s(1,3) = 0.75 \qquad v_R^s(1,4) = 0.96$$

$$v_R^s(2,3) = 0.92 \qquad v_R^s(2,4) = 0.79 \qquad v_R^s(3,4) = 0.71$$

and from (24)

$$v_{Q1,R}^s(1,2) = 1 \qquad v_{Q1,R}^s(1,3) = 0.9 \qquad v_{Q1,R}^s(1,4) = 1$$

$$v_{Q1,R}^s(2,3) = 1 \qquad v_{Q1,R}^s(2,4) = 0.99 \qquad v_{Q1,R}^s(3,4) = 0.82$$

and (25) yields

$$v^{s}_{Q1,R} = 0.95$$

and, finally, by (26),

$$con^{s}_{R}\,(Q1, Q2) = 1 \quad .$$

4. Concluding remarks

The proposed 'soft' consensus measure seems to reflect better than the conventional 'hard' ones the re human perception of the very essence of how consensus is to be understood in practice. It may be viewe as a step toward 'human consistent' formal tools that should help considerably to attain a high implementability of decision support systems (see Kacprzyk, 1986c, 1987).

Literature

Bezdek J., B. Spillman and R. Spillman (1977). "Fuzzy measures of preference and consensus in grou decision making". In K.S. Fu (ed.) Proc. 1977 IEEE Conf. on Decision and Control, 1303-1309.

Bezdek J., B. Spillman and R. Spillman (1978). "A fuzzy relation space for group decision theory Fuzzy Sets and Syst. 1, 255-268.

Bezdek J., B. Spillman and R. Spillman (1979). "Fuzzy relation spaces for group decision theory: a application." Fuzzy Sets and Syst. 2, 5-14.

Blin J.M. (1974). "Fuzzy relations in group decision theory". J. Cybern. 4, 17-22.

Blin J.M. and A.B. Whinston (1973). "Fuzzy sets and social choice." J. Cybern. 3, 28-33.

Farris D.R. and A.P. Sage (1975). "Introduction and survey of group decision making with applicatio to worth assessment". IEEE Trans. on Syst. Man and Cybern. SMC-5, 346-353.

Fedrizzi M. (1986). "Group decisions and consensus: a model using fuzzy sets theory" (in Italian). Rivi di mat. per le scienze econ. e soc. A.9, F.1, 12-20.

French S. (1981). "Consensus of opinion". Europ. J. Op. Res. 7, 332-340.

Fung L.W. and K.S. Fu (1975). "An axiomatic approach to relational decision-making in a fuzzy environment". In L.A. Zadeh et al. (eds.): Fuzzy Sets and Their Applications to Cognitive and Decision Processes. Academic Press, New York, 227-256.

Goodwin W.F. and W. Restle (1974). "The road to agreement: subgroup pressures in small group consensus processes." J. Pers. and Soc. Psych. 3, 500-517.

de Groot M.M. (1974). "Reaching a consensus". J. Amer. Stat. Ass. 69, 118-121.

Hare A.P. (1952). "A study of interaction and consensus in different sized groups". Am. Soc. Rev. 261-282.

Kacprzyk J. (1983). "Multistage Decision-Making under Fuzziness: Theory and Practice". Verlag TÜV Rheinland, Cologne.

Kacprzyk J. (1984). "Collective decision making with a fuzzy majority rule". Proc. WOGSC Congress. AFCET, Paris.

Kacprzyk J. (1985a). "Zadeh's commonsense knowledge and its use in multicriteria, multistage and multiperson decision making". In M.M. Gupta et al. (eds.) Approximate Reasoning in Expert Systems. North-Holland, Amsterdam (forthcoming).

Kacprzyk J. (1985b). "Some 'commonsense' solution concepts in group decision making via fuzzy linguistic quantifiers". In J. Kacprzyk and R.R. Yager (eds.): Management Decision Support Systems Using Fuzzy Sets and Possibility Theory. Verlag TÜV Rheinland, Cologne, 125-135.

Kacprzyk J. (1985c). "Group decision-making with a fuzzy majority via linguistic quantifiers". Part. I: A Consensory-like pooling. Cybernetics and Systems: an Inter. Journal 16, 119-129. Part II: A Competitive-like pooling. Cybernetics and Systems: an Inter. Journal 16, 131-144.

Kacprzyk J. (1986a). "Group decision making with a fuzzy linguistic majority". Fuzzy Sets and Syst. 18, 105-118.

Kacprzyk J. (1986b). "On some fuzzy cores and 'soft' consensus measures in group decision making". In J. Bezdek (ed.): The Analysis of Fuzzy Information. CRC Press, Boca Raton.

Kacprzyk J. (1986c). "Towards and algorithmic/procedural 'human consistency' of decision support systems: a fuzzy logic approach". In W. Karwowshi and A. Mittal (eds.): Applications of Fuzzy Sets in Human Factors. Elsevier, Amsterdam.

Kacprzyk J. (1987). "Towards 'human consistent' decision support systems through commonsense knowledge based decision making and control models: a fuzzy logic approach." Computers and Artificial Intelligence (to appear).

Kacprzyk J. and M. Fedrizzi (1986). "'Soft' consensus measures for monitoring real consensus under fuzzy preferences". Control and Cybernetics (to appear).

Kacprzyk J. and R.R. Yager, eds. (1985). "Management Decision Support Systems Using Fuzzy Sets and Possibility Theory". Verlag TÜV Rheinland, Cologne.

Kelly F.P. (1981). "How a group reaches agreement: a stochastic model." Math. Soc. Sci. 2, 1-8.

Kelly J.S. (1978). "Arrow Impossibility Theorems". Academic Press, New York.

Kline J.A. (1972). "Orientation and group consensus". Central States Speech J. 44-55.

Knutson J.J. (1972). "An experimental study of the effects of orientation behavior on small group consensus". Speech Mono. 159-165.

Kuzmin V.B. (1982). "Construction of Group Decisions in the Spaces of Non-fuzzy and Fuzzy Binary Relations". Nauka, Moscow (in Russian).

Kuzmin V.B. and S.V. Ovchinnikov (1980a). "Group decisions I: in arbitrary spaces of fuzzy binary relations". Fuzzy Sets and Syst. 4, 53-62.

Kuzmin V.B. and S.V. Ovchinnikov (1980b). "Design of group decisions. II: in arbitrary spaces of fuzzy binary relations". Fuzzy Sets and Syst. 4, 153-165.

Nurmi H. (1981). "Approaches to collective decision making with fuzzy preference relations". Fuzzy Set and Syst. 6, 187-198.

Regade R.K. (1976). "Fuzzy sets in communication systems and in consensus formation systems". J Cybern. 6, 21-38.

Regade R.K. (1977). "Profile transformation algebra and group consensus formation through fuzzy sets" In: M.M. Gupta, G.N. Saridis and B.R. Gaines (eds.): Fuzzy Automata and Decision Processes North-Holland, Amsterdam, 331-356.

Spillman B., J. Bezdek and R. Spillman (1979). "Coalition analysis with fuzzy sets". Kybernetes 8, 203 211.

Spillman B., R. Spillman and J. Bezdek (1979). "Development of an instrument for the dynamic measurement of consensus". Comm. Mono. 1-12.

Spillman B., R. Spillman and J. Bezdek (1980)". A Fuzzy analysis of consensus in small groups". In P.P. Wang and S.K. Chang (eds.): Fuzzy Sets Theory and Applications to Policy Analysis and Information Systems. Plenum, New York, 291-308.

Spillman B., R. Spillman and J. Bezdek (1982). "A dynamic perspective on leadership; development of fuzzy measurement procedure". Fuzzy Sets and Syst. 7, 19-33.

Tanino T. (1984). "Fuzzy preference orderings in group decision making". Fuzzy Sets and Syst. 12, 117 131.

Zadeh L.A. (1979). "A theory of approximative reasoning". In J.E. Hayes, M. Michie and L.I. Mikulic (eds.): Machine Intelligence 9, J. Wiley, New York.

Zadeh L.A. (1983). "A computational approach to fuzzy quantifiers in natural languages". Comp. & Maths. with Appls. 9, 149-184.

ASSUMPTIONS OF INDIVIDUAL PREFERENCES IN THE THEORY OF VOTING PROCEDURES

Hannu Nurmi
Department of Philosophy
University of Turku, SF-20500 TURKU, Finland

1. Introduction

The standard assumption in the group choice theory states that the individuals in the group have complete (connected) and transitive preference relations over the set of alternatives. In this paper we shall consider some alternatives to this assumption in an effort to find out whether a theory of group choice could be built on non-conventional basic assumptions concerning individual attitudes towards options from which the group has to make a choice. We shall be dealing with a specific class of group choice procedures, viz. voting procedures (VP's, for short). These are commonly used in determining the "socially best" alternatives either with or without preference ranking between them (for a description and analysis of the VP's mentioned in this paper, see Nurmi [6] and Riker [8]).

Over the past few decades a number of studies have shown that the social choice procedures in general and VP's in particular have serious shortcomings: there are circumstances and VP's resulting in Pareto dominated alternatives, others in which additional support would turn victorious alternatives into losers and still others where such alternatives are chosen that would be defeated by all the other alternatives in pairwise contests, to name just a few best-known shortcomings. Of particular interest is, therefore, the robustness of various negative results of VP theory vis-a-vis modifications of the assumptions concerning the individual preferences. In the following we shall concentrate on assumptions stating that the individuals have somewhat less specific opinions - and should, thus, be asked less specific questions - about the alternatives than the conventional assumptions of connected and transitive preference relation entails.

The impetus for investigating alternatives to the conventional assumption comes from two sources: (1) it has been argued that, despite the social choice theory results pointing to the contrary, the real world decision making outcomes seem quite stable (see e.g. Tullock [9], Nurmi [7]), and (2) experimental evidence seems to suggest that in some circumstances the individual preferences typically are not transitive (see e.g. Kahneman & Tversky [5], Grether & Plott [4]). Although the experiments have mainly focused on lotteries and their certainty equivalents leaving thus in principle open the possibility that in the social choice contexts similar phenomena would not necessarily emerge, the evidence gathered so far clearly warrants looking at least tentatively for non-conventional foundations of VP theory.

2. Asking for less than individual preference orderings

The least one can ask of a voter concerning a set X of alternatives is to indicate one alternative, either the one he deems best or the one he considers the worst. The former type of input is used in the plurality method, whereas the so-called negative voting utilizes the latter type of information. However, in negative voting the only sensible winning criterion would be the least number of negative votes. This, in turn, is bound to lead either to a large choice set or to several stages in a similar fashion as e.g. in Coombs´ procedure.

But obviously one could ask the voters to reveal a fixed number of their highest ranked alternatives, e.g. to indicate the three alternatives they consider best either with or without indicating their preference order among them. This procedure is particularly popular in voting bodies which have been given the task of nominating three office holders or - perhaps even more commonly - of indicating a collective preference order among the three alternatives considered as best by the body. An example of the latter variant is used in submitting to the nominating authority a proposal of a lower level body concerning the order of priority among the applicants to the office in question. The nominating officer may then have the option among the three candidates thus named or alternatively be entirely free to nominate anyone of the applicants. Obviously, in the latter case the importance of the priority order of the lower body may not be very important. But in either case it is of course important to determine whether there are non-arbitrary ways of coming up with a collective preference order concerning a subset of alternatives when the cardinality of the subset is fixed by the information asked of the voters.

2.1. Constructing a special preference order for a subset of alternatives

Among the methods discussed in the VP literature there are some which do not naturally lend themselves to constructing a social preference order. For example, the amendment procedure is such a one; it produces a social winner, but does not automatically give any ordering between the rest of the alternatives. Similarly, Schwartz procedure is primarily a method for reaching a social choice set.

But also among the methods that by their nature are capable of producing a social preference ordering, there are some that behave in a different manner when the voters are asked to give their entire preference orderings rather than to indicate their three alternatives or some other fixed number of highest ranked alternatives. If the voters are simply asked to list their three most-preferred alternatives without giving any order of priority, then the most natural way of choosing those three alternatives over which the social preference relation is to be constructed is to take the alternatives which have been mentioned by most voters in their lists of most preferred alternatives. Should this method be resorted to, then obviously if there i a majority alternative with respect to the voters' underlying preference orderings, this will not necessarily be among the three alterna tives that will be subjected to further consideration. Let us conside the following example.

Example 1. $|N| = 5$, $X = \{a,b,c,d\}$

1 person	1 person	1 person	2 persons
a	a	a	b
d	d	b	c
b	c	c	d
c	b	d	a

(N = the set of voters; $\underline{X}$ = the set of alternatives).

Now if each person sincerely reports his three most-preferred alterna tives, alternatives b, c and d will be chosen for further scrutiny an yet a has the majority of first ranks. This example shows that even though there is a majority alternative it may not be chosen because t the entire preference orderings of voters are not used. This possibil ity exists no matter which procedure is then utilized to obtain the social preference ordering over the three alternatives. This is simpl due to the fact that a, the majority alternative, is not among the three alternatives that the voters mention most often. In other words even though the method used in the last stage is such that it guarantees the choice of the majority candidate whenever one exists, the procedure as a whole may fail to accomplish this when the entire preference orderings of voters are taken into account. A fortiori, the example shows that no procedure used for determining the social preference ordering over the set of three alternatives obtained by asking persons to indicate their three most-preferred alternatives without their preferences over them, satisfies the Condorcet winning criterion when the entire preference orderings are considered. This example shows that in considering a fixed number of most-preferred alternatives only, one may lose the otherwise nice properties one's procedure might have. It should be observed that the problem here has nothing to do with utility-maximization on the group level. What is assumed is merely the individual preference orderings over the alternatives and nothing more. The feature shown in Example 1. is certainly a definite drawback for procedures which would otherwise necessarily choose the majority alternative and Condorcet winner when one exists. It is, however, worth emphasizing that this result is based on two assumptions: 1) that the voters have an ordering over the entire set of alternatives, and 2) that they are asked to name a fixed number of alternatives without indicating their preference over this set. In a sense the result is not all that surprising. What is says is that when the information about individual preferences is "positionalized" in an arbitrary fashion, the binary comparison criteria may give different results than when applied to non-reduced preferences.

What would happen then if in addition to naming three alternatives, the voters were asked to reveal their preferences over the indicated alternatives? Obviously this situation would immediately lead to further questions concerning the procedure used in aggregating the truncated preferences thus obtained. But regardless of the procedure utilized in this further processing of the preferences, we may observe that it now becomes possible that a Condorcet winning alternative will not be among the set of alternatives named by the voters. That is, it may happen that no voter names the Condorcet winning alternative either as his first, second or third ranked alternative even though there is one. The following example illustrates this peculiarity.

Example 2. $|N| = 3$, $X = \{a,b,c,d,e,f,g,h,i,j\}$

voter 1	voter 2	voter 3
e	g	h
d	f	i
a	j	c
b	b	b
c	c	a
f	a	e
g	e	d
h	d	j
i	h	f
j	i	g

Here b is the Condorcet winner, but all voters consider it worse than their third- ranked alternative. Hence, with sincere voting no voter includes b among his three best alternatives. So no matter which procedure is used to come up with the social choice after the preference lists have been given by the voters, the Condorcet winner is not among the winners.

Example 2. is one way of showing the crucial influence of those bodies or individuals who decide which individuals will be running. As extremely large candidate sets are impractical, these bodies may, by restricting the candidate set, exclude (inadvertently or otherwise) the Condorcet winner.

A glance at Example 2. also shows that by restricting the preference revelation to the three highest ranked alternatives one does not guarantee the exclusion of the Condorcet loser when such an alternative exists. In the above example j is the Condorcet loser and yet it is named by voter 2. The following example makes this point more conspicuous.

Example 3. $|N| = 5$, $X = \{a,b,c,d,e\}$

voter 1	voter 2	voter 3	voters 4 and 5
a	b	c	d
b	c	a	c
c	a	b	b
e	e	e	e
d	d	d	a

Here d, the Condorcet loser, is ranked first by more voters than any other alternative. Obviously, the restriction does nothing to eliminate Condorcet losers.

The above remarks do not assume that any particular preference aggregation method will be used once the restricted preference orders have been given by the voters. Obviously what we have said above concerning the general properties of the procedures applies mutatis mutandis also to situations where only a few alternatives are named by the voters. But can one work out a collective preference order over, say, three or four collectively best alternatives? The following methods have been used in practice:

(1). Count for each named alternative the number of its first ranks. If there is an alternative with more than 50 % of the first ranks, rank this first in the social preference order. If no such alternative can be found, the following scoring function is used: each alternative is given 1 point for each first rank it gets, 1/2 points for each second it gets and 1/3 points for each third rank. The points are added up for each alternative and the alternative with the largest total score is given the first rank in the social preference order. One then determines whether among the remaining k-1 alternatives there is one that is ranked first by more than 1/3 of the voters. If there is one, it is given the second rank in the social ordering. Otherwise the second ranked alternative is determined by the scores of alternatives as in the case of the first rank. In all cases the third rank is determined by the scores.

The method is used e.g. in making nomination proposals for chancellorships in Finnish state universities. More specifically, the consistoria or councils make their proposals concerning the person to be nominated as chancellor by indicating an order of preference among three candidates. The method described above is explicitly designed to guarantee "proportionality" in elections even though party or other kinds of lists are considered to be inapproriate. The nomination has to be made from the list of three candidates thus obtained, but the nomination decision-maker does not have to choose the first ranked candidate. In the particular case of university chancellors the nomination decision is made by the president of Finland. Thus although he is not completely constrained by the proposal produced by the collective body, the procedure is designed to indicate the preference of that body.

As was just said, this method is designed to guarantee some degree of proportionality in the sense that even if there is a large group of voters with identical preferences, it does not automatically dictate the social ordering apart from the first rank. We immediately observe that the method looks very much like the Borda count, but on closer inspection it is not equivalent to it. The present method is not reducible to any such scoring function that would give a points to the third ranked alternative, a+b to the second ranked one and a+2b to the first ranked one, as de Borda requires. Nonetheless this method has similar peculiarities to the Borda count. The following example sheds some light on them.

Example 4. $|N| = 10$, $X = \{a,b,c,d\}$

3 voters	3 voters	3 voters	1 voter
a	d	c	b
b	a	d	c
c	b	a	d
d	c	b	a

Suppose now that the above method were utilized so that for each rank an alternative is given 1 point, for the second rank 1/2 points, for the third rank 1/3 points and for the fourth rank 1/4 points. The total scores of the alternatives would then be:

a: $5\frac{9}{12}$

b: $4\frac{1}{4}$

c: $5\frac{3}{12}$

d: $5\frac{7}{12}$

Suppose now that b were left out of the contest for some reason or that the method were used to eliminate the alternative with the lowest total score and that the method were again applied to the set of remaining alternatives to produce the social ordering over three alternatives. We would then have the following preference configuration:

3 voters	3 voters	3 voters	1 voter
a	d	c	c
c	a	d	d
d	c	a	a

That is, the preferences are identical except that b has been erased from each preference order. Using the above method we get the following scores:

a: $5\frac{5}{6}$

c: $6\frac{1}{2}$

d: 6

In other words, the social preference order adc has been reversed to cda by the elimination of b, the alternative with the lowest score in the 4-alternative contests. There certainly does not seem to be much point in saying that cda is the "right" social preference order. Similar behaviour is characteristic of the Borda count as well as has been shown by Fishburn [3].

(2). The second method starts by assigning the alternative with the largest number of first ranks in individual ballots to the first rank in the social preference order. Thereafter, one adds up the number of first and second ranks given to various alternatives and assigns the alternative with the largest sum score to the second rank in the social preference order. The third rank is given to the alternative whose sum score when counting the number of first, second and third ranks is largest.

This method is used in similar contexts as the previous one, that is, in making nomination proposals. This time the offices to be filled are those of a bishop in the Lutheran church of Finland. In each district the entitled voters can vote for three candidates indicating their order of preference. The nomination proposal is then computed from the votes in the above fashion. This method is usually considered to be majoritarian in spirit, that is, no proportionality considerations are intended to enter these elections. In case there is an alternative that is ranked first by more than 50 % of the voters methods (1) and (2) rank it first, but in the absence of such an alternative marked differences may occur. Consider the following example.

Example 5. $|N| = 27$, $X = \{a,b,c\}$

11 voters	10 voters	6 voters
a	b	c
c	c	b
b	a	a

According to method (2) the social preference order is the following: a c b, because a has the largest number of first ranks, c the largest number of first and second ranks among b and c, and b then is ranked third.

On the other hand, method (1) would produce the following social preference order: b a c, because b has the largest score ($16\frac{2}{3}$), a has more than 1/3 of the first ranks and finally comes c.

If the number of persons with the preference order cba were 8 instead of 6, the social preference order determined by method (1) would become: c a b as now c would have the largest score ($18\frac{1}{2}$) and a would again have more than 1/3 of the first ranks which would leave b the third ranked alternative. We thus witness a complete reversal of the social preference even though not more than 2 persons have been added to the voting body.

The preceding discussion shows that if one wishes to guarantee the satisfaction of Condorcet-criteria or other related properties of social choices, then the restriction to a subset of alternatives does not seem a workable solution. If people are asked to reveal their top most alternatives only - with or without the preference order among them - the information on paired comparisons is lost. This in turn can lead to a situation where a Condorcet winner is not among the subset indicated by the voters. But what if the voters do not have a preference order over the set of alternatives to start with? All our previous results rest on this assumption. It may, therefore, be in order to consider the possibility that the voters view the alternative set in some other less structured fashion.

2.2. Results based on individual choice functions

The idea of assessing social choice procedures starting from the assumption that the voters do not necessarily have a complete and transitive preference relation over the set of alternatives, but instead have an individual choice function has recently been pursued by M.A. Aizerman and his collaborators. In the following we shall briefly restate some of their results trying to explicate their implications for the theory of voting procedures (see Aizerman & Aleskerov [1] and [2]).

To start with let us assume that the voters have an individual choice function C_i over the set of alternatives X so that for any subset X' of X the function C_i indicates the set X'' of best alternatives in i´s opinion, i.e.

$$X'' = C_i(X') \subseteq X', \text{ for all } X' \subseteq X.$$

We shall consider operators F transforming the n-tuples of C_i functions into choice functions having identical properties as the individual choice functions. More formally, we shall consider the largest closing classes of operators which means that our attention is on operators satisfying the following:

if $C_i(X) \in G$ for all i in N, then

$F(C_1(X),\ldots,C_n(X)) \in G$ where G is a subset of all possible choice functions.

Let us furthermore restrict our focus on choice functions - individual and social - that satisfy 1) locality, 2) sovereignty, 3) monotonicity, 4) neutrality and 5) anonymity. These are defined for choice functions in an analogous way to the context of choice rules based on individual preference orders. The first property, locality, requires that if in two choice situations concerning the same alternative set X, x belongs to the choice set of precisely the same voter set in each situation, then it must belong to the social choice set either in both situations or in either i.e. if for all $X' \subseteq X$ and $x \in X'$:

$$x \in C_i(X') \text{ if and only if } x \in C_i'(X'), \text{ for all } i, \text{ implies that}$$

$$x \in F(C_1(X'),\ldots,C_n(X')) \text{ iff } x \in F(C_1'(X'),\ldots,C_n'(X')),$$

then F satisfies locality. In other words, whether x belongs to the social choice set is determined solely by which individuals place it in their choice sets regardless of their attitude towards the other alternatives.

Sovereignty, in turn, requires that for any alternative in any subset of X, there is a n-tuple of individual choice functions such that this particular alternative is in the social choice set and an n-tuple of individual choice functions such that this alternative is not in the social choice set.

Monotonicity is defined in the usual way. It is a requirement that if for any X' an alternative x is in the social choice set in some choice situation and the set of voters whose individual choice set contains x is a subset of the individuals having x in their choice set in another choice situation where X' is considered, then x should also be in the social choice set in the latter situation. In other words if x is among the winners when X' is the alternative set, then it should remain among them if the set of individuals who have x in their choice set is either the same or contains the set of individuals choosing x in the first situation as its proper subset. Thus, monotonicity requires that additional support for x should not be harmful to it. Neutrality requires that if the voter set having x in their individual choice sets when X is considered is the same as the voter set having x' in their individual choice sets when X' is considered, then x belongs to the social choice set from X precisely when x' belongs to the social choice set from X'. In other words, the number of voters with various choice sets and that only should decide the social choice. Aizerman and Aleskerov [1] observe that neutrality thus understood is a combination of the independence of the context and the independence of alternatives. Indeed, it appears to be of questionable plausibility; certainly a violation of it would not be alarming as the following example shows.

Example 6. $|N| = 3$, $X = \{a,c\}$ $X' = \{A,C\}$

		from X	from X'
Individual choice sets:	voter 1	a	A,C
	voter 2	a	A,C
	voter 3	c	C

Here voters 1 and 2 have a and A in their choice sets in situations X and X', respectively. The neutrality property would now require that if $F(C_1(X),C_2(X),C_3(X)) = \{a\}$, then $F(C_1(X'),C_2(X'),C_3(X')) = \{A\}$. In other words, by neutrality the group should choose a from X if it chooses A from X' because the set of voters having a in their individual choice sets, viz. voters 1 and 2, is identical with the voter set having A in their individual choice sets. Yet it would not seem unreasonable to require that the choice from X should be a because two out of three voters would choose a and a only from X. But at the same time it would seem entirely plausible that C (and not A) be chosen from X' because all voters have C in their individual choice sets and no other alternative is so popular.

Anonymity, finally, requires that the permutation of the labels of individuals does not change the social choice. The properties 1) - 5) characterize social choice functions. In addition to them, we shall consider three further properties which may characterize individual choice functions as well. The first is heritage, which requires the following: for all subsets X' of X the choice from X' contains the intersection of the choice set from X and X', i.e. $C(X) \cap X' \subseteq C(X')$.

Concordance, in turn, requires that for any X_1 and X_2 the common elements chosen from X_1 and X_2 when considered separately are included in the choice set from $X_1 \cup X_2$, i.e.

$$C(X_1) \cap C(X_2) \subseteq C(X_1 \cup X_2) \text{ for all } X_1 \text{ and } X_2.$$

The independence of outcast variants, finally, states that if X_1 is such a subset of X_2 that no element of X_1 is in the choice set of X_2, then the removal of the elements of X_1 from X_2 should leave the choice set of X_2 intact, i.e.

$$X_1 \subseteq X_2 - C(X_2) \text{ implies that } C(X_2 - X_1) = C(X_2), \text{ where the}$$

minus sign is interpreted in the set-theoretic fashion.

Now Aizerman's and Aleskerov's theorem says that the intersection of those social choice functions that satisfy properties 1) - 5) above on the other hand, and the choice functions satisfying the heritage, concordance and independence of outcast variants both in individual and social choices, on the other, is empty. In other words, there are no such choice functions that satisfy all the above properties. If we do not require that the independence of outcast variants condition be satisfied by the social choice function, then there is exactly one social choice operator that has all the other properties mentioned above, viz. the "unanimity" operator which is defined as follows:

$$x \in F(C_1(X),\ldots,C_n(X)) \text{ iff } x \in C_i(X), \text{ for all } i \text{ in } N.$$

If, on the other hand, we would be willing to dispense with the property of concordance, then the other properties would be satisfied by a unique operator, viz. the following:

$$x \in F(C_1(X),\ldots,C_n(X)) \text{ iff there exists } i \text{ in } N \text{ such that } x \in C_i(X).$$

Another theorem of Aizerman and Aleskerov is of a nature analogous to the famous impossibility theorem of Arrow. It states that the class of those local choice functions that satisfy the heritage, concordance and independence of outcast variants both in individual and social choices coincides with dictator operators, i.e. operators with the following property:

$$x \in F(C_1(X),\ldots,C_n(X)) \text{ iff } x \in C_i(X) \text{ for a fixed individual } i.$$

A result of a more positive nature is one that states that if we are satisfied with the properties 1) - 5) and heritage only (the latter in the sense of both individual and social choices), then a class of operators exists that can be resorted to, viz. the class that Aizerman and Aleskerov call k-majority operators. When these operators are used all alternatives that have been named in the individual choice sets of at least k individuals are also in the social choice set.

What then are the implications of these results for the choice of voting procedures? First of all, the negative results seem to suggest that even if the assumption that the individuals have choice functions rather than preference orders over the alternative set was found to be justified, it still would not follow that a perfect procedure for aggregating individual choices could be found. Instead results analogous to the Arrow impossibility one would be encountered. Secondly, many of the properties or conditions featured in the preceding results seem to lack some of the normative significance that characterizes analogous properties when defined for procedures based on individual preference orders. For instance, property 1), locality, does not seem intuitively compelling. Surely this is partly due to reasons which are similar to those which make the positional voting procedures seem sometimes intuitively more reasonable than the binary ones. Also neutrality seems of somewhat questionable significance for similar reasons. On the other hand, the properties of heritage, concordance and the independence of outcast variants seem to capture something of what we could intuitively regard as the rationality characteristics of individual and social choices.

The over-all conclusion from the preceding survey of the problems encountered in trying to ask the voters something less than their preference order over the set of alternatives *in toto* suggests that more problems are created than solved by asking people to reveal their top-most preferences only (with or without ordering those alternatives). On the other hand, if it can safely be assumed that people do not ever have a preference order over the alternative but yet possess an individual choice function over the set of alternatives indicating for each subset the best elements in the voter's view, then the impossibility results analogous to that of Arrow are impending. If the properties of the heritage, concordance and independence of outcasts are regarded as rationality properties necessary to be preserved by both individual and social choices, then only dictatorial operators are available if we restrict ourselves to local operators. If, on the other hand, less stringent rationality requirements are imposed, then, of course, the normative significance of the possibility results is diminished. In short, the possibilities of finding good procedures by asking people less than their preference order over alternatives do not seem to be available.

3. Conclusion

To assume that the voters have somewhat less specific ideas about the alternatives than the preference orders will not be of much help in the avoidance of the negative results of VP theory. At least as far as the voters are allowed to indicate a fixed number of alternatives as their most preferred ones and the final choice is made from the set of alternatives thus obtained (either by plurality or some other VP), one can actually lose rather than gain nice properties that the VP's might otherwise have. This possibility is present regardless of whether the voters may indicate their preference order over the restricted set of alternatives or not. Aizerman's and Aleskerov's results show that the assumption according to which the individuals have choice functions instead of preference orders can also lead to rather negative results although one can question the general plausibility of some of the additional assumptions needed in the derivation of the results. Over all, then, the variations of the assumptions concerning individual preferences seem to suggest that the fact that all VP's have serious shortcomings is a rather robust invariance.

References

[1] Aizerman, M.A. and Aleskerov, F.T., "Local operators in models of social choice", Systems & Control Letters 3, 1-6 (1983)

[2] Aizerman, M.A. and Aleskerov, F.T., "Voting operators in the space of choice functions", California Institute of Technology, Social Science Working Paper 559 (1985)

[3] Fishburn, P.C., "Paradoxes of Voting ", American Political Science Review 68, 537-546 (1974)

[4] Grether, D.M. and Plott, C.R., "Economic theory of choice and the preference reversal phenomenon", American Economic Review 69, 623-638 (1979)

[5] Kahneman, D. and Tversky, A., "Prospect theory", Econometrica 47, 263-291 (1979)

[6] Nurmi, H., "Voting procedures: a summary analysis", British Journal of Political Science 13, 181-208 (1983)

[7] Nurmi, H., "Mathematical models of elections and their relevance for institutional design", Electoral Studies 5, 167-181 (1986)

[8] Riker, W.H., Liberalism against Populism, San Francisco: W.H. Freeman (1982)

[9] Tullock, G., "Why so much stability?", Public Choice 37, 189-202 (1981)